The Wadsworth Guide

to

MLA Documentation

The Wadsworth Guide

to

MLA Documentation

2009 MLA Update

Second Edition

Linda Smoak Schwartz

Coastal Carolina University

WADSWORTH
CENGAGE Learning

Australia • Brazil • Japan • Korea • Mexico • Singapore
Spain • United Kingdom • United States

WADSWORTH
CENGAGE Learning

The Wadsworth Guide to MLA Documentation: Second Edition
Linda Smoak Schwartz

Senior Publisher: Lyn Uhl

Acquisitions Editor: Kate Derrick

Development Editor: Leslie Taggart/
Vici Casana

Senior Assistant Editor: Kelli Strieby

Editorial Assistant: Beth Reny

Media Editor: Cara Douglass-Graff

Marketing Director: Jason Sakos

Marketing Coordinator: Ryan Ahern

Senior Marketing Communications
Manager: Stacey Purviance

Content Project Manager: Corinna Dibble

Senior Art Director: Jill Ort

Senior Print Buyer: Betsy Donaghey

Senior Rights Acquisition Specialist,
Image: Jen Meyer Dare

Senior Rights Acquisition Specialist,
Text: Katie Huha

Production Service: MPS Limited,
A Macmillan Company

Cover Designer: Dick Hannus

Compositor: MPS Limited, A Macmillan
Company

For product information and technology assistance, contact us at **Cengage Learning Customer & Sales Support, 1-800-354-9706**

For permission to use material from this text or product, submit all requests online at **www.cengage.com/permissions**
Further permissions questions can be emailed to **permissionrequest@cengage.com**

Library of Congress Control Number: 2010932596

ISBN-13: 978-1-111-34737-6
ISBN-10: 1-111-34737-9

Wadsworth
20 Channel Center Street
Boston, MA 02210
USA

Cengage Learning is a leading provider of customized learning solutions with office locations around the globe, including Singapore, the United Kingdom, Australia, Mexico, Brazil and Japan. Locate your local office at **international.cengage.com/region**

Cengage Learning products are represented in Canada by Nelson Education, Ltd.

For your course and learning solutions, visit **www.cengage.com**

Purchase any of our products at your local college store or at our preferred online store **www.cengagebrain.com**

Printed in the United States of America
1 2 3 4 5 6 7 14 13 12 11 10

To Albert Larry Schwartz; Robert Tracy Schwartz; Joe and Alice Smoak; Bob and Sylvia Schwartz; Catherine and Jim Eick; Rick and Rita Smoak; Julia, Paul, Jeanette, and Natalie Tucker; Barbara, Michael, Joshua, and Rachel Cheatham; and Leona and Nicholas Yonge for their unfailing support and understanding, and to my students at Coastal Carolina University, whose questions inspired the writing of this book.

[I]f I'd a knowed what a trouble it was to make a book I wouldn't a tackled it. . . .

—Mark Twain, *The Adventures of Huckleberry Finn*

May the Schwartz be with you.

—Mel Brooks et al., *Space Balls*

The Wadsworth Guide to MLA Documentation (formerly known as *The Harcourt Guide to MLA Documentation*) grew out of my desire to create a guide to MLA documentation that would be brief enough to be used as a supplement to a handbook or literature anthology, yet comprehensive enough to address all the documentation issues students might encounter in writing both general topic and literary analysis research papers. I wanted an MLA guide that would be suitable for the beginning student with virtually no experience using MLA-style documentation, yet sophisticated enough to be kept and used throughout the student's years in college and even into graduate school. I wanted a guide that would help students find sources in a university library and on the Internet. And I wanted a guide that would help students evaluate the research materials they found, make more sophisticated choices about what information to include in their papers, and successfully integrate the best information they could find into their papers.

The Wadsworth Guide covers the entire process of creating a research paper, including selecting and narrowing a topic; creating both a working outline and a working bibliography; finding and evaluating research materials in a library and online; taking notes; and writing, documenting, formatting, and revising a paper. It provides model citations for virtually any type of source a writer might need to include in the works-cited list of a documented paper.

Concise and easy to use, *The Wadsworth Guide* is ideally suited to freshman researchers who could purchase this text as a supplement to the handbook or literature anthology used in a first- or second-semester composition course and retain it for use as a reference throughout their college careers. This text is also suitable for any sophomore-, junior-, or senior-level course in which papers using MLA-style documentation are written. It is comprehensive enough to function as the primary text in classes devoted entirely to research and has been successfully classroom-tested in research seminars.

Those who used the second edition will find this updated edition thoroughly revised and expanded to include all of the changes in the *MLA Style Manual and Guide to Scholarly Publishing*, Third Edition (2008), and the *MLA Handbook for Writers of Research Papers*, Seventh Edition (2009).

Notable features of *The Wadsworth Guide to MLA Documentation*:

- Provides students and their instructor with four-month subscriptions to *InfoTrac® College Edition* (at the instructor's request); this online database gives students and faculty access to more than sixteen million full-text articles from over six thousand scholarly journals, popular magazines, and newspapers in a variety of fields. (Professors may order subscriptions for themselves and their students to *InfoTrac College Edition* as a supplement to this and other Wadsworth, Cengage Learning texts by contacting their local Wadsworth, Cengage Learning sales representatives.)
- Provides annotated model citations for the types of sources most frequently used by students documenting research papers (chapters 9–13)
- Explains how to find sources in a library as well as on the Internet (chapter 3)
- Explains how to use personal and library online subscription reference databases to search for sources (chapter 3) and how to document those sources (chapter 13)
- Includes an annotated list of print, library subscription, and free online reference databases (chapter 3)
- Includes a list of useful Web sites for newspapers, popular and news magazines, and television and radio stations (chapter 3)
- Explains how to evaluate both print and Internet sources (chapter 3)
- Covers word-processing strategies such as how to create a header, a hanging indent, and a superscript number
- Explains how to write and document general topic and literary analysis papers
- Features fully annotated general topic and literary analysis sample research papers (chapters 6 and 7)
- Explains how to quote from novels, short stories, plays, and poems as well as from the critics who analyze them (chapter 16)
- Takes illustrative materials from classic literary works with which most readers should be familiar or from critical analyses of familiar works
- Features three sample outlines (chapters 4, 6, and 7)
- Features four sample bibliographies—one of which is cross-referenced—and a sample entry from an annotated bibliography (chapters 6, 7, and 8 and works consulted)
- Gives a user-friendly checklist of exactly what information needs to be included in the citation after each model citation (chapters 9–13)
- Devotes a complete chapter to documenting various types of articles taken from scholarly journals, popular magazines, and newspapers (chapter 10)

- Clarifies many issues that often confuse beginning writers, such as the difference between scholarly journals and popular magazines and the correct way to cite the edition, section, and page numbers of variously formatted newspaper articles (chapter 10)

- Features model citations for many sources beginning writers have trouble documenting, such as telephone and personal interviews, letters, posters, maps, cartoons, comic strips, advertisements, films, television shows, radio shows, LP liner notes, compact disc booklets, and materials taken from literary anthologies and critical editions of literary works (chapters 9 and 11)

- Devotes an entire chapter to documenting materials taken from a wide variety of Internet sources (chapter 12)

- Explains how to cite materials from the CD-ROMs that supplement modern literary anthologies (chapter 12)

- Gives model citations for materials taken from print, microform, CD-ROM, DVD-ROM, and library and personal subscription databases and from free online encyclopedias, dictionaries, and reference databases (chapter 13)

- Explains the use of square brackets to change the case of letters, clarify pronouns, change verb tenses, give further explanation, and indicate errors in a source (chapter 17) and illustrates these strategies in the sample papers (chapters 6 and 7)

- Devotes an entire chapter to the use of the ellipsis (chapter 18) and illustrates the use of the ellipsis in both sample papers (chapters 6 and 7)

- Explains when, why, and how to use the bracketed ellipsis (chapter 18)

- Devotes an entire chapter to the issue of plagiarism from print as well as Internet sources (chapter 21)

My goal in writing *The Wadsworth Guide to MLA Documentation* was to make writing a research paper using MLA-style documentation as simple and as easy as possible. I hope you will enjoy using this text, and I look forward to hearing your suggestions for future editions.

Linda Smoak Schwartz

ACKNOWLEDGMENTS

This book summarizes, explains, and interprets the guidelines created by the Modern Language Association of America for documenting research papers. It is designed to guide undergraduate writers of both general topic and literary analysis research papers. This work is not an official publication of the MLA, however, and has not been endorsed by that organization. If you have any questions about the MLA documentation style not addressed in this book, you should consult the two official publications of the Modern Language Association of America:

MLA Handbook for Writers of Research Papers. 7th ed. New York: MLA, 2009. Print.

MLA Style Manual and Guide to Scholarly Publishing. 3rd ed. New York: MLA, 2008. Print.

I am grateful to my colleagues in the English, theater, business, psychology, and education departments and in the Honors Program at Coastal Carolina University who classroom-tested this text and encouraged me enormously in the writing process: Sarah Ellen Arnold, Maria K. Bachman, Elizabeth K. (Betsy) Barr, John P. Beard, Lee Bollinger, Donald O. Brook, Daniel J. Ennis, Veronica D. Gerald, Jacqueline L. Gmuca, Steven L. Hamelman, Linda P. Hollandsworth, Rebecca L. (Tommye) Imschweiler, Linda Cooper Knight, Peter C. Lecouras, David E. Millard, Donald J. Millus, R. Ray Moye, Steven J. Nagle, Sarah J. (Sally) Purcell, John Ramey, Nelljean M. Rice, S. Paul Rice, Penelope S. (Penny) Rosner, Julia Ann Ross, Karlene G. Rudolph, Sara J. Sabota, Sara L. Sanders, Clifford A. Saunders, Jill L. Sessoms, Glenda Y. Sweet, Suzanne W. Thompson, Jennifer J. Viereck, Randall A. Wells, and W. Horace Wood.

In addition, I am grateful to Margaret H. (Peggy) Bates, Margaret A. Fain, Allison Faix, Michael M. Lackey, Robert Stevens, Jeri L. Traw, and all of Coastal Carolina's wonderful librarians for technical assistance and moral support; to Nancy M. Nelson at Carolina Forest High School Media Center for helping me learn about materials and databases commonly cited by high school students; to Christopher D. Williams at Horry-Georgetown Technical College Library for helping me learn more about subscription reference databases; to Jean H. Ennis, Jack E. Flanders, and Vivien E. Ford for help with computer-related issues; to William E. Files, Caitlin Crawford-Lamb, and Jessica Lynn Piezzo for granting me permission to use their research papers or parts thereof; to Ken McLaurin for allowing me to use lines from his poems "The Bee Constellation," "Cancer," and "Storm Pit"; to Micheline B. Brown for her much-appreciated help with the index; to Albert Larry Schwartz for his much-appreciated help with the table of contents, the index, and countless other items related to the publication of this text; to Karen Moore, Julie McBurney, Melissa Gruzs, Kassandra Radomski, and most especially to Jon Davies and the production staff at Harcourt College Publishers for their excellent work on the first edition. For their help, encouragement, patience, and outstanding work on the second edition, I am grateful to Dickson Musslewhite, Steve Marsi, Laurie K. Runion, and Cynthia H. Lindlof. For their outstanding work on this updated edition, I am grateful to Vici Casana, Leslie Taggart, Ed Dionne, Corinna Dibble, Susan Warne, and the numerous other fine folks at Wadsworth, Cengage Learning who made this revised second edition a reality. Special thanks go to Vici Casana for her help in updating and proofreading this new edition.

Special thanks go to my colleagues at universities around the country who read the first and second editions of this text and offered their generous suggestions and encouragement at various stages of the revision process:

Margaret H. (Peggy) Bates, *Coastal Carolina University*

John P. Beard, *Coastal Carolina University*

Laura Campbell, *Cleary College*

Scott Douglass, *Chattanooga State Technical Community College*

Louie Edmundson, *Chattanooga State Technical Community College*

Margaret A. Fain, *Coastal Carolina University*

Allison Faix, *Coastal Carolina University*

Steven L. Hamelman, *Coastal Carolina University*

Anne Maxham, *Washington State University*

Valerie A. Reimers, *Southwestern Oklahoma State University*

Helen J. Schwartz, *Indiana University–Purdue University Indianapolis*

Jill L. Sessoms, *Coastal Carolina University*

Monalinda Verlengia, *College of the Desert*

Judith Williamson, *Sauk Valley Community College*

Lastly, I am grateful to Emily T. Cat—long-haired, black, white, and tan—who slept peacefully beside me as I worked late into the night on this and all the previous editions.

About the Author

Linda Smoak Schwartz teaches courses in American and British literature, modern and postmodern American poetry, and composition in the English Department at Coastal Carolina University, where she was Director of the Freshman Composition Program from 1982 until 1996. In addition, she directed Coastal's Sophomore Literature Program from 1992 until 1996. Her text *The Schwartz Guide to MLA Documentation* was published by McGraw-Hill in 1998. *The Harcourt Guide to MLA Documentation,* the first edition of this text, was published by Harcourt College Publishers in 2001 (and subsequently acquired by Thomson Wadsworth). The second edition of this text was published in 2004 by Thomson Wadsworth (now Wadsworth, a part of Cengage Learning). She lives in Conway, South Carolina, a charming Southern town ten minutes inland from Myrtle Beach and the white sand beaches of South Carolina's Grand Strand.

CONTENTS

CHAPTER 1

Why Do I Have to Write a Research Paper?

It's an unbelievably beautiful Monday, and having enjoyed a restful weekend just hanging out with your family or friends, you feel unusually energetic and happy when you wake up. You leave home and head to your first class of the day. Professor Smith enters the room smiling, and as the class begins, he announces the due date for the semester research paper and begins recommending topics you might want to consider.

You feel the energy and joy suddenly draining out of your body to be replaced with fear and dread. Four weeks to write the paper that may well determine whether you get the A you're determined to earn in this course. There's so much work you already have to do: midterm exams in almost every class, that trip to your best friend's wedding next week, the family barbecue at the lake, papers due in several other classes. How will you ever get everything done? "Why do I have to write a research paper?" you ask yourself.

Your professors will ask you to write research papers because they want to train you to become an independent scholar who can locate information in any library and on the Internet, assess the value and reliability of that information, combine what you have learned with your own original ideas, and present your conclusions in a clear and understandable style. Your professors know that the ability to successfully research any topic you need to know about will serve you well not only during your college years but also in whatever career you choose.

When you graduate from college and are hired for your first job or make a career change based on your recently acquired degree, it is likely that you will not know everything there is to know about the company you work for, the products it manufactures, or the services it provides. No doubt, you will have learned some strategies and skills during your college years that will be invaluable in whatever job you choose. However, it is likely that the company hiring you will give you some on-the-job training that will turn you into the knowledgeable, indispensable employee it hopes you will become.

In this highly technological modern world, what is true in January may have been disproved by March, so it will always be necessary for you to keep up with the latest developments in your field. You won't have your professors around to keep you informed about all these changes, so in the professional world you will have to become the independent scholar your professors were training you to become. Never forget that information is power. If you know a great deal about a subject, you become a valuable resource person to others who wish to learn about that subject. You become the employee most likely to get those promotions and raises.

Always remember, however, that the goal of research is not just to find out what others have written about a subject. Anyone can do that. The ultimate goal of research is to analyze a subject and present your own original analysis of it. The originality of thought you bring to your discussion of a topic you've researched is the magic ingredient that makes your presentation worth listening to or your paper or report worth reading.

CHAPTER 2

Using MLA and Other Styles of Documentation

Because you will undoubtedly be required to write numerous research papers if you plan to earn a degree from any college or university, you should be aware that there are numerous documentation styles you may be asked to use, depending on the subject for which you are writing a particular paper.

Modern Language Association (MLA) Style

Papers written for courses in the humanities (English, history, philosophy, religion, art, music, theater) are usually documented in the style recommended by the Modern Language Association of America (MLA).

This book summarizes the guidelines created by the Modern Language Association of America for writing and documenting general topic and literary analysis research papers. If you have any questions about the MLA documentation style not addressed in this book, you should consult the two official publications of the Modern Language Association of America:

MLA Handbook for Writers of Research Papers. 7th ed.

New York: MLA, 2009. Print.

MLA Style Manual and Guide to Scholarly Publishing. 3rd ed.

New York: MLA, 2008. Print.

The *MLA Handbook* is designed for the use of undergraduate writers of research papers, and the *MLA Style Manual* is designed to guide graduate students writing theses and dissertations and professors writing articles and books for publication. Look for them in your university library if you need more information than this guide includes.

The Modern Language Association also maintains a Web site through which you can order MLA publications and find information about the most recent updates of the MLA documentation guidelines: <http://www.mla.org>.

American Psychological Association (APA) Style

Professors in psychology, sociology, and education may require you to use APA-style documentation: <http://www.apastyle.org/pubmanual.html>.

American Psychological Association. *Publication Manual of the*

American Psychological Association. 6th ed. Washington:

American Psychological Association, 2009. Print.

Chicago Manual of Style (Chicago/CMS) Style

If you are preparing a manuscript for publication, you may need to use Chicago-style documentation, which uses the footnote/endnote method of documenting sources. Chicago style also has an author-date method. History professors sometimes require Chicago documentation. Web information is available at <http://www.press.uchicago.edu>.

The Chicago Manual of Style. 15th ed. Chicago: U of Chicago P,

2003. Print.

American Political Science Association (APSA) Style

Political science professors may ask you to follow the guidelines published by the American Political Science Association: <http://www.apsanet.org>.

Lane, Michael K. *Style Manual for Political Science.* 2nd rev. ed.

Washington: American Political Science Association, 2006.

Print.

Linguistic Society of America (LSA) Style

Linguistics professors may require you to submit papers documented according to the guidelines of the Linguistic Society of America. More information about these guidelines may be found on the LSA Web site: <http://www.lsadc.org>.

Council of Science Editors (CSE) Style

Science professors typically require you to use CSE-style documentation. Learn about it at <http://www.councilscienceeditors.org>.

Council of Science Editors. Style Manual Committee. *Scientific Style and Format: The CSE Manual for Authors, Editors, and Publishers.* 7th ed. Reston: Council of Science Eds., 2006. Print.

American Chemical Society (ACS) Style

Chemistry professors may require you to use ACS-style documentation. Learn about it at <http://pubs.acs.org>.

Coghill, Anne M., and Lorrin R. Garson, eds. *The ACS Style Guide: Effective Communication of Scientific Information.* 3rd ed. Washington: American Chemical Society, 2006. Print.

American Mathematical Society (AMS) Style

For papers in mathematics, follow the documentation guidelines of the American Mathematical Society at <http://www.ams.org>.

Swanson, Ellen. *Mathematics into Type.* Updated by Ellen Swanson and Arlene O'Sean. Updated ed. Providence, RI: American Mathematical Society, 1999. Print.

CHAPTER 3

Choosing a Topic and Finding Sources

Choosing an Appropriate Research Strategy

There is no one right way to research a subject. This text suggests some strategies you may find useful as you discover through the experience of gathering and evaluating information and writing papers what research strategies work best for you.

Consider creating a list of the tasks you must complete in the process of preparing the paper. Estimate how much time you will need to

- zero in on an interesting topic
- figure out what aspect of a subject you will research
- gather, read, and evaluate information
- move your paper from rough drafts to final draft
- prepare your works-cited list
- proofread and edit the final copy you will turn in to your professor

Creating a rough list of the tasks involved in preparing to write a research paper will reveal an important truth: Every task in life takes longer than you expect it will. Be realistic about the time it will take to write your paper. Hopefully this process will make it clear to you that if you wait until the night before the paper is due to begin your research, you won't be satisfied with the quality of the paper you'll be turning in.

Choosing a Topic

Some professors will give you a list of topics from which you may choose the one that most interests you. Others will assign each student a specific topic, and some professors will allow you to research and write about any subject that interests you. Try to choose a topic that truly engages your interest— ideally a topic you've always wanted to know more about but have not yet had the opportunity to spend any time researching. Choose a topic that will interest your readers as well, one that will teach them something they didn't know.

Consider surfing the Internet a bit to look for a subject that interests you. Or is there some topic you're studying in another course that you would like to learn more about? If you are writing a paper for an English class, check with your professor to see if a topic in history, psychology, biology, or marine science is acceptable. The research you do will enhance your understanding of the material you're studying in the other class while earning you a good grade in English.

Narrowing Your Topic

Once you have identified a topic that interests you, you need to think about the length of time you have available to work on the paper and the number of pages you are required to submit. One of your most important jobs will be to decide exactly what aspect of the topic you will research and what approach you will take to your subject. You will also need to find out how much information is available on your topic. If there are literally thousands of books and articles on your topic, that might be a clue that the topic you have chosen is too broad and needs to be narrowed down. On the other hand, if you find very few sources, you may need to consider broadening your topic or even choosing a different one.

Make sure you have chosen a topic that you can do justice to in the number of pages your instructor has assigned. It is better to analyze a small topic thoroughly than to cover a huge topic superficially.

Let's say you are interested in writing a paper dealing with horror movies. Could you fully discuss every conceivable aspect of horror movies in a double-spaced, typewritten ten-page research paper? Of course not. It would, in fact, be difficult to cover all the aspects of horror movies in a single book. A more manageable topic might be "An Analysis of Gary Oldman's Portrayal of Count Dracula in *Bram Stoker's Dracula*."

Creating a Working Outline to Guide Your Research

Creating a working outline can be a useful step in your research process. Make a rough list of the topics you think you will discuss in the paper to guide your research. Deciding what you plan to discuss in the paper before you begin your research will help you avoid wasting time reading sources that will provide no useful information. This outline will undoubtedly change as you find new sources and decide what you will cover in your paper. A working outline will help you decide if the order in which you are discussing materials in your paper is logical and whether your paragraphs contain enough supporting details. It will also help you eliminate repetitive or irrelevant material from your paper. If information does not support your thesis, it probably does not belong in your paper. Time spent developing and analyzing your working outline will help you move through the research and writing processes more efficiently.

Creating a Working Bibliography

As you find sources in your library or on the Internet that you expect will provide useful information on your topic, type into your computer (or record on note cards) the bibliographic citation for each source that will appear in your works-cited list if you decide to quote, paraphrase, or summarize material from that source. This list is called a working bibliography, and it will eventually become your works-cited list.

Take the bibliographical information directly from the source to make sure that it is correct. If you have taken bibliographical information from an online or card catalog or from an index, reference book, or other source in your library, compare it with the information provided in your original source to make sure your citation is accurate.

If information necessary for your citation (for example, the city of publication for a book entry) is missing in the source you are using but is available in an index, online catalog, card catalog, or other source, place that information in square brackets in your citation: [Detroit]: Gale, 1998.

Your working bibliography should be completed before you write the first draft of your paper so that you will know how to do the parenthetical citations correctly as you incorporate your quotations, paraphrases, and summaries into the text of your paper. To format parenthetical citations, you will need to know if you are citing from two authors with the same last name or if you are citing from two or more works by the same author.

The most efficient method of creating a working bibliography is to type the bibliographic entries into a computer. As you locate sources that you expect will provide useful information, create the bibliographic citations exactly as they will appear in your works-cited or works-consulted list. You can also cut and paste citations from your sources into your working bibliography, but be sure to change this raw bibliographical data to MLA format.

Your working bibliography may contain additional information not necessary for the works-cited list. You might consider placing this information in angle brackets (< >) or parentheses to remind yourself later that this information does not belong in the final version of your citation. At the end of each citation, be sure to include the library call number for books, the Web address (URL) for Internet sources, and exactly where you found the information about this source in case you need to locate the source again at a later date. Be scrupulously accurate when recording Web addresses; the slightest error will mean that your computer will not be able to return to the Web site.

If you need to return to a Web page for additional information, and your Web browser or search engine does not seem to recognize the URL you have typed into the search field, first check the URL to make sure you have not omitted, transposed, or mistyped any characters. If you have typed the URL accurately, but your browser still will not take you to the desired page, try deleting characters from the right of the URL and pressing Enter again. If the URL still does not get you where you need to go, try omitting all the characters to the right of the URL of the site's home page. If you can find the home page of the site, you should be able to find the page you need from there.

As you read your sources, check the footnotes, endnotes, parenthetical citations, and works-cited/consulted lists. Use the hypertext links in online sources. Each source you read is likely to lead you to other useful sources.

Your working bibliography will change as you delete sources that provided no useful information and add others that you intend to read. When you have finished writing the body of your paper, simply delete the unused sources and alphabetize those from which you quoted, paraphrased, or summarized information, and the working bibliography will become your works-cited list.

Another method is to write the bibliographic entries on note cards, which can be alphabetized easily when you are ready to type the entries into your computer. The cards for sources that did not provide useful information can be discarded. If you are using note cards for notes also, use a different color or size for the working bibliography.

You might prefer to create a handwritten list of sources. When you are ready to convert your working bibliography into your works-cited list, simply cross through sources you didn't cite, number the remaining entries in alphabetical order, and type them into your computer.

Your computer will alphabetize for you, but be sure to verify the ordering of the list before you submit it to your professor. Your computer is not getting the grade on the paper; you are.

Finding Sources in the Library

Attending an instructional session taught by a reference librarian is one of the easiest ways to learn how the library at your school operates and what resources it provides to assist you with your research. Most libraries also offer guided tours, workshops, maps, and handouts designed to help you find what you need.

Professional reference librarians are trained in locating research materials of all kinds and will be happy to help you learn how to find the materials you need for your research paper. Don't expect the librarians to do your work for you, however. Remember that you will write many research papers during your college career, so you need to learn how to find sources yourself. If this is the first time you've researched a topic in your school's library, however, be sure to ask for help until you learn what resources are available and how to use them.

Using Online and Card Catalogs

Most modern libraries have online catalogs that can be accessed through a library computer terminal or your personal computer. Check your library's Web site, or ask a librarian for information about how to access the online catalog and the online subscription reference databases from your dormitory room or home. If your library has both an online and a card catalog, ask a librarian whether all available sources are listed in both catalogs. In some cases, older materials are listed in the card catalog, and only the most recent acquisitions are listed in the online catalog. Or your library may be in the process of transferring the data in the card catalog to the online catalog. Ask a librarian whether you need to check both catalogs.

Finding Books

Online catalogs can typically be searched by author, title, author/title, subject, keyword, or call numbers. You may limit your search by year of publication, language, format (book, journal, videotape, LP, CD, DVD, CD-ROM, etc.), or place where you would expect to find the item (main collection, rare book collection, reserves, media collection, etc.). Look for a limit-search key on your screen.

If your school has a card catalog, you will find the books and other types of materials your library owns listed on bibliography cards stored in drawers. Sources are typically listed in three ways: by author, by title, and by subject.

Once you have determined the call number of the book you need, you can find the book on the library shelves. If your library has closed stacks, you will need to present a call slip containing the call number to a librarian at the checkout desk, and the book will be located and brought to you.

Finding Reference Books

Reference books have call numbers beginning with "Ref" and are typically shelved in a separate reference section of the library. Reference books (almanacs; general encyclopedias [*The New Encyclopaedia Britannica, Collier's Encyclopedia, The Encyclopedia Americana,* etc.]; subject-specific references

[*American Writers, British Writers, Dictionary of Literary Biography, Contemporary Literary Criticism, Facts on File, Congressional Quarterly Researcher,* etc.]; dictionaries [*The Oxford English Dictionary,* etc.]) cannot usually be checked out, so you must take notes from them in the library or photocopy the materials you need and read them later. Many of these print references are also available online. Check your library's Web site for a list.

Finding Reserve Books and Journal Articles

Professors will often put a number of books and/or journal articles on reserve in the library so that all students in a particular class will have access to the materials. Reserve materials can be checked out for library use only or sometimes for overnight use. You should be able to access the reserve lists for various professors through your library's Web site. If not, ask to see the reserve lists at the checkout desk. Most online catalogs will tell you whether an item is available, checked out, or on reserve.

Finding Articles in Periodicals: Scholarly Journals, Popular Magazines, and Newspapers

Scholarly journals, popular magazines, and newspapers are typically found in three separate areas of the library. Recently published copies will be shelved in a current periodicals section. Older materials are generally found either in a separate bound periodicals section of your library, in the regular stacks, or on microfilm full-text archives. Consult your library's periodicals list, which should be available through your school's online catalog or in print form or both. This guide to periodicals will tell you which scholarly journals, magazines, and newspapers your library subscribes to, when the library began receiving the subscriptions, whether there are any gaps in the subscriptions, and whether the material you need is located in the bound section, in the regular stacks, or on microfilm full-text archives. To retrieve information about a particular scholarly journal, popular magazine, or newspaper, type the title of the periodical into the search field of your school's online catalog.

Using Reference Databases to Search for Sources

You will need to use reference databases (also called *periodical indexes*) to find materials in scholarly journals, popular magazines, newspapers, and other sources relevant to your topic. Reference databases may be in print, online, on CD-ROM, or on microform. Some online reference databases may be freely used by anyone; others may be subscription databases available only to students and faculty of the university that pays for the subscription. Some databases give only citations, but the most useful databases will give citations, abstracts (paragraph-length summaries), and full-text reprints of research materials. Check your library's Web site to see which reference databases are available to you.

> The citations you find in the various reference databases are raw materials for your MLA-style bibliography. Although the database will give you all or most of the information you need to create your MLA-style citation, the information will not be given in the same format you will be expected to use on your works-cited page. In chapter 13 you will find model citations for full-text reprints taken from online, print, CD-ROM, DVD-ROM, and microform reference databases.

Using a Personal Subscription Database such as *InfoTrac® College Edition* to Search for Sources

InfoTrac College Edition, a typical personal subscription reference database, gives users access to full-text articles from the *New York Times* and from over six thousand scholarly journals and popular magazines. Your

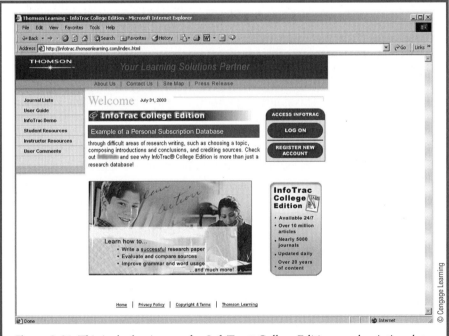

Figure 3.01 This is the log-in page for *InfoTrac® College Edition*, a subscription database. It tells that the database indexes articles from thousands of journals and that it is updated daily.

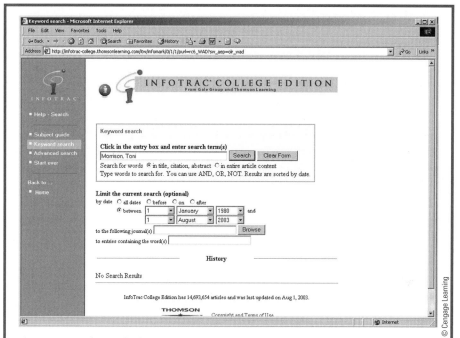

Figure 3.02 This is the basic search page of *InfoTrac College Edition*, a subscription database. Try an advanced search if you want to limit the number of sources retrieved or if you want to look only at sources related to a specific aspect of your topic.

instructor can order free subscriptions for you and your classmates to reference databases such as *InfoTrac College Edition* bundled with this or other Wadsworth-Cengage texts.

Let's suppose you have decided to write your paper on Toni Morrison's novel *Beloved*. Simply typing the author's name into the search box will retrieve several hundred journal and newspaper articles in which the works of Toni Morrison are discussed.

If you move to the advanced search screen of the database and use the pull-down menu, you can limit your search so that the database will retrieve only articles related to

Subject: *Toni Morrison*
Keyword: *Beloved*
only full-text articles
only articles published in refereed (peer-reviewed) journals
only articles published between specified dates (such as the last five years)
only articles published in the journals specified

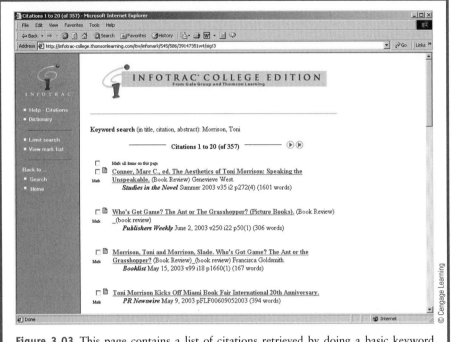

Figure 3.03 This page contains a list of citations retrieved by doing a basic keyword search for articles related to Toni Morrison using *InfoTrac College Edition*.

The database might retrieve a citation such as this:

"From the Seen to the Told": the construction of subjectivity in Toni Morrison's Beloved. (Critical Essay) Jeanna Fuston-White.

African American Review Fall 2002 v36 i3 p461(13) (8155 words)

The citation on the database screen (or on the printout if you print the screen) gives you all the information you need to format your MLA-style citation for this scholarly journal article if you should decide to quote, paraphrase, or summarize material from it in your paper.

The critical essay entitled " 'From the Seen to the Told': The Construction of Subjectivity in Toni Morrison's *Beloved*" (now formatted according to MLA guidelines) written by Jeanna Fuston-White was published in volume 36, issue 3, of *African American Review* in Fall 2002. The article began on page 461 and was 13 pages long, so it ended on page 473. Note that the quotation that is used as the title of the article is formatted in single quotation marks typed inside the double quotation marks in which the entire journal article is formatted. Note also that the title of Morrison's novel *Beloved* is italicized in the title of the journal article.

Your citation based on the above information would look like this:

Fuston-White, Jeanna. "'From the Seen to the Told': The Con-

    struction of Subjectivity in Toni Morrison's *Beloved*."

    African American Review 36.3 (2002): 461-73. *InfoTrac*

    College Edition. Web. 14 Aug. 2010.

See chapter 13 for a full discussion of citing materials accessed from personal and library subscription databases.

Using Online Library Subscription Databases to Search for Sources

Your library pays a fee to allow students and faculty access to a number of online subscription reference databases provided by services such as Info-Trac College Edition, EBSCOhost, and LexisNexis. These databases give bibliographical citations, abstracts (brief summaries), and full-text versions of millions of articles from scholarly journals, popular magazines, news-papers, books, dictionaries, encyclopedias, almanacs, subject-specific refer-ence books, and other valuable sources. These databases can be searched from a computer in the library or from your dormitory room or home as long as you have the appropriate passwords to prove that you are a student, faculty member, or staff member of the subscribing university. Ask your librarian how to access the subscription databases from computers outside the library. Some databases may be accessible only through a library computer.

Each reference database you use may offer different search options, so be sure to follow the directions the database search screens give you to learn how to perform a successful search. Be aware also that search pages for sub-scription databases can be set up differently at various libraries. If you have trouble searching a particular database, ask a librarian to help you.

Using *InfoTrac*® *OneFile* to Search for Sources

Let's suppose you want to find scholarly journal articles analyzing the works of William Faulkner and you decide to use the online library subscription database *InfoTrac OneFile* to begin your search. You might begin by pulling up the advanced search screen in the database and selecting *Subject* from the pull-down menu beside the first search box (because you want to search for materials written about William Faulkner, not materials written by William

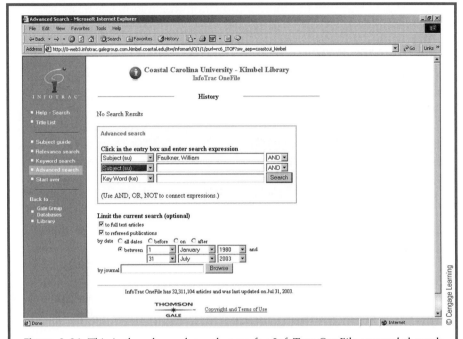

Figure 3.04 This is the advanced search page for *InfoTrac OneFile* accessed through Kimbel Library at Coastal Carolina University. The page is set to do a subject search for articles related to William Faulkner. The search is limited to full-text articles published between specified dates in refereed (peer-reviewed) journals.

Faulkner). Type *Faulkner, William* or *William Faulkner* into the search box beside the word *Subject*. Click on Search, and you should retrieve several hundred bibliographic citations relating to Faulkner.

Since scholarly journals publish book reviews as well as critical analyses, consider using the Boolean operator *NOT* to eliminate book reviews from the citation list the database retrieves. Simply select *NOT* from the pull-down menu next to *William Faulkner*, and type *book reviews* in the next search box. This time you will retrieve roughly one hundred fewer citations related to Faulkner. Or you can narrow your search even more by using a keyword from the title of one of Faulkner's short stories or novels to search just for articles relating to a particular work by Faulkner. If you search for

Subject: *Faulkner, William* or *William Faulkner* (Either way is fine.)

Keyword: *fury*

NOT: *book reviews*

you should get a list of twenty or more critical articles related to Faulkner's novel *The Sound and the Fury*.

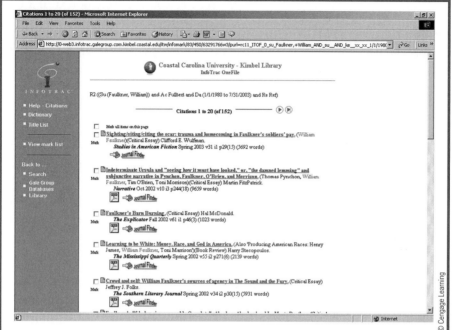

Figure 3.05 This page from *InfoTrac OneFile* displays the first twenty citations retrieved by doing a subject search for full-text articles related to William Faulkner published in refereed journals between specified dates. The third citation listed is a critical essay written by Hal McDonald entitled "Faulkner's 'Barn Burning.'" It was published in Fall 2002 in *The Explicator*, volume 61, issue 1. The article begins on page 46 of the journal and is three pages long, so it ends on page 48. The database offers a full-text HTML printout or a full-text PDF printout of this article.

You might also want to limit your search to

only full-text articles—only citations for articles available for full-text printout will be displayed

refereed—only articles published in peer-reviewed journals or magazines will be displayed

You can also limit your search to articles published in a single scholarly journal during a particular range of dates or to articles published in a selected group of journals during a specified range of dates.

If you already know the author and the title of the journal article you are looking for, you can do an author and a title search. And if you know the journal in which the article was published and the date of publication, you can limit your search by journal and date of publication as well as by author and title.

Beside each journal citation you might see the icon of a page of text. If a C (for *citation only*) appears inside the page icon, the database provides only a citation for that article. If an *A* (for *abstract only*) appears inside the page icon, the database provides only an abstract (brief summary) of the article. If no *C* or *A* appears inside the page icon, a full-text HTML version of the article can be displayed on your computer screen and read there, downloaded to your hard drive or to a disk, or printed. If you are using a library computer, you can e-mail the article to yourself and download or print it at home. If you e-mail the article, be sure to copy all the information you need for your works-cited entry into your preliminary bibliography before you move on to another article because you will not find all the information you need for your citation on the e-mailed version.

If the subscription database offers the option of printing a PDF (Portable Document Format) version of the document using Adobe® Reader®, you will see a page icon with *PDF* inside it underneath or beside the citation. If you choose this option, you can print the material exactly as it appears in the scholarly journal or other source. A PDF printout allows you to cite the exact pages of the original source in your parenthetical citations. (Information about downloading the latest version of Adobe Reader may be found at <http://www.adobe.com/products/acrobat/readstep2.html>.)

When you opt for the PDF printout of the article, the bibliographic citation for the article—which gives the name of the journal the article appeared in and the volume number, the issue number, the year of publication, and the inclusive page numbers of the article—and the name of the subscription database (*Info-Trac OneFile*) used to access the article will not appear on your printout, so be sure you have copied all the information required for your works-cited entry into your working bibliography before you leave the database screen. Print a copy of the page containing the citation information and attach it to your PDF printout so that you will be able to check the accuracy of the information in your citation when you are typing the final draft of your works-cited list.

Online Reference Databases: A Few to Consider

- *Academic Search Elite*—gives citations, abstracts, and some full-text reprints of articles from scholarly journals, popular magazines, newspapers, and other sources in the areas of social issues, science, business, humanities, literature, education, and others; an EBSCOhost database (*EBSCO* is an acronym for Elton B. Stephens Company. Do not spell out *EBSCO* when you cite from this database.)
- *America: History and Life*—gives citations and abstracts of articles published since 1964 in scholarly journals and books on topics relating to American and Canadian history from prehistory to modern times; no full-text reprints

- *Biography Resource Center/Complete Marquis Who's Who*—use to find full-text biographical sketches from Gale Group references and full-text biographical articles from periodicals; a Gale Group database

- *Books in Print*—gives information about books both in and out of print; may be searched by author, title, subject, publisher, publication date, or ISBN

- *Business NewsBank*—gives citations, abstracts, and full-text reprints of articles related to business (company performance analyses, etc.) published in newspapers, journals, trade publications, and broker research reports

- *Contemporary Authors*—biographical and bibliographical information on thousands of authors; an InfoTrac database

- *Contemporary Literary Criticism–Select*—gives biographical information and excerpts from literary criticism on contemporary authors taken from refereed scholarly journals and books; a Gale Group database

- *Custom Newspapers*—use to find recent articles in the *New York Times* and regional newspapers selected by individual libraries; an InfoTrac database

- *CQ Researcher* (*Congressional Quarterly Researcher*)—gives full-text reprints of articles on current events and social issues

- *DISCovering Authors*—gives citations, abstracts, and full-text articles about authors from scholarly journals, popular magazines, and subject-specific references such as *Dictionary of Literary Biography;* a Gale Group database

- *Electric Library* (*e-Library*)—gives citations and full-text reprints of articles from scholarly journals, magazines, newspapers, and books on current events, social issues, popular culture, and other areas

- *E*Subscribe*—use to access full-text reprints of *ERIC* (*Educational Resources Information Center*) documents related to the various fields of education

- *Expanded Academic ASAP*—gives citations, abstracts, and many full-text reprints of articles published in scholarly journals, popular magazines, and newspapers in fields such as literature, history, science, sociology, psychology, and anthropology (*ASAP* is an acronym for As Soon As Possible and is included in the names of a number of InfoTrac databases. Do not spell *ASAP* out when citing material from this database.)

- *Facts on File World News Archive*—use to find information related to historical events, people of historical significance, profiles of countries, and other world news issues from 1950 to 1979

- *Facts on File World News Digest*—use to find information related to current events, historical events, people of historical significance, profiles of countries, and other world news issues from 1980 to the present

- *General BusinessFile ASAP*—use to access company directory listings, broker research reports, business trade publications, and journal and newspaper articles related to business issues (finance, accounting, real estate, etc.); includes *Business Index* (indexes business-related magazines and journals), *Company Profiles* (gives information on thousands of companies), and *Investext* (full-text financial analyst reports) (*ASAP* is an acronym for As Soon As Possible. Do not write out *ASAP* when citing this InfoTrac database.)

- *General Reference Center*—gives citations, abstracts, and many full-text reprints of articles about current events, popular culture, sports, the arts, and the sciences from popular magazines, newspapers, and reference books; an InfoTrac database

- *Health Reference Center Academic*—gives citations, abstracts, and some full-text reprints of articles published in scholarly journals, popular magazines, and pamphlets in the fields of health and medicine; a Gale Group database

- *Health and Wellness Resource Center*—gives citations, abstracts, and full-text reprints of articles published in scholarly journals, popular magazines, and pamphlets relating to medicine, public health, occupational safety, fitness, nutrition, pregnancy, alcohol abuse, drug abuse, diseases, prescription drugs, and other health-related issues; an InfoTrac database

- *Historical Abstracts*—gives citations and abstracts of materials published since 1954 in scholarly journals and books on topics relating to world history (not including American and Canadian history); no full-text reprints

- *H. W. Wilson Select*—gives citations, abstracts, and some full-text reprints of articles from scholarly journals and popular magazines in numerous areas

- *InfoTrac OneFile*—searches all InfoTrac databases and gives citations, abstracts, and full-text reprints of articles from scholarly journals, popular magazines, and newspapers relating to literature, art, current events, education, health care, science, technology, sports, law, education, business, history, and many other areas

- *JSTOR*—gives full-text reprints of articles from scholarly journals related to anthropology, archaeology, botany, business, classical studies, ecology, economics, education, finance, general science, geography, history, history of science, language studies, literary studies, mathematics, philosophy, political science, population studies, sociology, statistics, African American studies, African studies, Asian studies, Latin American studies, Middle East studies, and Slavic studies

- *LexisNexis Academic Universe*—indexes materials in the following areas: *News* (articles from newspapers, scholarly journals, and popular magazines); **Reference** (a world almanac, biographies of well-known people, famous quotations, polls, surveys, and profiles of states and countries); **Business** (company news and financial information); **Medical** (information about health issues and medical research); **Legal Research** (state, federal, and international law; case law; information relating to patents; and legal career information)

- **LegalTrac**—use to find articles from law reviews and journals, specialty law and bar association journals, and legal newspapers related to state and federal legal cases, laws, and regulations; includes materials related to British Commonwealth, European Union, and international law; an InfoTrac database

- **Literature Resource Center**—gives full-text biographical information and critical evaluations of the works of thousands of authors; a Gale Group database

- **MagillOnLiterature**—use to access plot summaries, analyses of literary works, and other materials related to literary works and authors; an EBSCOhost database

- **MasterFILE Premier**—gives citations, abstracts, and some full-text reprints of articles from scholarly journals, popular magazines, newspapers, and other sources in the areas of business, education, the humanities, literary studies, the sciences, social issues, and other areas; an EBSCOhost database (*EBSCO* is an acronym for Elton B. Stephens Company. Do not spell out *EBSCO* when you cite from this database.)

- **MLA International Bibliography**—gives citations for scholarly journal articles and books in literature and linguistics; no full-text reprints (*MLA* is an acronym for Modern Language Association. You may use *MLA* when citing this database.)

- **NewsBank NewsFile Collection**—gives full-text reprints of articles published in American newspapers (Older reprints may be available on microfiche.)

- **Oceanic Abstracts**—gives citations and abstracts of articles in scholarly journals in oceanography and marine science; no full-text reprints

- **Opposing Viewpoints Resource Center**—use to access articles and primary documents related to social issues; includes links to full-text articles in popular magazines and newspapers and links to Web sites related to social issues

- **Project Muse**—gives full-text articles from scholarly journals in the humanities, the social sciences, and mathematics

- **ProQuest Direct**—gives citations and full-text reprints from scholarly journals, popular magazines, newspapers, and other sources related to a variety of vocational and technical subjects such as agriculture, computing, education, electronics, food service, health, hotel management, the military, nursing, office systems, public safety, and security

■ *ProQuest Literature Online*—gives full texts of literary works dating from AD 600 to the present, searchable dictionaries and encyclopedias of literary terms, and links to relevant literary Web sites

■ *ProQuest Newspapers*—gives full-text articles from more than three hundred American and international newspapers, including the *New York Times,* the *Los Angeles Times,* the *New York Daily News,* and the *Times* [London]

■ *PsychINFO*—gives bibliographic citations and abstracts (brief summaries) of scholarly journal articles, technical reports, dissertations, book chapters, and books on topics relating to psychology

■ *SIRS Knowledge Source*—gives citations and full-text reprints of articles published in scholarly journals, popular magazines, and newspapers; includes *SIRS Researcher*—full-text articles related to current events and social issues; *SIRS Government Reporter*—full-text historical documents and information by and about the U.S. government and its agencies; and *SIRS Renaissance*—full-text articles related to the arts, literature, and the humanities (*SIRS* is an acronym for *Social Issues Resources Series.* Use *SIRS* when citing this database.)

■ *UMI Periodical Abstracts*—gives citations and abstracts of articles from scholarly journals and popular magazines; gives transcripts of television news shows (*UMI* is an acronym for University Microfilms International. Do not spell *UMI* out when citing this database.)

■ *WorldCat*—gives bibliographic citations for books and other materials located in libraries throughout the world; an excellent place to find bibliographical information that is missing or unclear in your sources

■ *World History FullTEXT*—gives full-text articles related to anthropology, art, culture, economics, the military, politics, sociology, and world history; an EBSCOhost database

Print Periodical Indexes: A Few to Consider

■ *New York Times Index*—lists articles and reviews published in the *New York Times* newspaper

■ *Readers' Guide to Periodical Literature*—gives citations for articles in popular magazines and in some scholarly journals

■ *SIRS (Social Issues Resources Series)*—a loose-leaf print collection of full-text articles reprinted from American magazines and newspapers; each volume or series of volumes covers a specific topic such as Women, AIDS, Education, and Health; for recent materials consult the online version of this database

Free Sources of Information on the Web: A Few to Consider

- *AGRICOLA (Agricultural Online Access)* <http:// www.nal.usda.gov/>—gives citations for journal articles, reports, and books dealing with agriculture and related fields

- *American Presidents.org* <http://www.americanpresidents.org>—gives profiles, video archives, and research materials related to American presidents; based on C-SPAN's *American Presidents: Life Portraits*

- *American Universities* <http://www.clas.ufl.edu/au/>—provides links to home pages of an alphabetical list of American universities

- *American Writers.org* <http://www.americanwriters.org>—gives profiles, video archives, and research materials related to twentieth-century American writers; based on C-SPAN's *American Writers II: The 20th Century*

- *ERIC (Educational Resources Information Center)* <http:// eric.ed.gov>—provides access to bibliographic citations and abstracts for a variety of documents related to the various fields of education; gives citations and abstracts for articles published in scholarly journals in the fields of education, including teacher education, vocational education, adult education, language and linguistics education, and many other areas; full-text reprints of *ERIC* documents (*ED* followed by a six-digit identification number) are available in electronic form through *E*Subscribe,* an online library subscription service available at some libraries, on microfiche in some libraries, or in print form by request from *EDRS (ERIC Document Reproduction Service)* <http://www.edrs.com>; scholarly journal articles indexed by *ERIC* (*EJ* followed by a six-digit identification number) may be found in print journals owned by libraries, may be obtained through interlibrary loans, or may be purchased from reprint companies such as Ingenta <http://www.ingenta.com> or Institute for Scientific Information (ISI) <http://isidoc.com>

- *Federal Citizen Information Center* <http://www.info.gov>—a service provided by the Federal Citizen Information Center of the General Services Administration (GSA) for locating information related to the federal government and to consumer issues

- *Federal Web Locator* <http://www.infoctr.edu/fwl/>—useful for locating the Web sites of federal agencies

- *GPO Access (Government Printing Office Access)* <http:// www.access.gpo.gov>—use to access numerous databases to search for government documents

- *HighWire Press (HighWire Library of the Sciences and Medicine)* <http://highwire.stanford.edu>—offers free access to thousands of full-text journal articles in the biological, medical, physical, and social sciences
- *Internet Public Library* <http://www.ipl.org>—provides links to the Web sites of newspapers, journals, magazines, books, encyclopedias, dictionaries, and numerous other items of interest; sponsored by the University of Michigan
- *Internet Public Library: Literary Criticism* <http://www.ipl.org/div/litcrit>—provides links to literary criticism and author Web sites; searchable by names of authors, titles of works, and literary periods
- *Lakewood Public Library's Selection of Ready Reference Web Sites* <http://www.lkwdpl.org/readyref/>—provides links to a variety of Web sites relating to philosophy, psychology, religion, social sciences, languages, natural sciences, mathematics, technology, the arts, literature, rhetoric, geography, history, and others
- *LibraryHQ Site Source* <http://www.libraryhq.com/>—provides a searchable database of useful Web sites
- *Library of Congress* <http://www.loc.gov>—gives bibliographical information on every book and periodical published in the United States; an excellent place to find bibliographical information that is missing or unclear in your sources; provides links to *THOMAS* and other useful sites
- *NewsDirectory.com* <http://www.newsdirectory.com>—gives links to American newspapers by state and to international newspapers by country; gives links to magazines, television stations, universities, and governmental agencies
- *PubMed* <http://www.ncbi.nlm.nih.gov/PubMed/>—gives citations and abstracts for journals and books in medicine and related fields
- *THOMAS: Legislative Information on the Internet* <http://thomas.loc.gov>—use to locate historical documents and information related to all aspects of the federal government; named for Thomas Jefferson
- *Winsor School's Ready-Reference Using the Internet* <http://www.winsor.edu/academics/library_search.aspx>—gives links to information on a variety of topics organized from *A* to *Z;* maintained by the Winsor School, Boston

Newspaper Web Sites

Atlanta Journal-Constitution	<http://www.ajc.com>
Boston Globe	<http://www.boston.com/globe>
Chicago Sun-Times	<http://www.suntimes.com>

Chicago Tribune	<http://www.chicagotribune.com>
Christian Science Monitor	<http://www.csmonitor.com>
Daily Mirror [UK]	<http://www.mirror.co.uk>
Los Angeles Daily News	<http://www.dailynews.com>
Los Angeles Times	<http://www.latimes.com>
Miami Herald	<http://www.miamiherald.com>
New York Daily News	<http://www.nydailynews.com>
New York Times	<http://www.nytimes.com>
Times [London]	<http://www.timesonline.co.uk>
USA Today	<http://www.usatoday.com>
Village Voice	<http://www.villagevoice.com>
Wall Street Journal	<http://www.wsj.com>
Washington Post	<http://www.washingtonpost.com>

Magazine Web Sites

Entertainment Weekly	<http://www.ew.com>
Nation	<http://www.thenation.com>
New Yorker	<http://www.newyorker.com>
Newsweek	<http://www.newsweek.com>
People Weekly	<http://people.aol.com>
Prevention	<http://www.prevention.com>
Psychology Today	<http://www.psychologytoday.com>
Time	<http://www.time.com>
U.S. News & World Report	<http://www.usnews.com>

Television Web Sites

ABC News	<http://www.abcnews.go.com>
Arts and Entertainment Channel	<http://www.aetv.com>
BBC News	<http://bbc.co.uk>
Biography Channel	<http://www.biography.com>
CBS News	<http://www.cbsnews.com>
CNN	<http://www.cnn.com>
C-SPAN	<http://www.c-span.org>
Discovery Channel	<http://www.discovery.com>
Fox News	<http://www.foxnews.com>

History Channel	<http://www.historychannel.com>
Learning Channel	<http://www.tlc.discovery.com>
NBC News	<http://www.msnbc.com>
Public Broadcasting System	<http://www.pbs.org>

Radio Web Sites

KFI/Los Angeles	<http://www.kfi640.com>
National Public Radio	<http://www.npr.org>
NewsRadio 610/Miami	<http://www.newsradio610.com>
NewsRadio 1290/W. Palm Beach	<http://www.wjno.com>
WABC/New York	<http://www.wabcradio.com>

Finding Additional Sources Available in Most Libraries

You will also find rare books, government publications, pamphlet files, and audiovisual materials of various types in most libraries. Ask a librarian where these materials are located.

Considering an Interlibrary Loan

If your library does not own a book, pamphlet, government document, scholarly journal, magazine, or newspaper article you need and if the material cannot be accessed through the full-text reference databases, ask a librarian how to request the item from another library through an interlibrary loan.

Searching for Sources on the Internet

The World Wide Web is a giant network of hypertext connections to literally millions of electronic sites featuring texts, graphics, and sounds. Using a Web browser (such as Netscape Navigator or Microsoft Internet Explorer) and a search engine that indexes Web sites (such as Yahoo!, Google, or AltaVista), try a keyword search. Many search engines can be accessed by typing <http://www.nameofsearchengine.com> into the dialog box at the top of your Web browser screen and pressing Enter. Meta search engines, such as 37.com, search for materials using multiple search engines, remove duplicate listings, and generally identify the search engine from which a particular listing was retrieved. Different search engines will give you different results, so if you don't find the information you're looking for by using one search engine, try another. Additional information about search engines may be found at <http://searchengineguide.com> or <http://searchenginewatch.org>.

Electronic Addresses for Search Engines

Listed below are the URLs for some of the most popular search and meta search engines:

<http://www.yahoo.com>   <http://www.northernlight.com>
<http://www.google.com>   <http://dmoz.com>
<http://www.altavista.com>   <http://hotbot.com>
<http://www.askjeeves.com>   <http://www.dogpile.com>
<http://www.excite.com>   <http://www.37.com>
<http://www.webcrawler.com>   <http://www.search.com>
<http://www.lycos.com>   <http://www.megaweb.com>
<http://www.teoma.com>   <http://www.botbot.com>
<http://www.alltheweb.com>   <http://www.metaspider.com>
<http://www.go.com>

Angle brackets < > typed around an electronic address mean that all the characters typed between them should be considered a single unit with no spaces between the characters. If you accidentally type a space or mistype a character in a Web address, your browser will not find the address. Do not type the angle brackets into the search field of your Web browser or search engine.

The search engine's **Help** menu will give you timesaving tips on searching effectively. Be as specific as possible when doing a keyword search; otherwise, you will access numerous irrelevant sites and waste time. Even better is an exact-phrase search. Type quotation marks around a phrase you wish to find information on (for example, *female body image*). If you make a mistake, the search engine screen will give you advice about what to do to make your search more effective.

Using Boolean Operators: *AND, OR, NOT, NEAR*

Use the Boolean operators *AND, OR, NOT,* or *NEAR* to link words in a search. When you link terms with *AND* (*anorexia AND bulimia*), both terms must be present in the title for a successful hit; therefore, you are narrowing your search. Terms linked with *OR* (*anorexia OR bulimia*) will expand your search to include titles containing both or just one of the terms you have listed. Use *NOT* to eliminate any documents that contain the word typed after *NOT* (*anorexia NOT bulimia*). Some search engines allow you to use the word *NEAR* to locate documents in which two key terms appear close together. The plus and minus signs are generally equivalent to the terms *AND* and *NOT* (*anorexia + bulimia; anorexia − bulimia*).

Using Wild Cards or Truncation Symbols in a Search

Be sure to check the **Help** menu of whatever search engine you are using to see what types of operators and truncation symbols it requires. Also bear in mind that truncation symbols may only work in advanced searches. Your search engine may allow you to use an asterisk * to locate documents containing words beginning with specified letters. For example, *trou** would find documents whose titles contain words such as *troubadour, troupe, trousseau,* and *trout.* The asterisk is also useful for finding sources with non-American spellings in their titles (for example, *hon*r* should give you *honor* and *honour; Ka*mir* should give you *Kazmir* and *Kashmir*).

If you can't remember how to spell a keyword or an author's name, your search engine may allow you to type a question mark (*?*) or some other symbol, such as a dollar sign (*$*), in place of the letters you're unsure of. Thus *Brown?* should give you citations for *Brown, Browne,* and *Browning,* among others.

Don't forget to bookmark useful sites so that you can easily find them again. Bear in mind when surfing the Net that a site you find on Monday may be unavailable by Tuesday or the materials on the site may have been revised or updated. Therefore, to be safe, print a hard copy of any material you think will provide useful information. Add the appropriate MLA-style citation for each site you believe will be useful to your working bibliography while you have the material on your computer screen so that you can be sure you have all the information you will need if you decide later to quote, paraphrase, or summarize material from that site.

Bear in mind also that some Internet sites, such as e-mail discussion groups and online chat rooms, may not provide the type of information you would want to cite in a research paper, although they might provide useful links to more appropriate sources.

Evaluating Research Sources

My grandmother always believed everything she read in the local newspaper. She was sure that if something had been printed in a newspaper published in her hometown, it just had to be true. But if you walked into your local grocery store and saw a headline in a tabloid newspaper reading "Julia Roberts Abducted by Aliens," would you believe the article just because it was in print? You're intelligent enough to know that some disreputable newspapers make huge profits by printing exaggerations, half-truths, and just plain lies—hoping nobody will bother to sue them.

Let the Researcher Beware

The famous axiom *caveat emptor* means "let the buyer beware." A good rule of thumb in writing research papers is "Believe nothing you hear and only half of what you read."

One of your most important jobs as a researcher is to evaluate the material you read and to determine what is reliable information worthy to be quoted, paraphrased, or summarized in your paper and what is outdated, biased, or downright incorrect.

Print Sources versus Internet Sources

Before a scholarly book or textbook is published by a reputable publisher, it has typically been read and evaluated by expert consultants (called *peer reviewers*) who have assured the publisher that the material in the book is current, well researched, and reliable. Articles appearing in scholarly journals go through a similar rigorous peer-review process and normally will not be published unless they meet the high standards of the editorial staff of the journal. **Journals that publish only materials that have been evaluated by experts are called *refereed journals.*** Professional editors review articles written for popular magazines, newsmagazines, and newspapers, verifying the accuracy of the information presented and making sure that libelous information is not published.

On the other hand, anyone from a reputable scholar to a Web-savvy third grader can publish anything on the Internet. Information presented as part of a scholarly Web site maintained by expert researchers on the staff of a reputable university might prove more current than any information to be found in books or journals published on the same topic. Many authors maintain Web sites so that their readers can constantly access updated information on a particular subject. You might find excellent research materials in an online, peer-reviewed (refereed) scholarly journal. But you might also find online magazines and journals that publish any material submitted to them regardless of its accuracy or bias. You can find extremely liberal online magazines as well as extremely conservative magazines and just about anything in between.

Evaluating Print Sources

If a scholarly book has been published by a reputable publishing house, odds are good that it is a reliable source. But then again, not much in life is certain. If you are not sure about whether you should use information from a particular book, evaluate it using the print or online versions of *Book*

Review Index or *Book Review Digest.* Through these sources you can get a feel for the consensus among expert reviewers on the validity of the ideas presented in the book.

If an article has been published in a peer-reviewed (refereed) scholarly journal, you can be relatively sure that it contains reliable information. But always use your common sense to weigh what you are reading against what you are finding in your other sources. If the ideas in one article seem to contradict information in many of your other sources, consider discussing the source with your professor before you use information from it as the basis of your paper. In the area of literary criticism, for example, there are many interpretations of various literary works. Some may ring true to you, whereas others may seem totally unreasonable or just the opposite of what you think the work means. Ultimately, you must decide what information from your sources is valid enough to be incorporated into your paper.

Evaluating Internet Sources

Ask yourself the following questions when you are evaluating any source, but especially an Internet source:

(1) Author's credentials

- Who wrote this information, and what are this writer's credentials?
- Is the writer a child or an adult, a student or a professional researcher?
- What is the writer's position or title?
- For whom does this writer work?
- To whom is this writer loyal?
- What is this writer's purpose in making this information available on the Web?
- Does the site include an e-mail or postal address so that you can contact the author and ask questions?
- Is the author of this site trying to persuade you to buy something, to donate money to a particular organization, or to change your thinking or behavior in some way that would benefit the writer or the organization for which he or she works?
- Does the writer have a bias? For example, is the author a distinguished professor currently teaching political science courses at Harvard University who has published numerous scholarly journal articles and books on the Vietnam War? Or is the writer a veteran of the Vietnam War whose life was forever changed when he stepped on a mine that blew his legs off? Although the war veteran might have firsthand knowledge of certain events, might his version of the reality of the war be biased by his tragic experiences?

- Is the author presenting an unbiased, objective account of events? Or does this writer have a personal, political, or commercial agenda? Is the author's bias cleverly hidden or clearly obvious?

If no author is given, you have no way to evaluate the credentials or credibility of the writer. Think twice about citing information from such a site. And remember that students are not yet experts. Do not quote from student papers published on the Internet unless they have been published in refereed journals or unless you have your instructor's permission to do so.

(2) Timeliness

- How current is this information?
- When was this Web site created?
- When was the information it contains last updated?
- Could new information have been discovered since this Web site was updated?

In many fields, what is true on Monday has been disproved by Friday. If you are researching a scientific, medical, business, or technological topic, you should be careful to use the most current information available to you.

Even in the field of literary analysis, ideas about authors and interpretations of their works change. Although a critical interpretation of Prince Hamlet of Denmark, Shakespeare's most famous tragic hero, might be as accurate today as when it was written fifty years ago, in other cases, opinions and interpretations once accepted now seem outdated or absurd. For example, when Herman Melville first published *Moby Dick,* one reviewer described the book as "trash." Today Melville is considered a brilliant symbolist, and *Moby Dick* is considered one of the greatest American novels.

Because critical opinions of both authors and literary works change from decade to decade, you might want to think twice about quoting a critic who wrote his or her opinions fifty years ago unless you are certain that the critic's ideas are still valid and current.

(3) Credibility

- Can the information on the Web site be verified?
- Is there a list of works cited or consulted so that you can evaluate the sources from which the author took his or her information?
- Does the site include hypertext links to other sources through which the information presented on the site can be verified and additional information on the subject can be found?

Note the Last Two or Three Letters of the Domain Name in the Web Address

.com	a commercial site
.edu	an educational site
.gov	a county, state, or federal government site
.org	a nonprofit organization site
.mil	a military site
.net	a network management site
.au	an Australian site
.ca	a Canadian site
.uk	a British site

Commercial Sites: .com

Information found on commercial sites may be reliable or may simply be designed to sell you the goods that can be ordered through the site.

On amazon.com, for example, you can access not only information about the availability and price of a book, CD, or videotaped movie you might wish to purchase but also reviews written by Internet surfers just like you who have read the book, listened to the CD, or seen the movie. However, are the reviews you are reading as authoritative as a book review published in the *New York Times Book Review*, a CD review written by a professional columnist for *Musician Magazine* or *Rolling Stone,* or a movie review written by Roger Ebert for publication in the *Chicago Sun-Times* or *Roger Ebert's Movie Home Companion?*

Who wrote what you're reading? Is the author an expert on this subject? You'd be better advised to quote from well-known movie critic Roger Ebert's analysis than from an analysis written by a fellow Internet surfer who might be a professional house painter who enjoys watching movies in his spare time.

On the other hand, you can find highly useful information on reputable commercial sites such as those maintained by well-known magazines such as *Time* and *Newsweek* or by prestigious newspapers such as the *New York Times,* the *Los Angeles Times,* and the *Washington Post.*

Educational Sites: .edu

On educational sites, you might find scholarly projects created by knowledgeable professors who have published extensively in their fields of expertise and will provide you with highly reliable research materials.

Professors often maintain Web sites to keep students in a particular class informed about assignments and due dates for papers. They often post model papers written by themselves, by graduate assistants, or by former students to their Web sites to help their current students better understand what is expected in the papers they are writing for the class.

Don't assume, however, that professors post only excellent work on their Web pages. Many professors believe students learn how to write a good paper more effectively if they study flawed model papers. Thus, professors are just as likely to post examples of what not to do in a good paper as to post examples of ideal papers. If you're not hearing the class discussions, can you tell the difference between an ideal model paper and one that would have received a low or failing grade? Are you sure?

You might also be accessing a site created by a first-year graduate student instructor rather than by an experienced graduate instructor or professor.

Because anyone—even a child—can create a personal page on the Internet, you might be accessing a Web page created by a student as part of a class project or just for the fun of the experience. Can you tell if the information you're reading was posted by a senior marine science major who has done extensive research on water quality in local marshes or by a student in grammar, middle, or high school who is discussing a class assignment with classmates through the Internet?

Carefully evaluate the information you're reading before accepting it as reliable.

Government Sites: .gov

Information taken from sites maintained by city, county, state, or federal agencies is likely to be current, well researched, and highly reliable, but as always, compare what you are reading with information you are finding in your other sources and double-check anything that does not seem credible.

Nonprofit Organization Sites: .org

Does the organization sponsoring this site have a political agenda?

If you are reading information posted on the Web site of the National Rifle Association, an organization adamantly opposed to gun regulation, can you expect to find a fair representation of the position of those who favor gun regulations? Or if you are reading information posted on a site sponsored by PETA (People for the Ethical Treatment of Animals), would you expect the authors to support the use of live animals in scientific research? Does this site present information fairly and objectively? Does it present all sides of the issues under discussion?

A Source Evaluation Checklist

Look for the following indicators of an unreliable Web site:

- No author is identified. Therefore, you have no way of checking the credentials or possible biases of the writer.
- The author is a student. Students are not yet experts in their fields of study. Do not quote from student papers; quote from the work of experts.
- There is no evidence that the information presented has been reviewed and established as reliable by some sort of peer-review process. (The material has not been refereed.)
- You notice errors of fact. When you are doing research, you will see some basic information repeated from source to source, whereas other information will be specific to one particular source. If the source you are reading does not correctly present the information you know to be true, it is reasonable to assume that the new information on this site may be unreliable.
- The material on the Web page has not been recently updated and may not reflect the most current information available on the subject.
- The author's statements are not supported by convincing evidence or specific details.
- Opposing viewpoints are not acknowledged or addressed.
- The writer's tone is highly emotional (angry, spiteful, clearly biased) rather than calm and reasonable.
- The information presented seems exaggerated.
- No sources or hypertext links are given, so you have no way of checking the accuracy of the information or statistics presented on the site. For all you know, the author could be exaggerating or distorting the information or statistics.
- The writing on the Web site is sloppy. Sentences may be unclear or awkward. You notice misspelled words, incorrect grammar, and punctuation errors. Educated writers tend to be conscientious enough to revise awkward or unclear sentences and to check the accuracy of their spelling, grammar, and punctuation. If a writer has not bothered to check these aspects of the writing, how likely is it that he or she has checked the accuracy of the facts and opinions presented on the site?

Taking Notes

Copy directly quoted material exactly as it will appear in your paper if you decide to use it. Copy it in quotation marks with brackets used to specify any clarifications or changes you made in the text and with ellipses used to indicate any omissions not already obvious to your reader.

Photocopy or print as much as possible of the material you will read so you can annotate what you read and so you will have your sources available to check the accuracy of your quotations, paraphrases, and summaries as you incorporate them into the text of your first or later drafts.

Suppose you find a book or scholarly journal article you believe will contain just the information you need to incorporate into your paper. Photocopy the relevant pages in the book or article so that you can take them home, write sidebar annotations on them, and highlight useful information.

> Do not write on material that belongs to the library. Do not tear pages from materials that belong to the library. Be considerate of the needs of others who will need access to the materials you are using.

Just in case the title, author, or page numbers are cut off the pages when you photocopy from a source, write the bibliographical citation for the source on the first page of your photocopy before you allow the original version to leave your hands.

The most important thing to remember when you take notes from your sources is that you must clearly distinguish between quoted, paraphrased, and summarized material that must be documented in your paper and ideas that do not require documentation because they are considered general knowledge about that subject. As you do your research, you will also have original ideas about the subject that you will want to remember later when you write your first draft. Keep a list of your own ideas handwritten on note cards or on sheets of paper, or type them into your computer so that you can cut and paste them later.

In the margin beside each piece of information you write, type, or download into your notes, write or type some sort of letter, symbol, or word that will tell you later whether the material recorded there is

- a direct quotation (DQ)
- a paraphrase (P)
- a summary (S)
- general knowledge information (G)
- or your own original idea (MINE, or type angle brackets around your own ideas)

When you are ready to begin taking notes from your sources, sit down at your computer and type the bibliographic citation for that particular source onto the top of your page. As you read, type the page number from your source at the left margin so you will know later exactly what page in the source you took the notes from. When you have finished taking notes on that source, number and print the pages (just in case the hard drive on your computer or your backup disk fails before your paper is turned in). Always print out your work to be safe. Then clip your notes to the top of your photocopy or printout of the original materials. Later, when you are writing your first draft, your photocopy or printout will allow you to check the accuracy of your quotations, paraphrases, and summaries by comparing what you have written to the material in your original sources.

Typing or downloading materials you might want to quote, paraphrase, or summarize later into your computerized notes as you do your research will also allow you to cut and paste later, saving you the time it would take to retype handwritten materials from sheets of paper or note cards.

CHAPTER 4

Writing and Revising Your Paper

Writing the Paper

Read through all your notes right before you begin your rough draft so that the material will be fresh in your memory, and highlight things you might want to incorporate into your text. If you have kept a separate list of ideas that came to you as you did your research, those ideas will be the most important ideas expressed in your paper.

Avoid using an excessive number of quotations, paraphrases, and summaries in your paper. Although there is no hard-and-fast rule on this, two or three citations per page of text should be about right. Most of the paper should be your own analysis of the subject expressed in your own words.

Preparing a Final Outline for Your Paper

If your professor requires you to turn in an outline with your paper, simply convert your working outline into the format required by your professor.

Preparing a Topic Outline

A topic outline consists of parallel words or phrases and usually follows a format such as the one described here. Generally, if you have an A in such an outline, you should also have a B, and so on.

Caitlin Crawford-Lamb

Dr. Nelljean Rice

English 150: 10:00 TTH

15 April 2010

Title: Finding Shelter in the Storm: The Turbulent Influence of Society on the Body Image of Adolescent Girls

Thesis: Adolescent females are becoming more and more obsessed with body image issues, an obsession that often leads to emotional instability and eating disorders such as anorexia and bulimia.

   I. Definition of body image

      A. Healthy body image

      B. Unhealthy body image

  II. Societal influences on body image

      A. External influences

         1. Female gender role

            a. Overfeminized role

            b. Beauty defining worth

         2. "Lookism"

            a. Media input

            b. Cultural input

         3. Socialization of food worth

            a. Weight as a reference point

            b. Search for emotional nourishment

      B. Peer group influences

         1. Concern over weight as a unifying force

         2. Forum to gain acceptance and support from peers

 III. Physical consequences of unhealthy body image

      A. Anorexia nervosa

      B. Bulimia

Preparing a Sentence Outline

A sentence outline follows the same basic format as a topic outline. Simply substitute sentences for the words or phrases used in a topic outline.

Preparing a Controlling Sentence Outline

A simple way to create a final outline is to list the thesis for the paper, the topic sentences for each paragraph, and the conclusion sentence.

Thesis

The **thesis** is the controlling sentence for the entire paper. It typically explains what you will analyze, prove, or discuss in your paper. Although in some types of writing the thesis can be implied, it is usually stated near or at the end of the first paragraph.

Topic Sentence

A **topic sentence** is the controlling sentence for a particular paragraph within the essay. In certain types of writing, paragraphs have implied topic sentences. If this is the case, simply create for your outline the topic sentences that would be there if the paragraphs had them.

Conclusion Sentence

A **conclusion sentence** is the controlling sentence of the last paragraph of your essay. Often it is the first or last sentence in your concluding paragraph. It may restate the thesis in a slightly different way, may summarize what has been said in the essay, or may emphasize a final important idea you want to leave with your reader. The conclusion sentence brings a sense of completion to your essay.

A controlling sentence outline will help you make sure

- that all the information contained in your paper supports the thesis
- that each of your paragraphs is unified (covers a single idea)
- that your essay doesn't just stop abruptly but rather has a sense of closure
- that you are presenting the information in your essay in a logical pattern

(See William Files's controlling sentence outline in chapter 7.)

Thesis Statement:

Topic Sentence for Body Paragraph 1:

Topic Sentence for Body Paragraph 2:

Topic Sentence for Body Paragraph 3:

Topic Sentence for Body Paragraph 4:

Conclusion Sentence:

Preparing Your Works-Cited Page

Delete from your working bibliography any sources that provided no useful information. Alphabetize your sources by the authors' last names or, if no author was given, by the title (excluding *A, An,* and *The*). Your works-cited list is the last page of the paper, and that page should be numbered as part of your text. Remember to double-space everything on your works-cited page.

Revising Your Paper

When you have finished your first draft, revise, revise, revise, and then revise again. Let the paper sit overnight or, better still, for a day or two so you can read it with fresh eyes to look for problems.

Remember that your professor is looking for a clear presentation of your own analysis of the subject you have researched, not just a series of direct quotations, paraphrases, and summaries cut and pasted from your sources.

Reread the assignment sheets to see if you have forgotten anything you were required to include.

If your professor listed the criteria by which your paper will be evaluated, read them again and ask yourself if you have fulfilled your professor's expectations and formatting requirements.

Although the most important aspect of any paper is what you say in it (the content), your grade will most likely suffer if what you are trying to say is not clear to your reader. Excessively long or complicated sentences and mechanical, grammatical, punctuation, spelling, and typographical errors are not only distracting but also annoying to any reader, especially to a reader as well educated as your professor. In addition, such errors suggest that you are not conscientious about your work. When you see this sort of sloppiness in a source, it immediately suggests that you may not be able to rely on the accuracy of the research being presented. You want your reader to rely on the accuracy of your research; therefore, the presentation of your research is an important aspect of your paper.

Read your paper aloud to yourself or into a tape recorder, and listen to it so you can try to spot paragraphs that seem illogically organized or sentences that need clarification.

If you are having trouble with the paper, set up an appointment for a conference with your professor.

If your university provides a writing center or lab, make use of the help to be found there. If allowed by your professor, get classmates, friends, or relatives to read the paper and give you feedback. However, be sure to inform your professor about any help you received in writing the paper.

A Revision Checklist

- Is your paper interesting? Will others enjoy reading it?
- Will your paper teach your readers something they might not have known before about this subject, or are you just rehashing well-known information?
- Have you clearly stated or implied the thesis (main point/controlling idea) of your paper?
- Have you given enough supporting information to prove your thesis?
- Are the ideas presented in your paper logically organized?
- Does each paragraph in your paper have a clearly stated or implied topic (controlling) sentence?
- Are your paragraphs **unified**? Does everything in each paragraph specifically relate to the stated or implied topic sentence?
- Is the material in each paragraph **coherent**? Is there a logical reason for the order in which the sentences are presented? Did you use enough transitional words and phrases to clarify the relationships of the ideas to each other?
- Is your paper **unified**? Does everything in the paper specifically relate to the stated or implied thesis (controlling idea for the entire paper)?
- Is your paper **coherent**? Is there a logical reason for the order in which the paragraphs are presented? Did you use enough transitional words and phrases to clarify the relationships of the paragraphs to each other?
- Does your essay just stop, or does the concluding paragraph leave your reader with a sense of closure?
- Have you clearly identified and correctly documented all material taken from your sources?
- Have you eliminated any mechanical, grammatical, punctuation, spelling, or typographical errors?

CHAPTER 5

Formatting Your Paper

Use one-inch top, bottom, left, and right margins.

Double-space everything in your paper, including the quotations, the end-note page if you have one, and the works-cited or works-consulted page.

Use good quality white 8½-by-11-inch paper, and type or print only on one side.

Use a type size large enough to be easy to read, and make sure the print is not too light. A good choice in most fonts is 12-point type. Choose a font that looks professional and businesslike. Times New Roman, Arial, Courier, and Helvetica are good choices.

Indent all paragraphs one-half inch (on a computer) or five spaces (on a typewriter) from the left margin.

Indent all quotations that take up more than four lines when typed into your paper one inch (on a computer) or ten spaces (on a typewriter) from the left margin. Long quotations such as these are called *block* (or *set-off*) *quotations*.

Justify your lines only to the left margin, not to both margins.

Type your last name and the page number (Smith 4) in the top right corner of all pages, beginning with the outline if you are required to submit one. This can be done on your computer as a **header,** which will appear one-half inch from the top of each page. You will find the header option under the **View** menu in most word-processing programs.

If your instructor does not require a title page, type the following information flush left and double-spaced, beginning one inch from the top of the first page of your paper:

Your name	Jerome C. Smith
Your professor's name	Professor Jacobson
The course name: the time your class meets	English 102: 9:30 MWF
The day, month, and year your paper is due	15 February 2010

If your professor prefers a title page, center your title (not underlined, not in quotation marks, not in bold or italics) on a separate page. Next, center your

> ## Creating a Last Name and Page Header in Microsoft Word
>
> Click on the **View** menu. Click on **Header and Footer.** Click on the **Insert Page Number** button on the **Formatting** toolbar to add page numbering to your header. Click on the **Page Number Format** button on the toolbar for additional formatting options. Type your last name and one space before the number in the header area. Do not type a comma or any other mark between your name and the page number. The text you enter will be left aligned. To move the header to the right margin, press the **Tab** button twice. When the header looks the way you want it to, click on **Close** on the **Header and Footer** toolbar. For additional information about this process, click on the **Help** menu on the toolbar at the top of your screen.

name; your professor's name; the class name, number, and time; and the paper's due date in a double-spaced list below the title.

If your professor requires an outline at the beginning of your paper, type the four-line heading (double-spaced) on both the outline page and the first page of your paper and begin the last name and page number header (Smith 1) on the first page of the outline.

Double-space after the four-line heading, and center your title on the first page of the text of your paper.

Use a colon and one space to separate your title from your subtitle. If your title ends with a question mark, an exclamation point, or a dash, omit the colon between the title and the subtitle and use the more appropriate punctuation mark.

Capitalize the first and last words of both your title and your subtitle (no matter what parts of speech they are) and all other words, with the exception of

- articles (*a, an, the*)
- prepositions (*in, on, to, under, between, over, through,* etc.)
- the seven coordinating conjunctions (FANBOYS: *for, and, nor, but, or, yet, so*)
- the word *to* used in infinitives (*to* see, *to* run, *to* jump, etc.)

Capitalize the following parts of speech when used in a title:

nouns: tree, table, democracy, Mary, New York, Chicago, Wednesday, June

pronouns: he, she, it, they, you, your, everyone, anyone, someone, who, which, that

verbs: ran, jumped, danced, called, sat, is, are, were, rises, sets, comes, works, sees

adjectives: blue, large, happy, calm, biggest, best, hot, cold, smooth, rough

adverbs: too, very, happily, fast, high, rapidly, sweetly, kindly, often, rarely, usually

subordinating conjunctions and relative pronouns: words used to introduce subordinate or dependent clauses:

after	in order that	whatever
although	once	when
as	rather than	whenever
as if	since	where
as long as	so that	wherever
because	than	whether
before	that	which
even if	though	while
even though	unless	who
how	until	whoever
if	what	whose

Capitalize the word that follows a hyphen in a hyphenated word (American Executives Working in Spanish-Speaking Countries: Overcoming the Language Barrier).

Do not underline or place your title in quotation marks, bold, italics, or all capital letters.

Do not type a period after your title. If appropriate, your title or subtitle may end in a question mark or exclamation point.

The Story of Sarah Good: Guilty or Innocent?

Guilty or Innocent? The Story of Sarah Good

An Analysis of the Symbolism in Faulkner's *Absalom! Absalom!*

Eureka! Problem Solved at Last

Remember that the purpose of your title is to tell your reader exactly what you will discuss in your paper. The title should be very specific, fairly brief, and a phrase or a combination of words and phrases separated by a colon (unless your title ends with a question mark, exclamation point, or dash). With rare exceptions, your title should not be a sentence.

After your title, double-space and begin the text of your paper.

If you use an endnote page, number it as part of your text and place it after the last page of the body of your paper and immediately before the works-cited list. (See chapter 15 for information on how to format endnotes.)

The works-cited list is the last page of the paper, and that page should be numbered as part of your text. Center the title **Works Cited** or **Works Consulted** (not in all capital letters, not underlined, not in quotation marks, and not in bold or italics) one inch from the top of your page. Double-space after the title, and list your citations in alphabetical order using a hanging indent: first line flush with the left margin, all subsequent lines in the same entry indented one-half inch (on a computer) or five spaces (on a typewriter) from the left margin.

Use the **Hanging Indent** option in your computer's word processing program rather than the **Tab** function to create a hanging indent; using this option will prevent your text from scrambling if you need to add or delete materials in your citation. You will find the **Hanging Indent** option under **Format/Paragraph/Indentation/Special** menus in most word-processing programs. (See page 76 for more information on how to create a hanging indent.)

CHAPTER 6

Sample General Topic Research Paper

The Story of Sarah Good: Guilty or Innocent?

By Jessica Lynn Piezzo

Each student in Jessica Piezzo's English 101 class researched a person involved in the Salem witchcraft trials in Salem Village, Massachusetts, in 1692. Some students chose to write about one of the supposedly "afflicted" girls who made the accusations. Others wrote about the judges who sent those unfortunate enough to be convicted to their deaths. Jessica chose to discover what historians had to say about Sarah Good, one of the first three women accused of practicing witchcraft in Salem Village and the only one of those three to hang for her supposed allegiance to the devil. Jessica was interested in finding out whether Sarah Good was given a fair trial and why she was convicted and condemned to death. Jessica later presented the results of her research during an on-campus conference held at her university featuring presentations by students and faculty.

Although your professor may ask you to do so, MLA does not require you to format your thesis, topic sentences, and conclusion sentence in bold. In this text, bold is used simply to help you locate the controlling sentences in the model student essays.

Jessica Lynn Piezzo

Professor Schwartz

English 101: 9:30 MWF

14 April 2010

Title: The Story of Sarah Good: Guilty or Innocent?

Thesis: Although the court sentenced Sarah Good to death, she maintained her innocence, and it seems clear that she was falsely accused of being a witch.

  I. Reasons for the accusations of witchcraft in Salem

     A. Dr. Griggs's unfortunate diagnosis

     B. Bruce Watson's theory

        1. Religious factors

        2. Political factors

        3. Economic factors

        4. Social factors

     C. Mary Beth Norton's theory

        1. Different situation than most other cases

        2. Fear of Indian attacks

 II. Many lives destroyed

     A. 180 accused

     B. 144 arrested

    C. Giles Cory pressed to death

    D. Nineteen men and women hanged

    E. Six died in prison

III. Sarah's poverty a factor

    A. Cheated out of inheritance

    B. Left in debt after first husband's death

    C. Land confiscated to pay first husband's debts

    D. Married second husband, a ne'er-do-well

    E. Reduced to begging

IV. Tituba's false confession

    A. Sarah Good accused

    B. Sarah Osborne accused

V. Good's bad temper a factor

    A. Afflicted girls testified against her

    B. Disgruntled neighbors testified against her

    C. Husband testified against her

VI. Good's five-year-old daughter helped convict her

    A. Dorcas arrested, questioned, and imprisoned

    B. Dorcas accused mother

    C. Dorcas became mentally unstable

Piezzo 3

VII. Trial not fair

    A. Records show Hathorne's bias

    B. Good maintained innocence

VIII. Spectral evidence used against her

    A. Elizabeth Hubbard's accusation

    B. Constable's testimony

IX. Some evidence against Good proved false

    A. Broken knife incident

    B. Court ignored problem

X. Good defiant to the end

    A. Maintained innocence in last moments

    B. Irony of last words

XI. Reasons for Good's conviction

    A. Bad temper

    B. Poverty

    C. Powerlessness

Use one-inch
top, bottom,
left, and right
margins.

Double-space
your name,
your professor's
name, class
name and time,
and the paper
due date at the
top left margin
of the first page
of your outline
and on the first
page of the text
of your paper.

Jessica gives a
brief overview of
events that oc-
curred and some
possible causes
of the Salem
witch trials.

The first time
you cite from
an author, give
the full name.
Thereafter, give
only the last
name.

Your last name
and page num-
ber should ap-
pear as a header
one-half inch
from the top of
every page in
your paper.

Centered title
explains exactly
what will be
discussed in the
paper.

No page citation
is given for
Watson because
Jessica refers to
his article as a
whole.

Summary of
Norton's theory.
Author's name is
given at the be-
ginning, and the
page reference is
typed in paren-
theses before the
period of the last
sentence in the
summary.

Jessica Lynn Piezzo

Professor Schwartz

English 101: 9:30 MWF

14 April 2010

The Story of Sarah Good: Guilty or Innocent?

1   The Salem Witch Trials began in the middle of January

1692 when several young girls, including the daughter and

niece of Reverend Samuel Parris, began having bizarre fits and

were diagnosed by a local doctor as being bewitched. Many of

the "afflicted" girls were associated with prominent families

in Salem Village (now Danvers), Massachusetts. The girls'

inexplicable behavior and Dr. Griggs's unfortunate diagnosis

ultimately triggered the mass outbreak of witch hysteria in

Salem Village that remains the most famous incident of its

kind in American history. Bruce Watson notes that religious,

political, economic, and social issues were all important

factors in the cause of this outbreak. Mary Beth Norton, a

professor of history at Cornell University, notes that previ-

ous accusations of witchcraft in the New England area targeted

what she terms a few and never more than a dozen of "'the

usual suspects'"--people who had long been suspected by their

Piezzo 5

neighbors of practicing witchcraft. However, in Salem Village

and the surrounding towns, hundreds of people were accused, and

although some of those accused--Sarah Good and Sarah Osborne,

for example--were "'the usual suspects,'" many were respected

individuals who had never been suspected of any witchlike be-

havior before. She believes the hysteria may be explained by

fear of the Indian attacks that seemed to be moving closer

and closer to Salem Village at the time. One attack occurred

only twenty miles from Salem while the trials were being

held. Many believed that the devil and his minions were aid-

ing the Indians; therefore, anyone consorting with the devil

at that particular historical moment would have been seen

as a threat to the survival of the village (9). **The tragic**

events that took place in 1692 would destroy many lives--

including Sarah Good's--and change Salem Village forever.

2   The first formal accusations of witchcraft were made on

February 29, 1692, and the last trials resulting from those

accusations occurred in May of 1693. Norton notes that docu-

mented accusations against 180 people survive, but it is

likely that many others were accused as well. At least 144

inhabitants (38 men and 106 women) were arrested and spent a

Page reference for Norton paraphrased and quoted material placed in parentheses at end of last sentence and followed by a period.

Topic sentence for paragraph 1.

General knowledge information available uncited in many sources may be presented in the student's own words without citing a source.

Piezzo 6

considerable length of time in extremely harsh--in some cases lethal--prison conditions (4). An eighty-year-old man named Giles Cory was pressed (crushed) to death by heavy stones because he refused to enter a plea, apparently hoping to prevent his property from being confiscated. (The property of condemned people was forfeited to the state, and Cory did not want his children to lose their inheritance.) Six people died in prison (three women, one man, and two infants), and fourteen women and five men were hanged from a large tree on Gallows Hill. One of the nineteen executed was Sarah Good.

Although the court sentenced Sarah Good to death, she maintained her innocence throughout her trial, and it seems clear that she was falsely accused of being a witch.

3   **Sarah Good's poverty was one of the factors that led to her tragic end.** She was the daughter of a wealthy innkeeper named John Solart. After he drowned himself in 1672, an estate of approximately five hundred pounds was divided among his wife and his two sons. His seven daughters were not to receive their shares of the estate until they came of age. Mrs. Solart, however, soon remarried, and her inheritance and the shares destined for her daughters were turned over to the

Thesis statement explains what Jessica intends to prove in the essay.

Topic sentence for paragraph 3.

Piezzo 7

control of her new husband. As a result, Sarah and her sis-

ters never saw their shares of the inheritance. When Sarah's

first husband, Daniel Poole, died, he left her nothing but

debts. Those debts were left to be paid by Sarah and her sec-

ond husband, William Good, by all accounts a ne'er-do-well.

They were forced to forfeit most of their land to pay off

Poole's debts and then sold the rest to pay their living

expenses. Katherine Sutcliffe explains that by the 1690s,

Sarah, her husband, and their daughter were homeless and

"reduced to begging for work, food, and shelter from [their]

neighbors . . ." (1).

4   An Indian woman from Barbados named Tituba (a slave be-

longing to Rev. Samuel Parris), Sarah Good, and Sarah Osborne

were the first three women accused of practicing witchcraft

by the afflicted girls. After maintaining her innocence for

some time, Tituba eventually confessed to being a witch and

identified Sarah Good and Sarah Osborne as also being witches.

(Later Tituba claimed that her confession had been false--

beaten out of her by her master, Rev. Samuel Parris.) **Because**

of Tituba's false confession, Sarah Good was one of the first

women actually brought to trial.

Jessica summarizes general background information about Sarah Good. Because this information is available uncited in many sources, Jessica can summarize it in her own words without giving a source.

The pronoun *her* in the source is changed in square brackets to *their*.

Ellipsis indicates that words after *neighbors* were omitted.

Topic sentence for paragraph 4.

5   **Sarah's bad temper helped convict her of witchcraft.** She

is described by Frances Hill as a pushy, middle-aged, foul-

tempered outcast who smoked a pipe. If there were witches in

Salem Village, she was sure to be one of them (36). When

Sarah begged for food and shelter for herself and her family,

she was often turned away by her neighbors. According to

Richard Weisman, Sarah often responded by "scolding and curs-

ing as a means of retaliation against unresponsive neigh-

bors," and this behavior provided evidence for the court and

"generated a wealth of negative testimony" against her (56).

In addition to the testimony of the afflicted girls, at least

seven people who had witnessed Sarah's disturbing behavior

while begging testified against her in court. Ironically, one

of those people was her own husband. Although he testified

that he had never witnessed his wife practicing witchcraft,

he told the court that he feared Sarah "'either was a witch

or would be one very quickly'" (qtd. in Weisman 56). He said

that she treated him badly and described her as "'an enemy to

all good,'" apparently oblivious to the pun on his name (qtd.

in Weisman 56).

Topic sentence
for paragraph 5.

Paraphrase from
Frances Hill
begins with the
author's name
and ends with
a page reference
in parentheses.

No ellipses are
needed when
you quote only
short phrases
from a source.

Single quotation
marks inside
double quota-
tion marks show
that the quoted
words were in
double quota-
tion marks in
the source.

Abbreviation
qtd. informs the
reader that the
quoted words
are those of
Sarah Good's
husband and
were not written
by Weisman.

Piezzo 9

Topic sentence
for paragraph 6.

6   **Dorcas Good, Sarah's five-year-old daughter, also helped convict her mother.** Dorcas was accused of witchcraft and arrested, and in her terrified confession, she indicated that her mother was indeed a witch. Sarah's young daughter spent nine months chained in a prison cell. Accused witches were kept in chains because the Puritans believed the chains would prevent their specters (the devil in human form) from flying about doing evil deeds. Dorcas never recovered from the trauma of her experience. In 1710 her father said, " '[S]he hath ever since been very chargeable, having little or no reason [with which] to govern herself' " (qtd. in Breslaw 171). By "chargeable" he meant that she was a great deal of trouble and expense to him because she was unable to take care of herself and had to be looked after for the rest of her life. As a result of her experience in prison, she never became a responsible member of her society. Dorcas's father was in later years paid thirty pounds by Massachusetts as reparation for the loss of his wife's life and his daughter's sanity.

Square brackets are used to change the lowercase *s* in the source to a capital *S* because the first word in a grammatically complete sentence must begin with a capital letter.

Topic sentence
for paragraph 7.

7   **By today's standards Sarah did not receive a fair trial.** Magistrates John Hathorne and Jonathan Corwin came to Salem Village on March 1, 1692, to examine the accused witches.

Piezzo 10

Sarah Good was the first of the accused to be questioned by

Hathorne. It is obvious from the recorded testimony that

Hathorne believed Sarah was a witch:

A full-sentence lead-in to a quotation ends with a colon.

Block quotation is indented one inch from the left margin. Double quotation marks in the source are retained in the quotation.

      "Sarah Good, what evil spirit have you familiar-

ity with?"

      "None." Sarah answered defiantly.

      "Have you made no contract with the devil?"

      "No."

      "Why do you hurt these children?"

      "I do not hurt them. I scorn it."

      "Who do you employ then to do it?"

      "I employ nobody."

      "What creature do you employ then?"

      "No creature, but I am falsely accused."

      "Why did you go away muttering from Mr. Parris

his [sic] house?"

Latin word *sic* in square brackets explains that error appeared in source and was not Jessica's typing error.

Explanatory information is added to the quotation in square brackets.

      "I did not mutter but I thanked him for what he

gave my child [a reference to Sarah's daughter,

Dorcas Good]."

      "Have you made no contract with the devil?"

Citation is placed after the period that ends the block quotation.

      "No." (qtd. in Hill 43)

Piezzo 11

Throughout her trial, Sarah remained defiant and never confessed to being a witch.

⁸   **Highly questionable spectral evidence was also used to convict Sarah Good.** Elizabeth Hubbard, at seventeen one of the oldest of the afflicted girls, claimed that she saw Sarah standing on the table in the home of Dr. Griggs "naked-breasted and bare-legged and that if she had something to do it with she would kill her" (Hill 66). Samuel Sibley, a Salem inhabitant who was present at the time, "struck with his staff where she pointed," and Elizabeth told those present that he had struck Sarah's back (Hill 66). The next day in court, the constable testified that Sarah's forearm was bloody. This was considered evidence that Sarah Good's specter had been struck by Sibley's staff at Dr. Griggs's house--even though at the time Elizabeth, who was the only person present who could actually see the supposed specter, had told those present that the staff had hit Good's back. No one apparently noticed this important discrepancy in relation to the location of Sarah's supposed injury by Sibley, an injury received while her physical body was not only chained up but locked in a prison cell.

Topic sentence for paragraph 8.

If the author is not named in the sentence, the name must appear in the parenthetical citation with no comma between the name and page number.

A dash is created by typing two hyphens with no spaces before, between, or after them. See page 77 for instructions on how to create a single-line dash.

Piezzo 12

Topic sentence
for paragraph 9.

9   **Some of the spectral evidence in Sarah Good's trial was**
clearly proved to be false. According to Katherine Sutcliffe, a girl cried out during the trial that Sarah Good's specter was stabbing her with a knife. Although part of a broken knife was found in the girl's possession, a young man in the court-room stated that he had broken that same knife and had thrown it away "in the presence of the afflicted girls." He showed the constable the matching part of the broken knife as proof that he was telling the truth (1). The girl, who had clearly lied about her supposed injury at the hand of Good, was sim-ply told not to lie again, and the discovery that she had lied to the court had no effect whatsoever on the outcome of the trial. The members of the Court of Oyer and Terminer were clearly interested in finding evidence to convict Sarah, not in making sure she got a fair trial. As one historian put it, " '[T]here was no one in the country around against whom popu-lar suspicion could have been more readily directed, or in whose favor and defense less interest could be awakened' " (qtd. in Sutcliffe 1).

Summary of in-
formation from
Sutcliffe begins
with the author's
name and ends
with a page
reference in
parentheses.

Jessica gives her
interpretation
of the informa-
tion she has
summarized
from Sutcliffe.

Lowercase *t* in
source changed
to capital *T* in
square brackets
indicates that
words were
omitted before
there in the
source; there-
fore, no ellipsis
is needed.

10   **Sarah Good was sentenced to death by hanging on June 29,**
1692. She was executed on July 19. At her execution, she

Topic sentence
for para-
graph 10.

Piezzo 13

showed no remorse, which only further convinced the people

of Salem Village that she was indeed a witch. On the way to

Gallows Hill, where the condemned witches were hanged, a min-

ister by the name of Nicholas Noyes attempted to get a con-

fession out of Sarah Good. She responded, " 'You are a liar.

I am no more a witch than you are a wizard, and if you take

away my life God will give you blood to drink' " (qtd. in

Sutcliffe 1). Ironically, Nicholas Noyes died some time later

from an internal hemorrhage. As Good had predicted, he died

with blood in his mouth (Sutcliffe 1).

11   What really happened in Salem Village, Massachusetts,

remains a mystery. The tragedy that occurred over three hun-

dred years ago intrigues historians to this day. Most of the

evidence that was presented against Sarah was hearsay, which

would never have been allowed in a courtroom today. It seems

clear, however, that no amount of evidence could have proven

that Sarah Good was innocent, for in the minds of the towns-

people and the judges, she had been guilty from the start.

In the end, Sarah Good lost her life not because she had been

practicing witchcraft but because she was ill-tempered, poor,

and powerless.

Single quotation marks inside double quotation marks show that the quoted words were in double quotation marks in the source.

Conclusion sentence: Jessica explains why she believes Good was executed.

Piezzo 14

Works Consulted

Historical docu-
ment published
in a book and
accessed through
an online schol-
arly project.

Boyer, Paul, and Stephen Nissenbaum, eds. "Examination of

Sarah Good." *The Salem Witchcraft Papers: Verbatim Tran-*

scripts of the Legal Documents of the Salem Witchcraft

Outbreak of 1692. Vol. 2. New York: Da Capo, 1971. *Salem*

Witch Trials Documentary Archive and Transcription Proj-

ect. Ed. Benjamin C. Ray and Bernard Rosenthal. Elec-

tronic Text Center, Alderman Lib., U of Virginia. Web.

10 Apr. 2010.

Book in a series.

Breslaw, Elaine G. *Tituba, Reluctant Witch of Salem: Devilish*

Indians and Puritan Fantasies. New York: New York UP,

1996. Print. American Social Experience Ser. 35.

Web page with
no author given
from an online
scholarly project.

"The Examination of Sarah Good, March 1, 1692." *Famous*

American Trials: Salem Witchcraft Trials 1692. Ed.

Douglas O. Linder. UMKC School of Law, Sept. 2009. Web.

11 Apr. 2010.

Scholarly journal
article.

Gould, Philip. "New England Witch-Hunting and the Politics of

Reason in the Early Republic." *New England Quarterly*

68.1 (1995): 58–82. Print.

Book.

Hill, Frances. *A Delusion of Satan: The Full Story of the*

Salem Witch Trials. New York: Da Capo, 1997. Print.

Piezzo 15

Linder, Douglas O. "An Account of Events in Salem." *Famous American Trials: Salem Witchcraft Trials 1692.* Ed. Douglas O. Linder. UMKC School of Law, Sept. 2009. Web. 8 Apr. 2010.

Norton, Mary Beth. "Finding the Devil in the Details of the Salem Witchcraft Trials." *Chronicle of Higher Education* 21 Jan. 2000: B4+. Web. 10 Apr. 2010.

"Overview of the Salem Witch Trials." *Salem Witch Trials Documentary Archive and Transcription Project.* Ed. Benjamin C. Ray and Bernard Rosenthal. Electronic Text Center, Alderman Lib., U of Virginia, 2002. Web. 11 Apr. 2010.

"The Salem Witch Trials 1692: A Chronology of Events." *Salem Web.* Salem Office of Tourism and Cultural Affairs, 2007. Web. 10 Apr. 2010.

Sutcliffe, Katherine. "Biographies of Key Figures in the Salem Witchcraft Trials: Sarah Good." *Famous American Trials: Salem Witchcraft Trials 1692.* Ed. Douglas O. Linder. UMKC School of Law, Sept. 2009. Web. 12 Apr. 2010.

Web page with author given from an online scholarly project.

Article from an online scholarly newspaper.

Web page with no author given from an online scholarly project.

Web page with no author given.

Web page with author given from an online scholarly project.

Full-text monthly magazine article accessed through an online library subscription database.

Watson, Bruce. "Salem's Dark Hour: Did the Devil Make Them

    Do It?" *Smithsonian* Apr. 1992: 116-30. *Expanded Academic*

    ASAP. Web. 11 Apr. 2010.

Book.

Weisman, Richard. *Witchcraft, Magic, and Religion in 17th*

    Century Massachusetts. Amherst: U of Massachusetts P,

    1984. Print.

CHAPTER 7

Sample Literary Analysis Research Paper

An Analysis of the Character Biff Loman in *Death of a Salesman*

By William E. Files

William Files was asked to analyze a character from a short story or play studied during the semester in his English 102 class. He chose to analyze Biff Loman from Arthur Miller's classic play *Death of a Salesman*.

Tips for Writing a Literary Analysis Paper

1. Analyze literary works in present tense.
2. Identify the author, genre, and title of the work in the first sentence of your essay.
3. Write in a relatively formal style. Do not use contractions or slang in a literary analysis essay unless you are quoting.
4. Analyze the work; do not just summarize the plot. Summarize only enough of the work to allow your reader to understand your analysis.
5. Do not plagiarize. Credit to your sources ideas and interpretations not original with you and precise wording taken from the sources you have read.
6. Use an ellipsis (three spaced periods) when you omit words, phrases, or sentences from a quotation if the omission is not already obvious.
7. Quotations from the short story, play, poem, or novel you are analyzing should be taken from your textbook (or from whatever text of the work you are using as your primary source), not from your secondary sources (articles and books in which literary critics have analyzed the work).
8. Double-space your outline, the text of your paper, and your works-cited list.
9. Format your thesis, topic sentences, and conclusion sentence in bold only if your professor asks you to do so. Formatting controlling sentences in bold is not an MLA requirement. In this text, bold is used simply to help you locate the controlling sentences in the model student essays.

William E. Files

Professor Schwartz

English 102: 9:30 MWF

19 April 2010

Outline

Title: An Analysis of the Character Biff Loman in *Death of a Salesman*

Audience: General Audience

Word Count: 1,243

Thesis: Biff achieves what eludes every other character in this story—a change in identity and a casting off of his father's old image of him.

Topic Sentence 1: Biff's first life-changing experience drastically alters his opinion of his father.

Topic Sentence 2: In the present and back at home, Biff tells his father that he is going to see Bill Oliver, for whom he claims to have once worked as a salesman, to ask for a loan to start a business of his own selling sporting goods.

Topic Sentence 3: When Biff realizes what a waste his life has been, he feels the need to confront his father.

Files 2

Topic Sentence 4: His father's death changes Biff, allowing him to become fully himself with no one else's imposing sense of the world weighing him down.

Conclusion Sentence: Having at last escaped the tenacious grasp of his father's dreams and illusions, Biff Loman can finally be his own person and live out his own dreams and destiny, unburdened with his father's false guidance.

Honor Pledge: Except as documented on my works-cited page, I received no help on this essay other than a discussion with my brother Michael about the play and its characters and editing assistance from Professor Schwartz.

Use one-inch top, bottom, left, and right margins.

Double-space your name, your professor's name, class name and time, and paper due date at the top left margin of your paper.

Your name and page number should appear as a header one-half inch from the top of the page.

William E. Files

Professor Schwartz

English 102: 9:30 MWF

19 April 2010

An Analysis of the Character Biff Loman

in *Death of a Salesman*

Centered title explains exactly what will be discussed in the paper.

Author, genre, and title of work should be identified in the first sentence of a literary analysis essay.

1   Arthur Miller's play *Death of a Salesman* tells the story of Willy Loman, a salesman living in Brooklyn, New York, and his family. At the heart of the play is the strained relationship between Willy and his eldest son, Biff. In Willy's world, the qualities that will get a man ahead in life are his good looks and his charm, so he tells his boys, "[T]he man who makes an appearance in the business world, the man who creates personal interest, is the man who gets ahead. Be liked and you will never want" (Miller 1784). He is so obsessed with Biff's good looks and masculine charm that he builds him up to be a successful businessman and expects nothing short of that. Biff has always been imbued with the values of his father and the goal of monetary success, but after a series of illuminating though traumatic events, he finally begins to develop his own identity and values separate

Analyze literary works in the present tense.

If the author is not named in the lead-in to the quotation, the name must be placed in the parenthetical citation.

No ellipsis is needed to show the already obvious omission of words at the beginning of the quoted sentence because the lowercase *t* in the source is changed in square brackets to a capital *T*, informing the reader that *the* was not the first word in the quoted sentence.

Files 4

Thesis statement. The purpose of this essay is to present evidence to convince the reader that this thesis statement is true.

Topic sentence for paragraph 2.

Paraphrase of Helterman's analysis begins with the critic's name and ends with the page in a parenthetical citation, which is placed before the period ending the sentence.

The first time you refer to an author, give the name in full. Thereafter, give only the last name of the author.

A single-line dash is created by typing two hyphens with no spaces before, between, or after them, then typing the word that follows the hyphen and hitting the space bar.

A quotation lead-in ending in *that* needs no punctuation after the word *that*.

from his father's. **In the end, Biff achieves what eludes every other character in this story—a change in identity and a casting off of his father's old image of him.**

2   **Biff's first life-changing experience drastically alters his opinion of his father.** Prior to his graduation from high school, Biff makes plans to attend the University of Virginia on a full football scholarship. His graduation is imperiled, however, when he fails his senior math course. Biff goes to Boston to ask his father to talk to the math teacher for him. Jeffrey Helterman suggests that Biff, following his father's example, believes that having his father convince his math teacher to pass him would be easier than taking the class again during the summer and is therefore the correct choice (93). When Biff gets to Willy's hotel room, he finds his father with a scantily clad woman and thus discovers Willy's infidelity. This is a real turning point for Biff, and he begins to view his father as a liar, a fake, and a phony. Helterman also points out that

> Willy never stops selling himself, and selling means improving the product—making it sound better than it is. His reports of his selling trips, even

Files 5

Long, block quotation is indented one inch from the left margin. No quotation marks are used because the material was not in quotation marks or blocked in the source and because the blocking identifies the material as a quotation.

on his best days, are always exaggerations, the

step to outright lies is only a small one, and

Hap inherits this trait from his father. Biff goes

along with Willy's petty cheating until he dis-

covers that Willy has cheated even on his own

wife. (93)

From this point forward Biff looks at his father through dis-

illusioned eyes and starts to see that his father's way is

skewed. Biff's burning of his tennis shoes symbolizes his

throwing away his plans to go to the University of Virginia,

thereby dashing Willy's hopes for his son to become a suc-

cessful businessman.

Topic sentence for paragraph 3.

3   **In the present and back at home, Biff tells his father**

that he is going to see Bill Oliver, for whom he claims to

have once worked as a salesman, to ask for a loan to start a

sporting goods business. Biff knows he does not have any in-

terest or real skill in the business world, yet he does this

to please his father. As Karl Harshbarger points out, Biff

deludes himself into believing that he can succeed in a sports

equipment business by getting a loan from Bill Oliver. He

lies to himself to build up his confidence that he can create

Paraphrase of Harshbarger's analysis begins with the critic's name and ends with the page citation.

Files 6

this new business career for himself, even though the thought

of a nine-to-five job in the business world fills him with

horror (44). When his attempted meeting with Oliver turns out

to be a complete failure, it finally dawns on Biff what a

An exclamation point or question mark ending quoted material is placed inside the closing quotation marks and before the parenthetical citation.

phony and a loser he is and "what a ridiculous lie my whole

life has been!" (Miller 1819). Harshbarger explains:

> Oliver's rejection, in fact, has a stunning effect
>
> on Biff. He can tell Happy, "I'm all numb, I
>
> swear," and he talks about what happened in Oliver's
>
> office *with great tension and wonder*" [emphasis
>
> Harshbarger's]. After having evaluated Biff's past,
>
> we can see that this event repeats a chronic prob-
>
> lem for Biff: the surfacing of the knowledge that
>
> he is not a man, that he is a failure. (44)

Double quotation marks from the original source are retained in a block quotation.

Bracketed material explains that italicized words appeared in the source and were not italicized by William.

The parenthetical citation is typed after the period that ends a block quotation.

Topic sentence for paragraph 4.

4   **When Biff realizes what a waste his life has been, he**

feels the need to confront his father. After meeting Happy at

a restaurant, Biff tries to explain to him that the Loman

family is caught in a web of deceit, but Happy, like his fa-

ther, refuses to hear what Biff is trying to tell him. When

Willy shows up, he tells the boys he has been fired. Biff

wastes no time trying to tell his father about his experience

William explains the changes he finds in Biff's behavior as he analyzes this scene.

with Oliver, but Willy won't listen, so Biff gives up and instead tells Willy what he wants to hear—that he has another appointment with Oliver the next day. A now more realistic Biff realizes, however, that having stolen a gold pen from Oliver's desk, he cannot go back to see Oliver again. At this point, Willy starts having flashbacks to the Boston incident and goes to the bathroom to escape from Biff and the guilt he feels about ruining his beloved son's life. The boys leave their father alone in the restaurant, setting the stage for the final confrontation of the play.

5   Later that night, Biff comes home and explains to Willy that it would be best for them to never see each other again. Biff cannot, until the final moments of his time with Willy, articulate his contempt for Willy's life of illusions. He tries once again to explain that he is "not a leader of men," that he is in fact "a dime a dozen" (Miller 1833). Willy denies this self-assessment and tells Biff once again how great he can be. Willy refuses to see the truth, and this frustrates Biff to the point that he breaks down and sobs, asking Willy to forget him. However, as Neil Carson points out, "Willy has too much emotional capital tied up in his dreams

No ellipses are needed when you quote short phrases from the source.

Short quotation begins with the critic's name in lead-in and ends with the page reference, which is placed before the period that ends the sentence.

Files 8

of Biff's magnificence, and he prefers to sacrifice his life rather than his illusion" (56). He has in mind one last business deal: to cash in on his twenty-thousand-dollar life insurance policy by killing himself. This will set Biff up financially, transferring his unfulfilled dream of business success onto his son. Willy drives out into the night and crashes his car, killing himself. At the funeral, however, Biff assures his brother Happy, "I know who I am . . . " (Miller 1836). **His father's death has changed Biff, allowing him to become fully himself with no one else's imposing sense of the world weighing him down.**

Ellipsis (three spaced periods) indicates that one or more words were omitted at the end of a quotation that appears to be a complete sentence but contained additional words in the source.

Topic sentence for paragraph 5.

6   The traumatic discovery of his father's infidelity in Boston, the eye-opening meeting with Bill Oliver, and the reality of his father's suicide take Biff to a new awareness. These events change his view of himself, his father, and the world. Traumatic events in life often give people new insight that helps them become more aware of themselves and of their surroundings. **Having at last escaped the tenacious grasp of his father's dreams and illusions, Biff Loman can finally be his own person and live out his own dreams and destiny, unburdened with his father's false guidance.**

Conclusion sentence reminds reader of the main point of the essay.

Files 9

Works Cited

Book in a series. Series name (not italicized) appears after the medium of publication and includes the number of the book if there is one (Gale Author Ser. 2.).

Carson, Neil. *Arthur Miller.* New York: Grove, 1982. Print. Grove Press Modern Dramatists.

Book. When a title that should be italicized falls inside another title that should be italicized, italicize the primary title, but do not italicize the secondary title. In this entry the title of Harshbarger's book is italicized, but the title of Miller's play is not.

Article from a literary reference book. Give full bibliographic information for reference books that have not been frequently updated.

Harshbarger, Karl. *The Burning Jungle: An Analysis of Arthur Miller's* Death of a Salesman. Washington: UP of America, 1977. Print.

Helterman, Jeffrey. "Arthur Miller." *Twentieth-Century American Dramatists.* Pt. 2. Ed. John MacNicholas. Vol. 7 of *Dictionary of Literary Biography.* Detroit: Gale, 1981. 86-111. Print.

Miller play from a literary anthology.

Miller, Arthur. *Death of a Salesman. Literature: An Introduction to Fiction, Poetry, Drama, and Writing.* Ed. X. J. Kennedy and Dana Gioia. 11th ed. New York: Longman-Pearson, 2010. 1772-1836. Print.

Files 10

Additional Works Consulted

Centola, Steven. "Family Values in *Death of a Salesman*."

CLA *Journal* 37.2 (1993): 29-41. Print.

> Scholarly journal article.

Dudar, Helen. "A Modern Tragedy's Road to Maturity." *New York Times* 25 Mar. 1984, late ed., sec. 2: 1+. Print.

> Article from a Sunday *New York Times*. That the article jumped from page 1 to another page in the newspaper is indicated by the plus sign (sec. 2: 1+.).

Hogan, Robert. "Arthur Miller." *American Writers: A Collection of Literary Biographies*. Ed. Leonard Unger. Vol. 3. New York: Scribner's, 1974. 145-69. Print.

> Article from a literary reference book that has not been frequently updated.

Lawrence, Stephen A. "The Right Dream in Miller's *Death of a Salesman*." *College English* 25.4 (1964): 547-49. Print.

> Scholarly journal article.

"Miller, Arthur." *Encyclopaedia Britannica Online*. Encyclopaedia Britannica, 2010. Web. 7 Apr. 2010.

> Article from an online encyclopedia.

"Miller, Arthur." *Encyclopedia Americana*. 2003 ed. Print.

> Article from a general encyclopedia.

Miller, Arthur, Robert Falls, and Brian Dennehy. "An American Classic: A Half-Century Anniversary." Interview by Paul Solman. *NewsHour with Jim Lehrer*. PBS. 10 Feb. 1999. *PBS*. Web. 7 Apr. 2010. Transcript.

> Transcript of a television interview accessed from a Web site.

Parker, Brian. "Point of View in Arthur Miller's *Death of a Salesman*." *University of Toronto Quarterly* 35.2 (1966):

Files 11

144-57. Rpt. in *Arthur Miller: A Collection of Critical Essays*. Ed. Robert W. Corrigan. Englewood Cliffs, NJ: Prentice, 1969. 95-109. Print.

Ribkoff, Fred. "Shame, Guilt, Empathy, and the Search for Identity in Arthur Miller's *Death of a Salesman*." *Modern Drama* 43.1 (2000): 48- . *InfoTrac OneFile*. Web. 6 Apr. 2010.

Thompson, Terry W. "Miller's *Death of a Salesman*." *Explicator* 60.3 (2002): 162-63. *InfoTrac OneFile*. Web. 6 Apr. 2010.

Scholarly journal article reprinted in an essay collection. If you believe that your readers (especially if some of your readers will be students) may not know where a city of publication is located, give the postal abbreviation for the state.

Scholarly journal article from an online library subscription database. Because the database gave only the first page of an article clearly longer than one page, based on the printout of the article, William cited the first page followed by a hyphen, one space, and a period.

Scholarly journal article taken from an online library subscription database. The database gave the page reference for this article as "p162(2)," which means that the article began on page 162 and was two pages long.

CHAPTER 8

Preparing Your Bibliography

General Guidelines for Preparing Your Bibliography

The word **bibliography** literally means a list of books used to prepare a paper. Because modern researchers typically use many nonprint as well as printed sources to prepare research papers, the titles **Works Cited** and **Works Consulted** are more appropriate. In this discussion, the general term **bibliography** is used to refer to either a works-cited or a works-consulted list.

The bibliography is titled **Works Cited** if it lists only the sources from which you quoted, paraphrased, or summarized in the paper.

It is titled **Works Consulted** if it lists not only the sources from which you quoted, paraphrased, or summarized but also other sources that you read but from which you did not cite materials.

If you want to inform your instructor about all the works you used in preparing the paper, whether or not you cited from them, prepare a works-consulted list and include all the works that provided useful information. Do not include sources you used to find the materials you actually read. For example, if you used the *New York Times Index* to find a useful article in the *New York Times*, cite the article, not the index you used to find the article. (See works-consulted lists on pages 60–62 and 293–94.)

A third option is to give both a works-cited list containing the sources from which you cited material and a second list entitled **Additional Works Consulted** in which you list sources you read but from which you did not take cited information. (See William Files's works-cited/additional works-consulted lists on pages 72–74.)

Works are listed alphabetically by the author's last name or, if no author is given, by the first significant word of the title, excluding *A, An,* and *The*.

The first line of each entry should be typed flush with the left margin. If the entry contains more than one line, indent each line after the first line one-half inch (on a computer) or five spaces (on a typewriter) from the left margin. This is called a *hanging indent*.

Creating a Hanging Indent in Microsoft Word

To create a hanging indent, highlight or select the material you want to appear in hanging indent format. Then go to the **Format** menu at the top of your screen. Go to **Paragraph.** Under **Indentation,** go to **Special** and click on the arrow beside **(none)** to reveal the options. Highlight **Hanging.** Click on **OK.** Your first line should now be flush with the left margin of your text, and all subsequent lines in the same entry should be indented one-half inch from the left margin. If there is no typewritten text after the material you have formatted with a hanging indent, all the text you type thereafter will appear in hanging indent format.

Removing a Hanging Indent in Microsoft Word

To remove a hanging indent, highlight or select the material you want not to appear in hanging indent format. Then go to the **Format** menu at the top of your screen. Go to **Paragraph.** Under **Indentation,** go to **Special** and click on the arrow beside **Hanging** to reveal the options. Highlight **(none).** Click on **OK.**

Use the **Hanging Indent** option in your computer's word processing program rather than the **Tab** function so that your citation will not become scrambled if you need to add or delete material or make other corrections.

Double-space the entire works-cited list.

The works-cited list is the last page of your paper, and that page should be numbered as part of your text. If you use an endnote page, number it as part of your text and place it before the works-cited list.

Center the title **Works Cited** or **Works Consulted** (not in all capital letters, not underlined, not in quotation marks, and not in bold or italics) one inch from the top of the page. Double-space between the title and first entry in your list.

If publication information does not appear on the title page or copyright page (on the back of the title page), look for it in your library's online catalog or in other sources, such as *WorldCat* or the Library of Congress online catalog <http: www.loc.gov>, and give the information in square brackets to show that the information is known but was not given in your source: Boston: Houghton, [2009].

If publication information is unavailable (does not exist), use the following abbreviations so your reader will know that you would have given the information if it had been available. Note that MLA recommends leaving no

Creating a Dash in Microsoft Word

To create a dash, type two hyphens with no spaces before, between, or after them; type the word that follows the dash; and press the Space Bar. If this process does not create a single dash out of the two hyphens, go to the **Format** menu. Click on **AutoFormat.** Click on **Options.** Check the box beside **Hyphens (--) with dash (—).** Click on **OK.** Consult the **Help** menu on the toolbar at the top of your screen for additional information about formatting dashes.

Either of the following examples is acceptable.

```
He was--let there be no mistake about it--the guilty

    person.
```

```
He was—let there be no mistake about it—the guilty

    person.
```

spaces in the abbreviations *n.p.* and *n.d.* but leaving one space after the *n.* in *n. pag.*

- **No place of publication given:** N.p.: Houghton, 2003.
- **No publisher given:** Boston: n.p., 2003.
- **No date of publication given:** Boston: Houghton, n.d.
- **No pages given for a book entry:** Boston: Houghton, 2003. N. pag.
- **No pages given for a journal entry:** *College English* 52.4 (1992): n. pag.

Spacing of Punctuation Marks

You may leave one space after commas, semicolons, colons, end periods, question marks, and exclamation points as is the practice in material prepared for publication, or you may leave one space after internal punctuation marks (commas, semicolons, and colons) and two spaces after end marks (periods, question marks, and exclamation points).

Shortening Numbers

When citing inclusive page numbers in a bibliographic entry, give the complete numbers for any number between one and ninety-nine: 4–5, 12–17, 22–24, 78–93.

You may shorten numbers over ninety-nine if they fall within the same range (e.g., 200–299, 300–399, 1400–1499) or if the second number will be clear to your reader when shortened. Numbers such as these are clear: 107–09, 245–47, 372–78, 1002–09, 1408–578, 1710–12.

Shortening would be unclear for numbers such as these, so give the complete numbers: 87–127, 287–305, 397–405, 956–1023, 1714–1823.

Preparing an Annotated Bibliography

If your professor asks you to prepare an annotated bibliography, alphabetize your citations by author or by the first significant word of the title (excluding *A, An,* and *The*) if no author is known. Follow each citation with a brief summary of the contents of the source. Here is a sample entry from an annotated bibliography:

Norton, Mary Beth. "Finding the Devil in the Details of the

　　　Salem Witchcraft Trials." *Chronicle of Higher Education* 21

　　　Jan. 2000: B4+. Web. 25 Apr. 2010.

Mary Beth Norton, a professor of history at Cornell University, notes that previous accusations of witchcraft in the New England area targeted what she terms a few and never more than a dozen of what she calls "'the usual suspects'"—people who had long been suspected of practicing witchcraft by their neighbors. However, in Salem Village and the surrounding towns of Essex County, Massachusetts, hundreds of people were accused, and although some of those accused were "'the usual suspects,'" many had never been suspected of any witchlike behavior before. She believes the hysteria may be explained by fear of the Indian attacks that were occurring at the time. In fact, there was an attack only twenty miles from Salem Village while the trials were being held. Many believed that the devil and his minions were aiding the Indians; therefore, anyone consorting with the devil at that particular historical moment would have been seen as a threat to the survival of the village.

Citing Titles Correctly in a Works-Cited List

Capitalize the first and last words of the title and subtitle and all other words with the exception of

- articles (*a, an, the*)
- prepositions (*in, on, to, under, between, over, through,* etc.)
- the seven coordinating conjunctions (FANBOYS: *for, and, nor, but, or, yet, so*)
- the word *to* used in infinitives (*to* see, *to* run, *to* jump, etc.)

Converting All Titles to MLA Style

Follow the MLA-style capitalization rules described here for all titles and subtitles cited in your paper—even though those rules may not have been followed on the title page of the book, journal article, popular magazine article, or newspaper article that you are citing. If a quotation is used as part of a title, capitalize the words in the quotation according to MLA guidelines. If the first line of an untitled poem is used as the title, however, format the title just as it appears in the poem.

On the title page of a book, the title is typically formatted in a larger font than the subtitle and may be in all capital letters and in bold, bold italic, or some other font style that contrasts with whatever is used to format the subtitle. For example, a title and subtitle might look like this on the title page:

LITERATURE

AN INTRODUCTION TO

FICTION, POETRY, AND DRAMA

In your works-cited list, you would format the title shown above as follows, adding the colon between the title and subtitle and italicizing the entire title and the period that follows the title:

Literature: An Introduction to Fiction, Poetry, and Drama.

Online reference databases often format all titles and subtitles in bold, capitalizing all significant words in the title but using lowercase letters for all words in the subtitle with the exception of proper nouns used for names of persons or titles of books.

The title of a journal article is formatted in *InfoTrac OneFile* like this:

`American Tragedy: At 50, Willy Loman is still our favorite`
`failure.`

Reformatted according to MLA guidelines, this title would look like this:

`"American Tragedy: At Fifty, Willy Loman Is Still Our Favorite`
`Failure."`

Note that in MLA format, numbers that can be expressed in one or two words are spelled out.

A title of a journal article in *InfoTrac College Edition* is formatted like this:

`"From the Seen to the Told": the construction of subjectivity`
`in Toni Morrison's Beloved.`

Reformatted according to MLA guidelines, this title would look like this:

`"'From the Seen to the Told': The Construction of Subjectivity`
`in Toni Morrison's Beloved."`

You should also format the titles of entries from encyclopedias and dictionaries according to MLA guidelines for titles.

An entry in an encyclopedia might be formatted like this:

`TEMPLE ARCHITECTURE`

Reformatted following MLA guidelines, the title would look like this:

`"Temple Architecture."`

Italicizing Titles in a Works-Cited List

Italicize the titles of works that were published as separate entities and additional items listed here. In a works-cited list, also italicize the period after the italicized title. If a title ends with a question mark or exclamation point, also italicize that punctuation mark (e.g., *Absalom! Absalom!*).

In the text of your paper, do not type a period after an italicized title unless the title falls at the end of a sentence. The following titles should be italicized.

a book	*The Scarlet Letter*
a play	*Death of a Salesman*
a poem published as a separate work	*Paradise Lost*
a scholarly journal	*College English*
a popular magazine	*Time*
a newspaper	*New York Times*
a pamphlet	*Carolina Bays: A Wastewater Treatment Program*
a film	*The Hurt Locker*
a television or radio program	*Star Trek: The Next Generation*
a record album (LP)	*Abbey Road* (The Beatles)
a compact disc or audiocassette	*Lucky Town* (Bruce Springsteen)
a digital videodisc (DVD)	*Harry Potter and the Chamber of Secrets*
a painting	*Mona Lisa* (Leonardo da Vinci)
a sculpted work	*David* (Michelangelo)
a ship	HMS *Titanic,* USS *Yorktown*
a plane	*Enola Gay*
a spacecraft	*Apollo 13,* USS *Enterprise*
a ballet	*Swan Lake* (Tchaikovsky)
an opera	*The Magic Flute* (Mozart)
a symphony identified by title	*Eroica* (Beethoven)
a Web site	*Famous American Trials*
an online database	*LexisNexis Academic*

Using Quotation Marks around a Title in a Works-Cited List

Use double quotation marks around the title of a work too short to be published as a separate entity. The examples below are formatted with a period falling inside the end quotation marks, as these titles would appear in a works-cited or works-consulted list.

In the text of your paper, do not type a period at the end of a title in quotation marks unless the title falls at the end of the sentence. Remember that periods are always typed inside end quotation marks (as shown below).

a short story	"A Rose for Emily."
an essay	"Self-Reliance."
a short poem	"Stopping by Woods on a Snowy Evening."
a chapter in a book	"Writing and Revising Your Paper."
a lecture	"The American Scholar."
a scholarly journal article	"Scarlet A Minus."
an article in a popular magazine	"Weight Training Made Easy: Tooling Up."
a newspaper article	"Ruling May Cut Medical Costs."
a definition in a dictionary	"Enigma."
an article in a reference book	"Romanticism."
an encyclopedia article	"Frost, Robert Lee."
one episode of a television series	"The House." (one episode of *The Waltons*)
a song on an LP, CD, or audiocassette	"Born to Run." (Bruce Springsteen)
a page in a Web site	"The Salem Witch Trials."

Titles Not Italicized or in Quotation Marks in the Text of a Paper

Capitalize but do not italicize or use quotation marks around the following titles when you refer to them in the text of your paper:

names of sacred writings	the Bible, the Koran, the Upanishads
names of parts of sacred writings	Old Testament, New Testament, Gospels
versions of sacred writings	King James Version, Revised Standard Version
titles of books of the Bible	Exodus, Psalms, Matthew, Revelation
political documents	the Constitution, the Declaration of Independence

acts and laws	Bioterrorism Act of 2002
treaties	Treaty of Paris
societies	Society for the Prevention of Cruelty to Animals
buildings	Empire State Building
monuments	Washington Monument
conferences	College English Association Conference
workshops	Writing Center Workshop: Editing with Ease
series of books	Gale Author Series
high school or college courses	Composition and Literature, History 101

Italicizing Titles of Published Editions of Sacred Works

Italicize the title of a particular published edition of a sacred work just as you would any other book title in your works-cited or works-consulted list. (For more information on formatting sacred works in your works-cited list, see chapter 9.)

The Holy Bible: Revised Standard Version. Ed. Herbert G. May
and Bruce M. Metzger. New York: Oxford UP, 1962. Print.

The Koran. Trans. J[ohn] M[edows] Rodwell. London: Dent; New
York: Dutton, 1909. Print.

The New English Bible with the Apocrypha. Pocket ed. New York:
Oxford UP, 1970. Print.

The Talmud of the Land of Israel. Trans. Jacob Neusner. Chicago: U of Chicago P, 1987. Print.

The Upanishads: Breath of the Eternal. Trans. Swami Prabha-
vananda and Frederick Manchester. Hollywood: Vedanta,
1947. Print.

Formatting the Names of Parts of a Work in the Text of a Paper

In the text of your paper, do not capitalize, do not italicize, and do not type quotation marks around the names of parts of works:

chapter 7	afterword
act 2	bibliography
scene 5	works-cited list
stanza 12	list of works cited
introduction	works-consulted list
preface	table of contents
foreword	index

Formatting the Names of Parts of a Work in a Works-Cited List

If you are identifying a part of a work (introduction, preface, foreword, or afterword) in your works-cited list, capitalize the word, but do not italicize it or type quotation marks around it.

Moore, Harry T. Preface. *Graham Greene: The Entertainer.* By

   Peter Wolf. Carbondale: Southern Illinois UP; London: Fef-

   fer, 1972. x–xii. Print. Crosscurrents: Modern Critiques.

Formatting First Lines of Poems as Titles in a Works-Cited List

If the first line is used as the title of a poem, reproduce the line as it appears in the poem, using capitals and lowercase letters as used in your source. For example, the title of an Emily Dickinson poem would be formatted like this:

Dickinson, Emily. "My life had stood—a Loaded Gun." *Concise*

   Anthology of American Literature. Ed. George McMichael et

   al. 5th ed. Upper Saddle River, NJ: Prentice, 2001. 1139.

   Print.

Formatting Titles Containing Quotations

Follow standard MLA capitalization rules for titles when you use a quotation as part of your title or subtitle.

"'And That Has Made All the Difference': An Analysis of Frost's 'The Road Not Taken.'"

Formatting Titles Falling inside Other Titles

If a title or quotation that should be placed in quotation marks appears within the title of an article or essay you are citing, use single quotation marks around the title of the short story, poem, essay, or quotation, and use double quotation marks around the title of the article or essay.

"Symbols of Decay in Faulkner's 'A Rose for Emily.'"

If an essay or journal article title contains the title of a work that should be italicized (novel, play, work of art, etc.), use double quotation marks around the essay title and italicize the secondary title.

"Female Characters in Faulkner's *The Sound and the Fury*."

"Symbolism in Shakespeare's *Romeo and Juliet*."

If a book title contains the title of another work that should also be italicized, italicize the main title but not the secondary title.

A Reader's Guide to Moby Dick.

Twentieth Century Interpretations of Death of a Salesman.

CHAPTER 9

Citing Books and Parts of Books

Citing Books

Annotated Citation for a Book with One Author

Author's full name, last name first, followed by a period.

Title and subtitle italicized, followed by a period. Italicize the period.

City of publication, followed by a colon and one space. Give the postal abbreviation for the state only if the city is not well known or could be confused with another city.

Sundquist, Eric J. *Faulkner: The House Divided.* Baltimore:

Johns Hopkins UP, 1983. Print.

Publisher, followed by a comma. Shorten the names of well-known publishers, but give the full name of a university press, using *U* for *University* and *P* for *Press*.

Year of publication, followed by a period.

Medium of publication, followed by a period.

A Book with One Author

Cash, Jean. *Flannery O'Connor: A Life.* Knoxville: U of
Tennessee P, 2002. Print.

Richardson, William C. *Emily Dickinson: Her Life and Poetry.*
3rd ed. New York: Random, 1994. Print.

Wittenberg, Judith Bryant. *Faulkner: The Transfiguration of*

    Biography. Lincoln: U of Nebraska P, 1979. Print.

1. Give the author's name exactly as it appears on the title page, inverted for alphabetizing. Do not omit initials or shorten first or middle names to initials.

2. You may use initials if they appear on the title page: Eliot, T. S. You may clarify initials in square brackets if you think the clarification would be useful to your reader: Eliot, T[homas] S[tearns].

3. Place an essential suffix after the inverted name, preceded by a comma: Russell, John E., Jr. or Smith, Wilson R., IV.

4. Omit degrees or other titles (*PhD, Sister, Saint, Sir, Lady*).

5. If the author uses a pen name, you may give the author's real name in square brackets after the pseudonym: Twain, Mark [Samuel Langhorne Clemens].

6. Give both the title and the subtitle of a book. Use a colon between the title and subtitle. If there is a question mark, exclamation point, or dash after the main title, omit the colon.

7. Italicize the title and subtitle, including the period that follows the title: *Sylvia Plath: A Critical Study.*

8. If the title ends with a question mark or exclamation point, omit the usual end period and italicize the final punctuation mark: *Absalom! Absalom!*

9. Give the first city of publication listed on the title page.

10. Give the state, province for Canadian cities, or country only if the city is not well known or could be confused with another city: for example, Upper Saddle River, NJ; Charleston, SC; Charleston, WV; Rome, GA; Rome, NY; Rome, It.; Cambridge, MA; Cambridge, Eng.

11. Omit the state if the publisher's name identifies it: Baton Rouge: Louisiana State UP, 2003.

12. If you give the state, use the standard postal abbreviation without periods. Use MLA-recommended abbreviations for countries (*Eng.* for *England, It.* for *Italy*) and provinces of Canada (*ON* for *Ontario, QC* for *Québec*). (See abbreviations for states, Canadian provinces, and countries in chapter 22.)

13. Shorten the publisher's name to one significant word: Houghton Mifflin Co. becomes Houghton; W. W. Norton and Co., Inc. becomes Norton; McGraw-Hill, Inc. becomes McGraw, and so on. Give the full name of a university press, however, using the abbreviations *U* for *University* and *P* for *Press:* U of Chicago P, Yale UP. (See chapter 23 for more on shortening publishers' names.)

14. You need not give a publisher for a book published before 1900: London, 1878.

15. Give the most recent publication date listed on the title page or copyright page (the back of the title page). If no date of publication is given, give the most recent copyright date listed. If no date of publication or copyright can be found, use *n.d.* in place of the date.

16. List the medium of publication (*Print*), followed by a period.

Two or More Books by the Same Author

Smith, Charles R. *Robert Frost's Poetry.* 2nd ed. New York:

  Random, 1994. Print.

---. *Symbolism in Robert Frost's Poetry.* New York: Harper,

  1995. Print.

---, ed. *The Writing Style of Robert Frost: A Collection of*

  Critical Essays. Boston: Houghton, 1995. Print.

---, trans. *A Young Reader's Guide to the Poetry of Robert*

  Frost. By John T. Collins. Englewood Cliffs, NJ: Prentice,

  1997. Print.

1. Three hyphens used in place of the author's name mean the book was written by the same author cited in the previous entry, not that no author is known. If no author is known, begin the entry with the title.

2. Type a comma, one space, and the appropriate abbreviation after the three hyphens to indicate that the person is an editor (*ed.*), translator (*trans.*), or compiler (*comp.*) rather than an author.

3. List two or more books by the same person alphabetically by the first significant word of the title, excluding *A, An,* and *The.*

A Book with an Editor instead of an Author

Yeazell, Ruth Bernard, ed. *Henry James: A Collection of*

  Critical Essays. Englewood Cliffs, NJ: Prentice, 1994.

  Print. New Century Views.

A Book with an Author and an Editor

Whitman, Walt. *Complete Poetry and Selected Prose.* Ed. James E.

Miller, Jr. Boston: Houghton, 1959. Print. Riverside Editions.

Miller, James E., Jr., ed. *Complete Poetry and Selected Prose.* By

Walt Whitman. Boston: Houghton, 1959. Print. Riverside

Editions.

1. If you are citing material written by the author, begin your entry with the author's name and place the editor's name after the title, preceded by the abbreviation *Ed. (Edited by).*
2. If you are primarily citing material written by the editor, however, such as the introduction, explanatory materials, or notes, give the editor's name first, followed by the abbreviation *ed. (editor)* or *eds. (editors)* for more than one editor. After the title, type *By* and give the author's name.

A Book with Two Authors

Harrison, Samuel W., and Benjamin R. Wright. *Movies in the*

Twentieth Century. Cambridge, MA: Harvard UP, 1994. Print.

1. Give the authors' names in the same order in which they appear on the title page. Invert only the name of the first author listed.
2. If both authors have the same last name, give both names in full.

A Book with Three Authors

Peabody, Charles T., Robert N. James, Jr., and Sylvia W.

Samuels. *Ernest Hemingway: The Early Years.* Rev. ed.

New York: St. Martin's, 1993. Print.

1. Give all three names in the same order in which the names appear on the title page.
2. Invert only the name of the first author.

A Book with Four or More Authors

Glenn, Cheryl, et al. *Hodges' Harbrace Handbook.* 17th ed. 2009

MLA Update ed. Boston: Wadsworth-Cengage, 2010. Print.

```
Glenn, Cheryl, Robert K. Miller, Suzanne Strobeck Webb, and

    Loretta Gray. Hodges' Harbrace Handbook. 17th ed. 2009 MLA

    Update ed. Boston: Wadsworth-Cengage, 2010. Print.
```

1. Give the name of the first author listed, and then type *et al.,* which means "and others." Note that *al.* is an abbreviation of the Latin word *alii;* therefore, it is always followed by a period.
2. If you prefer, you may give the names of all the authors in the order in which they are given on the title page. Invert only the name of the first author listed.
3. In the model citations above, note that *Hodges' Harbrace Handbook* was published by Wadsworth, which is an imprint of Cengage Learning. When the names of two publishers appear on the title page, check the copyright page to see whether one of the publishers is an imprint or division of the other publisher. If this is the case, give a shortened name for the imprint or smaller company (Wadsworth Publishing should be shortened to Wadsworth), type a hyphen, and give a shortened name for the larger company (Cengage Learning should be shortened to Cengage). Thus, you would give the publisher for the book cited above as Wadsworth-Cengage. (See page 93 for more information about how to cite publishers' imprints.)

A Book with Four or More Editors

```
Gross, Seymour, et al., eds. The Scarlet Letter: An Authori-

    tative Text, Essays in Criticism and Scholarship. By

    Nathaniel Hawthorne. 3rd ed. New York: Norton, 1988.

    Print. Norton Critical Editions.

Gross, Seymour, Sculley Bradley, Richmond Croom Beatty, and

    E. Hudson Long, eds. The Scarlet Letter: An Authoritative

    Text, Essays in Criticism and Scholarship. By Nathaniel

    Hawthorne. 3rd ed. New York: Norton, 1988. Print. Norton

    Critical Editions.
```

1. Give the name of the first editor listed, and then type *et al.,* which means "and others." Note that *al.* is an abbreviation of the Latin word *alii;* therefore, it is always followed by a period.

2. If you prefer, you may give the names of all the editors in the order in which they are given on the title page. Invert only the name of the first editor listed.

A Book with a Corporate Author

American College of Sports Medicine. *ACSM's Exercise Manage-*

   ment for Persons with Chronic Diseases and Disabilities.

   2nd ed. Champaign, IL: Human Kinetics, 2003. Print.

1. If the name of a foundation, committee, council, association, commission, university, society, or other type of organization is given on the title page and if no individual authors or editors are identified, cite the name of the organization as author.
2. Omit the article *A*, *An*, or *The* if it appears in the name of the organization. *The American Mathematical Society* would be cited as *American Mathematical Society*.
3. Cite the organization as the author even if the same organization is listed as the publisher of the book.

A Book with No Author Given

Broadcasting and Cable Yearbook 2002-2003. New York:

   Broadcasting and Cable, 2002. Print.

1. If no author is given on the title page, begin your citation with the title of the book, italicized and followed by a period, also italicized.
2. Alphabetize the work by its title, ignoring the article *A*, *An*, or *The* if it begins the title.
3. Give the city of publication, the publisher, and the date of publication or most recent copyright date, followed by a period.
4. Give the medium of publication, followed by a period.

An Edition Other Than the First

Sydney, Beatrice E. *A Study of James Joyce.* 2nd ed. Boston:

   Little, 2002. Print.

1. If the book is not a first edition, give the edition number specified on the title page—*2nd ed., 3rd ed., 4th ed., Rev. ed.* (for *Revised edition*),

Abr. ed. (for *Abridged edition*)—after the title. Use MLA-recommended abbreviations for edition numbers. (See chapter 22 for a list.)

2. If an editor's, translator's, or compiler's name appears after the title, give the edition number after the editor's, translator's, or compiler's name.

Annotated Citation for a Book in a Series

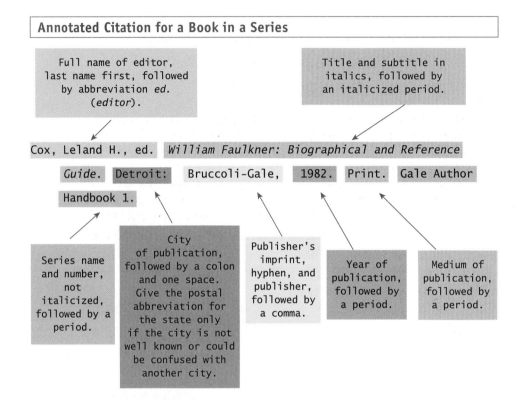

A Book in a Series

Wilson, C. Philip, Charles C. Hogan, and Ira L. Mintz, eds.

    Fear of Being Fat: The Treatment of Anorexia Nervosa and

    Bulimia. New York: Aronson, 1983. Print. Classical

    Psychoanalysis and Its Applications.

1. If the book you are citing is part of a series of books, the series name and sometimes a series number will be given above the title of the book or on the page opposite the title page (called the *half-title page*).

2. Give the name of the series (not italicized or in quotation marks) at the end of the listing, after the medium of publication and followed by a period. Use the MLA abbreviation *Ser.* for *Series*: Penguin Classics Ser.

3. If a series number is given, type it immediately after the series name, inside the period: Gale Author Handbook 2.

A Book with More Than One Publisher Listed on the Title Page

Wolf, Peter. *Graham Greene: The Entertainer.* Carbondale:

    Southern Illinois UP; London: Feffer, 1972. Print.

    Crosscurrents: Modern Critiques.

1. If a book has been published by different publishers (usually in two different countries) and both are listed on the title page, list both in the order in which they are given on the title page; put a semicolon after the first publisher listed. Then give the date of publication or most recent copyright date. Check the copyright page to make sure that the publishers listed are not two offices of the same publisher or that one publisher is not a division or an imprint of the other, larger publisher.

2. Give the medium of publication. Then give the series title (if there is one).

A Publisher's Imprint

Meyer, Michael. *Thinking and Writing about Literature.* Boston:

    Bedford-St. Martin's, 1995. Print.

1. Publishers often group the various categories of books they publish under special names called *publishers' imprints*. If the name of a publisher's imprint appears on the title page along with the publisher's name, type the imprint name, a hyphen, and the publisher's name (e.g., Bedford-St. Martin's, Vintage-Random, Washington Square-Pocket, Perennial-Harper, Collier-Macmillan, Wadsworth-Cengage). Check the copyright page to determine whether you are dealing with two completely different publishers who might have published the book (usually in different countries) or with an imprint (or smaller division) of a larger company.

2. In the model citation above, *Thinking and Writing about Literature* was published by Bedford Books, which is an imprint of St. Martin's Press, Inc. Always give the name of the imprint before the name of the larger publisher.

3. You will find additional information about publishers, including a list of the imprints of a particular publisher, in references such as *Literary Market Place* and *Books in Print*, which should be available in your university library in print, online, or in both formats.

A Multivolume Work

Smith, Raymond C. *The Novels of Thomas Hardy.* 4 vols. Boston:

Little, 1988-93. Print.

1. List the author (name inverted), the title (italicized), the editor's name if there is one, the edition number if the work is not a first edition, and the total number of volumes in the work.
2. If you cite material from several volumes of a multivolume work, identify the volume you used in your in-text parenthetical citation: (Smith 2: 345).
3. Give the inclusive dates if the volumes were published over a period of years: 1955-62. If the work is still in progress, give the number of volumes currently available (2 vols. to date). Give the date the first volume was published, and type a hyphen, one space, and a period (1996- .).
4. Give the medium of publication, followed by a period.

One Volume of a Multivolume Work

Dixon, Murphey R. *George Eliot: A Biography.* 2nd ed. Vol. 2.

Oxford, Eng.: Oxford UP, 1992. Print. 4 vols.

1. If you used only one volume, give the volume number after the title, editor if there is one, and edition number if there is one.
2. Give publication information only for the volume you used.
3. If you wish, you can give the total number of volumes and inclusive publication dates (1992–96) after the medium of publication.

A Translation

Sophocles. *Oedipus the King.* Trans. Francis Storr. Ed. T. E.

Page and W. H. D. Rouse. London: Heinemann, 1912. Print.

The New Testament: An Expanded Translation. Trans. Kenneth S.

Wuest. Grand Rapids, MI: Eerdmans, 1961. Print.

1. If you are primarily referring to the work rather than to the translator of the work, cite the author of the work (if given) and the italicized title of the work, followed by an italicized period and one space.
2. Then type the abbreviation *Trans.* (*Translated by*), and give the name of the translator.

3. If both a translator and an editor are listed on the title page, as in the first entry above, list the names after the title in the order in which they appear on the title page.

A Religious Text

The Holy Bible: Revised Standard Version. Ed. Herbert G. May

and Bruce M. Metzger. New York: Oxford UP, 1962. Print.

The Koran. Trans. J[ohn] M[edows] Rodwell. London: Dent;

New York: Dutton, 1909. Print.

The New Testament: An Expanded Translation. Trans. Kenneth

S[amuel] Wuest. Grand Rapids, MI: Eerdmans, 1961. Print.

The New Testament with Psalms and Proverbs: Contemporary

English Version. New York: Amer. Bible Soc., 1995. Print.

The Talmud of the Land of Israel. Trans. Jacob Neusner.

Chicago: U of Chicago P, 1987. Print.

Tyndale, William, trans. *Tyndale's New Testament.* New Haven,

CT: Yale UP, 1989. Print.

The Upanishads: Breath of the Eternal. Trans. Swami Prabha-

vananda and Frederick Manchester. Hollywood: Vedanta,

1947. Print.

1. Cite a published edition of a religious work just as you would any other published book listed in your works-cited list.
2. Italicize the title of the work and the period that follows the title.
3. Italicize the version if it is the subtitle of the work (e.g., *The Holy Bible: Revised Standard Version.*).
4. If the work already has a subtitle, give the version (if there is one) after the title, capitalized but not italicized, followed by a period and one space.
5. If the title page lists both an editor and a translator, give the names after the title in the order in which they appear on the title page.
6. If the full names of the editor(s) or translator(s) are given on the copyright page or in an online catalog, you may supply information missing

on the title page in square brackets if you think it would be useful to your reader (e.g., Trans. Kenneth S[amuel] Wuest.).

7. If you are primarily discussing the work of the editor or translator, give that person's name at the beginning of the citation, followed by the abbreviation *ed.* (*editor*) or *trans.* (*translator*), as in the Tyndale entry above.

8. Give the city of publication, publisher, and date of publication or most recent copyright date. End with the medium of publication.

9. If the citation begins with the title, alphabetize it in your works-cited list by the title, ignoring the article *A*, *An*, or *The* at the beginning of the title.

Citing Parts of Books

A Chapter in a Book

Crews, Frederick. "Psychological Romance." *The Sins of the Fathers: Hawthorne's Psychological Themes.* New York: Oxford UP, 1966. 3-26. Print.

An Introduction, Preface, Foreword, or Afterword

Feal, Rosemary. Foreword. *MLA Handbook for Writers of Research Papers.* 7th ed. New York: MLA, 2009. xiii-xv. Print.

Johnson, Thomas H. Introduction. *The Complete Poems of Emily Dickinson.* Ed. Johnson. Boston: Little, 1960. v-xi. Print.

Miller, James E., Jr. Introduction. *Complete Poetry and Selected Prose.* By Walt Whitman. Ed. Miller. Boston: Houghton, 1959. xix-liii. Print. Riverside Editions.

Graff, Gerald. Preface. *Beyond the Culture Wars: How Teaching the Conflicts Can Revitalize American Education.* By Graff. New York: Norton, 1992. vii-x. Print.

Frost, Robert. "The Figure a Poem Makes." Preface. *Collected Poems.* By Frost. New York: Holt, 1939. v-ix. Print.

1. Give the author of the introduction, preface, foreword, or afterword.

2. Capitalize but do not italicize or use quotation marks around the name of the appropriate part: *Introduction, Preface, Foreword,* or *Afterword.*

3. If the introduction, preface, foreword, or afterword has a title, give it in double quotation marks. Then give the name of the part (not italicized or in quotation marks), followed by the title of the book (italicized).

4. Type the word *By* after the book title, and give the full name of the author of the book if different from that of the writer of the introduction, preface, foreword, or afterword and not given in the book title.

5. If the author of the book also wrote the introduction, preface, foreword, or afterword, type the word *By* after the title of the book and give only the author's last name.

6. Type *Ed.* (*Edited by*), and give the name of the editor (if there is one) after the name of the author.

7. If the editor of the book also wrote the part, type the word *By* after the title of the book and give the author's full name, followed by a period and one space. Then type the abbreviation *Ed.,* and give the editor's last name, followed by a period and one space.

8. Give the city of publication, publisher, and date of publication or most recent copyright date, followed by a period and one space.

9. Give the first and last page numbers of the introduction, preface, foreword, or afterword as they appear in the source (usually in small Roman numerals), followed by a period.

10. Give the medium of publication, followed by a period.

Citing Anthologies and Works in Anthologies

An Edited Anthology

You would typically cite an entire anthology only if cross-referencing a number of works from the same anthology. Each short story, essay, poem, play, or novel you have used from the anthology must be cited individually, as in the following model citations (unless you are cross-referencing). For more on creating a cross-referenced bibliography, see page 101. For an example of a cross-referenced bibliography, see the works-consulted list on pages 293–94.

```
Kennedy, X. J., and Dana Gioia, eds. Literature: An Introduc-

    tion to Fiction, Poetry, and Drama. 8th ed. Interactive

    ed. New York: Longman, 2002. Print.
```

McMichael, George, et al., eds. *Concise Anthology of American Literature.* 5th ed. Upper Saddle River, NJ: Prentice, 2001. Print.

McMichael, George, J. C. Levenson, Leo Marx, David E. Smith, Mae Miller Claxton, and Susan Bunn, eds. *Concise Anthology of American Literature.* 5th ed. Upper Saddle River, NJ: Prentice, 2001. Print.

Annotated Citation for a Short Story in an Anthology

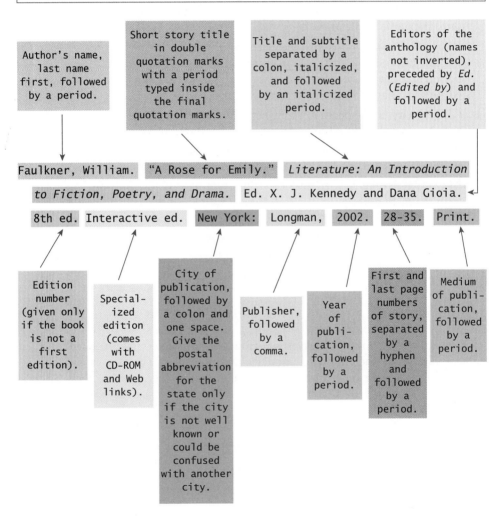

A Short Story, Poem, or Essay in an Anthology

Crane, Stephen. "The Open Boat." *Literature: An Introduction*
   to Fiction, Poetry, and Drama. Ed. X. J. Kennedy and Dana
   Gioia. 8th ed. Interactive ed. New York: Longman, 2002.
   197–215. Print.

1. Give the author or authors of the work. Invert the name of the first author listed.
2. Type double quotation marks around the title of the short story, poem, or essay, with a period typed inside the final quotation marks.
3. Italicize the title of the anthology and the period that follows.
4. Type the abbreviation *Ed.* (*Edited by*), and give the name(s) of the editor(s) of the anthology. If two editors are listed, do not type a comma after the first editor's name (Ed. X. J. Kennedy and Dana Gioia.).
5. If the anthology is not a first edition, specify the edition number or type using the suggested MLA abbreviation (*2nd ed., Rev. ed., Abr. ed.*) listed in chapter 22. If you are using a specialized edition of a text, such as an interactive edition (one with a CD-ROM and Web links), specify the type of edition.
6. Give the city of publication, the publisher, and the date of publication or most recent copyright date listed on the copyright page, followed by a period and one space.
7. Give the first page and last page numbers of the story, poem, or essay, separated with a hyphen and followed by a period.
8. End with the medium of publication and a period.

A Play in an Anthology

Williams, Tennessee. *The Glass Menagerie. Literature: An Intro-*
   duction to Fiction, Poetry, and Drama. Ed. X. J. Kennedy
   and Dana Gioia. 8th ed. Interactive ed. New York: Longman,
   2002. 1951–2000. Print.

1. Give the author(s) of the play. Invert the name of the first author listed.
2. Italicize the title of the play and the period that follows it.
3. Italicize the title of the anthology and the period that follows it.

4. Type the abbreviation *Ed.* (*Edited by*), and give the name(s) of the editor(s) of the anthology. If two editors are listed, do not type a comma after the first editor's name (Ed. X. J. Kennedy and Dana Gioia.).

5. If the anthology is not a first edition, specify the edition number or type using the MLA abbreviation (*2nd ed., Rev. ed., Abr. ed.*) listed in chapter 22. If you are using a specialized edition of a text, such as an interactive edition (one with a CD-ROM and Web links), specify the type of edition.

6. Give the city of publication, the publisher, and the date of publication or most recent copyright date listed on the copyright page, followed by a period and one space.

7. Give the first page number of the play, type a hyphen, and give the last page number, followed by a period.

8. End with the medium of publication and a period.

A Novel in an Anthology

Twain, Mark [Samuel Langhorne Clemens]. *The Adventures of*

   Huckleberry Finn. Concise Anthology of American Literature.

   Ed. George McMichael et al. 5th ed. Upper Saddle River, NJ:

   Prentice, 2001. 1196–1380. Print.

1. Give the author or authors of the novel. Invert the name of the first.

2. If the author uses a pen name, you may give the author's real name in square brackets after the pseudonym.

3. Italicize the title of the novel and the period that follows it.

4. Italicize the title of the anthology and the period that follows it.

5. Type the abbreviation *Ed.* (*Edited by*), and give the name(s) of the editor(s) of the anthology. If two editors are listed, do not type a comma after the first editor's name (Ed. X. J. Kennedy and Dana Gioia.).

6. If the anthology is not a first edition, specify the edition number or type using the MLA abbreviation (*2nd ed., Rev. ed., Abr. ed.*) listed in chapter 22. If you are using a specialized edition of a text, such as an interactive edition (one with a CD-ROM and Web links), specify the type of edition.

7. Give the city of publication, the publisher, and the date of publication or most recent copyright date listed on the copyright page, followed by a period and one space.

8. Give the first page number of the novel, type a hyphen, and give the last page number of the novel, followed by a period.

9. End with the medium of publication and a period.

Cross-Referencing Works from an Anthology

When citing several literary works from the same anthology, avoid unnecessary repetition in your works-cited list by cross-referencing. If you quote lines from an essay, a short story, a poem, a play, and a novel all collected in the same anthology, give a complete bibliographical citation for the anthology; then cross-reference each of the literary works by following the guidelines listed here. List the cross-referenced citations in alphabetical order by last name of the author or editor (or by title if no author/editor is known).

A Poem

Dickinson, Emily. "Success is counted sweetest." McMichael

    et al. 1125.

An Essay

Emerson, Ralph Waldo. "Self-Reliance." McMichael et al. 655-72.

A Short Story

Hemingway, Ernest. "The Short Happy Life of Francis Macomber."

    McMichael et al. 1822-44.

An Entire Anthology

McMichael, George, et al., eds. *Concise Anthology of American*

    Literature. 5th ed. Upper Saddle River, NJ: Prentice,

    2001. Print.

A Play or Novel

Miller, Arthur. *Death of a Salesman.* McMichael et al. 1931-95.

1. Give the author(s) of the essay, short story, poem, play, or novel.

2. Give the title of an essay, short poem, or short story in double quotation marks followed by a period typed inside the final quotation marks.

3. Italicize the title of a book-length poem, play, or novel and the period that follows it.

4. If one particular literary work (but not the contents of the entire anthology) was translated from a foreign language into English, type *Trans.* (*Translated by*) after the title of the work, and give the name of the translator, followed by a period (Trans. James T. Woods.).

5. Give the last name of the editor(s) of the anthology and the first and last pages of the essay, short story, poem, play, or novel, followed by a period. Do not type a period or comma between the name of the editor(s) of the anthology and the page numbers of the work. A period is needed only if you use the Latin phrase *et al.* (*et alii,* which means "and others") after the name of the editor because *alii* is always abbreviated (McMichael et al. 24-46.).

6. If you list two or more works by the editor of this anthology in your works-cited list, type a comma after the editor's name and give the full or a short form of the title after the editor's name and before the inclusive page numbers of the work. No comma follows the title.

Citing Essays

An Essay Written for a Collection of Essays

Martin, Samuel A. "Willy Loman: A Modern Tragic Hero." *Arthur*

    Miller: A Collection of Essays. Ed. Glenn T. Richardson.

    Boston: Houghton, 1992. 72-84. Print.

Cross-Referencing Essays from a Collection of Essays

When you are citing several essays from the same essay collection, avoid unnecessary repetition in your works-cited list by cross-referencing. For example, suppose you cite information from three scholarly essays analyzing twentieth-century American poetry. Give a complete bibliographical citation for the entire collection; then cross-reference each of the essays you used by following the guidelines given here. List the cross-referenced citations in alphabetical order by the last name of the author or editor (or by the title if no author/editor is known).

Daniels, Kate. "The Demise of the 'Delicate Prisons': The
    Woman's Movement in Twentieth-Century American Poetry."
    Myers and Wojahn 224-53.

Hirsch, Edward. "Helmet of Fire: American Poetry in the 1920s."
    Myers and Wojahn 54-83.

Myers, Jack, and David Wojahn, eds. *A Profile of Twentieth-*
    Century American Poetry. Carbondale: Southern Illinois UP,
    1991. Print.

Ullman, Leslie. "American Poetry in the 1960s." Myers and
    Wojahn 190-223.

1. Give the author or authors of the essay. Invert the name of the first.
2. Give the title of the essay in double quotation marks with a period inside the final quotation marks. If there is a title that should also be in quotation marks within the essay title, place the secondary title in single quotation marks.
3. If one particular essay (but not the entire collection) was translated from a foreign language into English, type *Trans.* (*Translated by*) after the title of the essay and give the name of the translator (Trans. Robert K. Moore.).
4. Give the last name(s) of the editor(s) of the essay collection (not followed by a comma) and the first and last page numbers of the essay, separated by a hyphen and followed by a period.
5. If you list two or more works by the editor(s) of this collection in your works-cited list, put a comma after the name(s) of the editor(s) and give the full or a short form of the title after the name(s) of the editor(s) and before the inclusive page numbers for the essay. No comma follows the title.

Myers and Wojahn, *Profile* 190-223.

Myers and Wojahn, *Study* 205-10.

Citing Reprinted Essays, Articles, and Excerpts

A Scholarly Journal Article Reprinted in an Essay Collection

Seltzer, Mark. "*The Princess Casamassima:* Realism and the Fan-
    tasy of Surveillance." *Nineteenth-Century Fiction* 35.4
    (1981): 506-34. Rpt. in *Henry James: A Collection of*

> *Critical Essays.* Ed. Ruth Bernard Yeazell. Englewood
>
> Cliffs, NJ: Prentice, 1994. 98-117. Print.

1. Tell your reader where and when the article was first printed. The original publication information is usually given at the bottom of the first page of the article.
2. Then type *Rpt. in* (*Reprinted in*), and give full publication information on the essay collection you actually used.

An Essay from a Book Reprinted in an Essay Collection

> Porter, Carolyn. "Gender and Value in *The American.*" *New Essays*
>
> *on* The American. Ed. Martha Banta. Cambridge: Cambridge
>
> UP, 1987. 99-125. Rpt. in *Henry James: A Collection of*
>
> *Critical Essays.* Ed. Ruth Bernard Yeazell. Englewood
>
> Cliffs, NJ: Prentice, 1994. 39-59. Print.

1. Tell your reader where and when the material was first printed. The original publication information is usually given at the bottom of the first page of the article.
2. Then type *Rpt. in* (*Reprinted in*), and give full publication information on the essay collection you actually used.
3. Note that the title of the novel *The American* is not italicized in the title of the essay collection (*New Essays on* The American). When a title that is italicized falls inside another title that is italicized, the primary title is italicized (the title of the collection), but the secondary title is not (the title of the novel discussed in the essay collection).

What Is a Critical Edition?

A critical edition typically contains the text of a literary work, such as a novel or play, and a collection of excerpts from historical documents, reviews, scholarly journal articles, and books in which the work is analyzed.

A Scholarly Journal Article Reprinted in a Critical Edition

Abel, Darrel. "Hawthorne's Hester." *College English* 13.4 (1952):

    303-09. Rpt. in *The Scarlet Letter: An Authoritative Text,*

    Essays in Criticism and Scholarship. By Nathaniel Hawthorne.

    Ed. Seymour Gross et al. 3rd ed. New York: Norton, 1988.

    300-08. Print. Norton Critical Editions.

1. Give the full name of the author, last name first. If more than one author is listed, give the names in the order in which they appear on the title page of the article, inverting only the name of the first author.

2. Type double quotation marks around the title of the article, and place a period inside the final quotation marks.

3. Italicize the title of the journal, and type one space but no period after it.

4. Omit articles such as *The* at the beginning of the journal title, but retain *The* at the beginning of the title of the journal article and the book.

5. Give the volume number, a period, and issue number in Arabic numerals followed by one space, and type parentheses around the year of publication. Type a colon and one space after the end parenthesis, and give the first page number of the article, type a hyphen, and give the last page number, followed by a period.

6. If no volume number is given, use the issue number in place of it.

7. The original publication information on the journal in which the material was originally published is usually given at the bottom of the first page of the reprinted material.

8. Type *Rpt. in* (*Reprinted in*), and give the title and subtitle of the critical edition, separated by a colon, italicized, and followed by a period and one space.

9. Type *By,* and give the full name of the author of the literary work being analyzed, followed by a period.

10. Type *Ed.* (*Edited by*), and give the name of the editor(s) of the critical edition, followed by a period.

11. If the critical edition is not a first edition, give the edition number (abbreviated following MLA guidelines as described in chapter 22).

12. Give the city of publication, the publisher, and the date of publication or most recent copyright date, followed by a period and one space.

13. Give the first and last page numbers of the material as printed in the critical edition, separated by a hyphen and followed by a period.

14. Give the medium of publication, followed by a period.

15. Give the name (and number if there is one) of the series of which the critical edition is a part (e.g., Gale Author Handbook 2) last, not italicized, followed by a period.

A Chapter from a Book Reprinted in a Critical Edition

Crews, Frederick. "The Ruined Wall." *The Sins of the Fathers: Hawthorne's Psychological Themes.* New York: Oxford UP, 1966. 136-53. Rpt. in *The Scarlet Letter: An Authoritative Text, Essays in Criticism and Scholarship.* By Nathaniel Hawthorne. Ed. Seymour Gross et al. 3rd ed. New York: Norton, 1988. 361-71. Print. Norton Critical Editions.

1. Give the author of the book, name inverted for alphabetizing.
2. Give the title of the chapter in double quotation marks, followed by a period typed inside the end quotation marks.
3. Give the title and subtitle of the book in which the chapter was originally published, separated by a colon, italicized, and followed by a period.
4. Give the city of publication, the publisher, and the date of publication or most recent copyright date, followed by a period and one space.
5. Give the first and last pages of the chapter as originally published, separated by a hyphen and followed by a period and one space.
6. The original publication information for the book in which the chapter was originally published is usually given at the bottom of the first page of the reprinted chapter.
7. Type *Rpt. in* (*Reprinted in*), and give the title and subtitle of the critical edition, separated by a colon, italicized, and followed by a period.
8. Type *By,* and give the full name of the author of the literary work being analyzed, followed by a period.
9. Type *Ed.,* the name(s) of the editor(s) of the critical edition, and a period.
10. Give the edition number (abbreviated following MLA guidelines) if the critical edition is not a first edition.
11. Give the city of publication, the publisher, and the date of publication or most recent copyright date, followed by a period and one space.

12. Give the first and last page numbers of the chapter as printed in the critical edition, separated by a hyphen and followed by a period.

13. Give the medium of publication, followed by a period.

14. Give the name (and number if there is one) of the series of which the critical edition is a part (e.g., Norton Critical Editions), not italicized, followed by a period.

An Excerpt from a Chapter in a Book Reprinted in a Critical Edition

Male, Roy R. "[Transformations: Hester and Arthur.]" *The Scarlet Letter: An Authoritative Text, Essays in Criticism and Scholarship.* By Nathaniel Hawthorne. Ed. Seymour Gross et al. 3rd ed. New York: Norton, 1988. 325-35. Norton Critical Editions. Excerpt from *Hawthorne's Tragic Vision.* Austin: U of Texas P, 1957. 102-17. Print.

1. Give the author of the excerpted book, name inverted for alphabetizing.

2. Give the title of the excerpt from the book in double quotation marks, followed by a period typed inside the final quotation marks.

3. In the Male entry, the square brackets indicate that the title of the reprinted excerpt from a chapter in Male's book was created by Seymour Gross et al. rather than by the author of the material. Gross and his coeditors created their own title for the material they used from Male's book because they used only a small part of Male's chapter. If Gross et al. had reprinted an entire chapter or almost all of a chapter from the book, they would have used Male's chapter title.

4. Give the title and subtitle of the critical edition, separated by a colon, italicized, and followed by a period.

5. Type *By,* and give the full name of the author of the literary work being analyzed, followed by a period.

6. Type *Ed.* (*Edited by*), and give the name of the editor or editors of the critical edition, followed by a period.

7. Give the edition number (abbreviated following MLA guidelines) if the critical edition is not a first edition.

8. Give the city of publication, the publisher, and the date of publication or most recent copyright date, followed by a period and one space.

9. Give the first and last page numbers of the material as printed in the critical edition, separated by a hyphen and followed by a period.

10. Give the name (and number if there is one) of the series of which the critical edition is a part (e.g., Norton Critical Editions), not italicized, followed by a period and one space.

11. Type *Excerpt from* and give the title and subtitle of the book in which the material was originally published, separated by a colon, italicized, and followed by a period.

12. Give the city of publication, the publisher, and the date of publication or most recent copyright date, followed by a period and one space.

13. Give the first and last page numbers of the material as originally published, separated by a hyphen and followed by a period and one space.

14. The original publication information for the book in which the material was originally published is usually given at the bottom of the first page of the reprinted material.

15. Give medium of publication, followed by a period, last.

CHAPTER 10

Citing Periodicals

What Is a Periodical?

A periodical is a source that is published periodically (at regular intervals). Most scholarly journals are published quarterly (four times per year), although some are published more or less frequently. Popular magazines are usually published every week (weekly), every two weeks (biweekly), every four weeks (monthly), or every two months (bimonthly). Newspapers are usually published every two weeks (biweekly), once a week, twice a week, or daily.

Citing Scholarly Journal Articles

Annotated Citation for an Article from a Scholarly Journal with Continuous Pagination

Author's full name, last name first, followed by a period.

Title and subtitle, separated with a colon and typed in double quotation marks with a period typed inside the final quotation marks. Novel title italicized.

Adams, Jenny. "Marketing the Medieval: The Quest for Authentic History in Michael Crichton's *Timeline*." *Journal of Popular Culture* 36.4 (2003): 704-23. Print.

Volume number, followed by a period and no space, and the issue number, followed by one space.

Year of publication in parentheses, followed by a colon.

First page, a hyphen, and last page of article (second number shortened if appropriate), followed by a period.

Medium of publication, followed by a period.

Journal title italicized (not followed by a period).

An Article from a Scholarly Journal with Continuous Pagination

Adams, Jenny. "Marketing the Medieval: The Quest for Authentic
History in Michael Crichton's *Timeline*." *Journal of Popular Culture* 36.4 (2003): 704-23. Print.

Koolish, Lynda. "'To Be Loved and Cry Shame': A Psychological
Reading of Toni Morrison's *Beloved*." *MELUS* 26.4 (2001):
169-96. Print.

Lawson, Andrew. "'Spending for Vast Returns': Sex, Class, and
Commerce in the First *Leaves of Grass*." *American Literature* 75.2 (2003): 335-65. Print.

Ribkoff, Fred. "Shame, Guilt, Empathy, and the Search for
Identity in Arthur Miller's *Death of a Salesman*." *Modern Drama* 43.1 (2000): 48-55. Print.

1. In a journal published quarterly, the volume for a particular year will contain four issues. If the first issue of the year ends with page 275, and the next issue begins with page 276, the journal has continuous pagination.
2. Give the full name of the author, last name first. If more than one author is listed, give the names in the order in which they appear on the title page of the article, inverting only the name of the first author.
3. Type double quotation marks around the title of the article, and place a period inside the final quotation marks.
4. Italicize the title of the journal, and type one space but no period. Omit articles such as *The* at the beginning of the journal title, but retain *The* at the beginning of the title of the journal article.
5. Type the volume number in Arabic numbers, a period, and one space. Then type the issue number and one space, and type parentheses around the year of publication. Type a colon and one space after the end parenthesis, and give the first page number of the article, type a hyphen, and give the last page number, followed by a period.
6. You may omit the month (May 1994) or season (Fall 1995) if the journal's pages will be numbered continuously when all the issues are bound together into one volume at the end of the year. However, if you believe this information will be helpful to readers or if your

professor asks you to do so, MLA allows you to include the month, or season in your entry: 34.1 (Jan. 2002): 48-62.

7. If no volume number is given, use the issue number in place of the volume number.

8. End with the medium of publication and a period.

9. If a title or quotation that should be in quotation marks appears within the title of the article you are citing, use single quotation marks around the title of the short story, poem, essay, or quotation, and use double quotation marks around the title of the journal article. Note that the period falls inside both the single and the double quotation marks in the title below.

"Naturalism in Crane's 'The Open Boat.'"

10. Italicize the title of a novel or play or the name of a work of art that appears in the title of a journal article.

Rose, Jacqueline. "*Hamlet*--the *Mona Lisa* of Literature."

Critical Quarterly 28.2 (1986): 35-49. Print.

An Article from a Scholarly Journal without Continuous Pagination

Rector, Liam. "The Cultural, the Religious, and the War Wars."

American Poetry Review 32.3 (2003): 45-46. Print.

1. If the journal begins each issue published during the year with page 1, be sure to give the issue number as well as the volume number.

2. Give the full name of the author, last name first. If more than one author is listed, give the names in the order in which they appear on the title page of the article, inverting only the name of the first author.

3. Type double quotation marks around the title of the article, and place a period inside the final quotation marks.

4. Italicize the title of the journal. Do not type a period after the title.

5. After the title, type the volume number, a period and no space, the issue number, one space, the year of publication in parentheses, a colon and one space, and the first and last page numbers of the article, separated by a hyphen and followed by a period. End with the medium of publication and a period.

Finding the Volume and Issue Number of a Bound Journal Article

If you are using a bound journal, make sure you have found the correct volume and issue numbers for the article you are citing. There may be several volumes and many issues of the journal together in the same binding. The table of contents for each issue of the journal will give the journal title, the volume number, the issue number, the date of publication, and a list of all the articles contained in that particular issue. Make sure that your article is listed in the table of contents for the volume and issue you are citing.

An Article from a Journal Published in More Than One Series

Voigt, Ellen Bryant. "Syntax: Rhythm of Thought, Rhythm of

Song." *Kenyon Review* ns 25.1 (2003): 144-63. Print.

If a journal has been published in more than one series, give the series designation—*2nd ser., 3rd ser., os* (*old* or *original series*), or *ns* (*new series*) (not capitalized)—between the title of the journal and the volume and issue numbers. Do not type a period after *os* or *ns*.

A Special Issue of a Scholarly Journal

Walden, Daniel, ed. *The World of Chaim Potok*. Spec. issue

of *Studies in American Jewish Literature* 4.1 (1984):

1-123. Print.

1. Give the full name of the editor of the special issue, last name first, followed by the abbreviation *ed.* (*editor*). If more than one editor is listed, give the names in the order in which they appear on the title page, inverting only the name of the first editor. If four or more editors are listed, either give all the names or give only the first name, followed by *et al.* (*and others*): Frankel, Laura, et al., eds.
2. If no editor is identified, begin the entry with the title of the special issue, italicized and followed by a period.
3. Type *Spec. issue of* and the italicized title of the journal (but no period).
4. Type the volume number, a period, the issue number, and one space.

5. Follow with the year of publication in parentheses, a colon, and one space.

6. Type the first and last page numbers of the entire issue, a period, the medium of publication, and a period.

7. If the special issue was published as a book, begin with the editor's name and the italicized title of the book. Then give the city of publication, publisher, year, and the medium of publication. Then type *Rpt. of spec. issue of,* the journal's name (italicized), its volume and issue numbers (separated by a period), the year of publication (in parentheses), a colon, a space, and the first and last page numbers of the issue.

Walden, Daniel, ed. *The World of Chaim Potok*. Albany: State

U of New York P, 1985. Print. Rpt. of spec. issue of

Studies in American Jewish Literature 4.1 (1985): 1-123.

An Article in a Special Issue of a Scholarly Journal

Kremer, S. Lillian. "Dedalus in Brooklyn: Influences of *A

Portrait of the Artist as a Young Man* on *My Name Is Asher

Lev.*" *The World of Chaim Potok*. Spec. issue of *Studies in

American Jewish Literature* 4.1 (1985): 26-38. Print.

1. Give the full name of the author of the article, last name first. If more than one author is listed, give the names in the order in which they appear on the article's title page, inverting only the name of the first author.

2. Give the article's title and subtitle in double quotation marks with a period inside the final quotation marks. Note that in the model citation above, the titles of the novels of Joyce and Potok are italicized within the title of the journal article.

3. Give the italicized title of the special issue, followed by a period. If there is an editor of the special issue, type *Ed.* (*Edited by*) and give the name, first name first.

4. Type *Spec. issue of* and give the italicized title of the scholarly journal (not followed by a period).

5. Type the volume number, a period, the issue number, and one space.

6. Give the year of publication in parentheses, followed by a colon and a space.

7. Give the first and last page numbers of the article, separated by a hyphen and followed by a period. End with the medium of publication and a period.

Citing Popular Magazines

Annotated Citation for an Article from a Popular Monthly or Bimonthly Magazine

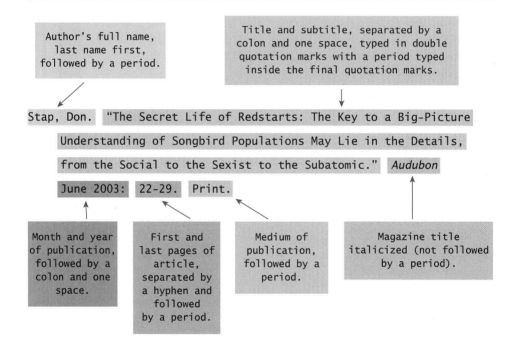

Author's full name, last name first, followed by a period.

Title and subtitle, separated by a colon and one space, typed in double quotation marks with a period typed inside the final quotation marks.

Stap, Don. "The Secret Life of Redstarts: The Key to a Big-Picture Understanding of Songbird Populations May Lie in the Details, from the Social to the Sexist to the Subatomic." *Audubon* June 2003: 22-29. Print.

Month and year of publication, followed by a colon and one space.

First and last pages of article, separated by a hyphen and followed by a period.

Medium of publication, followed by a period.

Magazine title italicized (not followed by a period).

An Article from a Popular Monthly or Bimonthly Magazine

Hawass, Zahi. "Egypt's Forgotten Treasures." Photographs by Kenneth Garrett. *National Geographic* Jan. 2003: 74-87. Print.

Wilson, Jennifer. "Made in the USA: A Factory Tour Is a Whimsical Way to Answer the Age-Old Question 'Where Does This Come From?'" Photographs by Alison Miksch. *Better Homes and Gardens* May 2003: 180-83. Print.

1. Give the full name of the author, last name first. If more than one author is listed, give the names in the order given on the title page of the article, inverting only the name of the first author listed.
2. Give the title and subtitle of the article in double quotation marks, followed by a period typed inside the final quotation marks.

3. If additional contributors to the article are listed (usually at the end of the article), type *With, Reported by, Photographs by,* or whatever is appropriate after the title, and list the names (not inverted) in the order in which they are given in the article.

4. If the author of the article also took the photographs, after the title type *Photographs by* and the author's last name.

5. Give the italicized title of the magazine (**not** followed by a period).

6. Type the month and year of publication, a colon, and a space. Abbreviate all months except May, June, and July. (See chapter 22.)

7. Do not give the volume and issue numbers even if they are listed.

8. Give the first and last page numbers of the article, separated by a hyphen and followed by a period.

9. End with the medium of publication and a period.

An Editorial from a Popular Monthly or Bimonthly Magazine

Allen, Bill. "From the Editor." Editorial. *National Geographic*

    May 2003: 8. Print.

1. Give the author's name, last name first. If no author is given, begin the citation with the title (in quotation marks). Then type *Editorial* (capitalized but not in italics or quotation marks), followed by a period.

2. Give the italicized title of the magazine (not followed by a period).

3. Give the month and year of publication, followed by a colon and one space. Abbreviate all months except May, June, and July. (See chapter 22.)

4. Give the first page number of the article, a hyphen, and the last page number, followed by a period.

5. Give the medium of publication, followed by a period.

An Article from a Popular Weekly or Biweekly Magazine

Eisenberg, Daniel, and Maggie Sieger. "The Doctor Won't See

    You Now: The Soaring Cost of Malpractice." Reported by

    Dody Tsiantar, Anne Berryman, Paul Cuadros, and Michael

    Peltier. *Time* 9 June 2003: 46-60. Print.

Hasnain, Ghulam. "On Osama bin Laden's Trail: Searching the

    Badlands for the World's Most-Wanted Terrorist." *Time*

    24 Mar. 2003: 43. Print.

1. Give the full name of the author, last name first. If more than one author is listed, give the names in the order given on the title page of the article, inverting only the name of the first author listed.

2. Give the title and subtitle of the article in double quotation marks with a period typed inside the final quotation marks.

3. If additional contributors to the article are listed (usually at the end of the article), type *With, Reported by,* or whatever is appropriate after the title, and list the names (not inverted) in the order given in the article.

4. If the author of the article also took the photographs for the article, after the title type *Photographs by* and the author's last name.

5. Give the italicized title of the magazine (not followed by a period).

6. Type the day, month, and year (with no commas), a colon, and a space.

7. Give the first page number of the article, a hyphen, and the last page number, followed by a period.

8. End with the medium of publication and a period.

An Interview Published in a Popular Weekly or Biweekly Magazine

Miller, Arthur. "Rebirth of a Salesman: Arthur Miller Talks

about Fifty Years of a Classic." Interview by Jack Kroll.

Newsweek 22 Feb. 1999: 51. Print.

1. Give the full name of the person interviewed, last name first.

2. Give the title and subtitle of the interview (if any) in double quotation marks with a period typed inside the final quotation marks.

3. Type *Interview by,* the full name of the interviewer, and a period.

4. Give the italicized magazine title (not followed by a period).

5. Type the day, month, and year (with no commas), a colon, and a space.

6. Give the first page number of the interview, a hyphen, the last page number, and a period.

7. End with the medium of publication and a period.

A Signed Editorial from a Popular Weekly or Biweekly Magazine

Kelly, James. "How We Rediscovered a Founding Father."

Editorial. *Time* 7 July 2003: 8. Print.

A Signed Opinion Piece from a Popular Weekly or Biweekly Magazine

Klein, Joe. "Blessed Are the Poor--They Don't Get Tax Cuts."

   Opinion piece. *Time* 9 June 2003: 25. Print.

An Article in a Series from a Popular Weekly or Biweekly Magazine

Wright, Evan. "From Hell to Baghdad." Photographs by Wright.

   Rolling Stone 10 July 2003: 52-61. Print. Pt. 2 of a

   series, The Killer Elite, begun 26 June 2003.

---. "The Killer Elite." Photographs by Wright. *Rolling Stone*

   26 June 2003: 56-68. Print. Pt. 1 of a series, The Killer

   Elite.

1. Give the full name of the author, last name first. If more than one author is listed, give the names in the order given on the title page of the article, inverting only the name of the first author listed.
2. Give the title and subtitle of the article in double quotation marks with a period typed inside the final quotation marks.
3. If additional contributors to the article are listed (usually at the end of the article), type *With, Reported by, Photographs by,* or whatever is appropriate after the article title, and list the names (not inverted) in the order given in the article.
4. Give the italicized title of the magazine (not followed by a period).
5. Give the day, month, and year, followed by a colon and one space.
6. Give the first page number of the article, a hyphen, the last page number, and a period.
7. Give the medium of publication and a period.
8. If the articles in the series were all written by the same author or authors and appear under the same title, cite all the parts of the series in one bibliographical citation, listing different dates and page numbers separated by a semicolon: 15 Apr. 2003: 27-32; 22 Apr. 2003: 56-62.
9. If each part of the series bears a different title or the same title with a different subtitle, list each article in the series in a separate entry. At the end of each entry, give the number of the article in the series (*Pt. 2 of a series*), followed by a comma and the title of the series (not in italics or quotation marks). For each new part of the series, type *begun* and the date the first part of the series was published, followed by a period.

A Special Issue of a Popular Weekly or Biweekly Magazine

Koepp, Steve, and Christopher John Farley, eds. *The Amazing*

   Adventures of Ben Franklin. Spec. issue of *Time* 7 July

   2003: 1-108. Print.

Koepp, Steve, Janice Simpson, and Howard ChuaEoan, eds. *Gulf*

   War II. Spec. issue of *Time* 31 Mar. 2003: 1-198. Print.

1. Give the full name of the editor of the special issue (if known), last name first, followed by the abbreviation *ed.* (*editor*). If more than one editor is listed, give the names in the order given on the title page, inverting only the name of the first editor listed.
2. If no editor is identified, begin the entry with the title of the special issue, italicized and followed by an italicized period.
3. Type *Spec. issue of,* and give the italicized title of the magazine (not followed by a period).
4. Give the day, month, and year of publication (not separated by commas), followed by a colon and a space.
5. Give the first and last page numbers of the entire issue, separated by a hyphen and followed by a period.
6. End with the medium of publication and a period.

An Article in a Special Issue of a Popular Weekly or Biweekly Magazine

McGeary, Johanna. "Inside Saddam's Head." Reported by Douglas

   Waller, Adam Zagorin, Aparisim Ghosh, Helen Gibson, Bruce

   Crumley, Scott MacLeod, and Simon Robinson. *Gulf War II.*

   Ed. Steve Koepp, Janice Simpson, and Howard ChuaEoan.

   Spec. issue of *Time* 31 Mar. 2003: 56-59. Print.

Stacy, Schiff. "Making France Our Best Friend: If Not for a

   Superstar Diplomat Who Charmed All of Paris, America Might

   Have Lost Its War for Independence." *The Amazing Adventures*

   of Ben Franklin. Ed. Steve Koepp and Christopher John Far-

   ley. Spec. issue of *Time* 7 July 2003: 70-73. Print.

1. Give the full name of the author, last name first. If more than one author is listed, give the names in the order given on the title page of the article, inverting only the name of the first author listed.

2. Give the title and subtitle of the article in double quotation marks with a period typed inside the final quotation marks.

3. If additional contributors to the article are listed (usually at the end of the article), type *With, Reported by, Photographs by,* or whatever seems appropriate after the title, and list the names (not inverted) in the order given in the article. If four or more persons are listed, either give all the names or give only the first name listed, followed by *et al.* (*and others*).

4. Give the title of the special issue, italicized and followed by a period.

5. Type *Spec. issue of,* and give the italicized title of the magazine (not followed by a period).

6. Give the day, month, and year (not separated by commas), followed by a colon and a space.

7. Type the first page number of the article, a hyphen, the last page number, and a period.

8. End with the medium of publication and a period.

Citing Newspaper Articles

Citing the Sections of a Newspaper

Newspapers use various methods of identifying the sections, a situation that complicates citing newspaper sections correctly.

- **Section Letter and Page Number Given on Each Page: natl. ed.: C10.**
  If each page of the newspaper gives a section letter followed by a page number, give the edition (if there is one), followed by a colon and one space. Then give the section letter and page number, followed by a period. Type a plus sign and a period after the page number if the article skips to another page: natl. ed.: C10+.

- **Page Number and Section Letter Given on Each Page: city ed.: 10C.**
  If each page of the newspaper gives a page number followed by a section letter, give the edition (if there is one), followed by a colon and one space. Then give the page number and section letter exactly as they appear on the page of the newspaper. Type a plus sign and a period after the section letter if the article skips to another page: city ed.: 5B+.

- **Numbered Sections: late ed., sec. 5: 7.**
  If the sections of the newspaper are numbered, give the edition (if there is one), followed by a comma and one space. Type the

(continues)

> ## Citing the Sections of a Newspaper (continued)
>
> abbreviation *sec.*, one space, and the section number, followed by a colon and one space. Then give the page number, followed by a period. Type a plus sign and a period after the page number if the article skips to another page: late ed., sec. 5: 7+.
>
> ■ **Lettered Sections Not Given on Pages: western ed., sec. C: 7.**
> If the sections of the newspaper are lettered, but only the page numbers are given on the pages of the newspaper, give the edition (if there is one), followed by a comma and one space. Type the abbreviation *sec.*, one space, and the section letter, followed by a colon and one space. Then give the page number, followed by a period. Type a plus sign and a period after the page number if the article skips to another page: western ed., sec. C: 7+.

A Newspaper Article with an Author Given and Numbered Sections

Flinn, R. S. "Can't Find a Summer Job? Blame All the Layoffs."

New York Times 29 June 2003, late ed., sec. 1: 3+. Print.

Ligos, Melinda. "As Graduates Look for Work, the Engineer Is

Standing Tall." New York Times 29 June 2003, late ed.,

sec. 10: 1+. Print.

1. Give the name of the author or authors of the article, first author's name inverted for alphabetizing. List the names of the authors in the order given in the article if more than one author is given.
2. Give the title of the newspaper article in double quotation marks (followed by a period typed inside the final quotation marks).
3. Italicize the title of the newspaper, omitting articles such as *The*. Do not type a period after the title of the newspaper.
4. If the city is not named in the title of the newspaper, give it in square brackets (not italicized) after the title along with the MLA-recommended abbreviation for the state, Canadian province, or country if the city is not well known or could be confused with another city. (See chapter 22 for abbreviations.) You need not specify the city of publication for well-known, nationally published newspapers such as *USA Today* or the *Wall Street Journal*.
5. Give the day, month, and year of publication (not separated by commas), followed by a comma and one space. Abbreviate all months except May, June, and July (see chapter 22).

6. If several editions of a newspaper are printed each day, give the edition you are using (in lowercase: *natl. ed., city ed., late ed.*) because different editions contain different articles, and the same article might be on a different page in a different edition. Look for the edition on the front-page masthead near the title of the newspaper.

7. After the edition (if there is one), type the abbreviation *sec.* and give the section number, followed by a colon and one space.

8. Give the page number of the article, followed by a period.

9. If the article begins on one page and skips to another (e.g., it begins on page 3 and continues on 12), give the first page number, a plus sign, and a period: 3+.

10. End with the medium of publication and a period.

Annotated Citation for a Newspaper Article with an Author Given and Lettered Sections

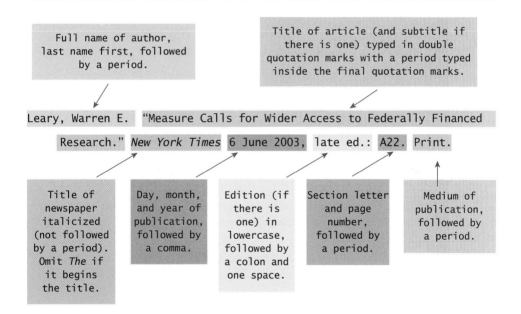

A Newspaper Article with an Author Given and Lettered Sections

Berry, John M. "Fed Again Cuts Interest Rates." *Washington Post*

26 June 2003: A1+. Print.

Sampson, Pamela. "Scientists Announce Discovery of Solar

System Similar to Ours: Find Raises Chance of 'Another

Earth.'" *Sun News* [Myrtle Beach, SC] 4 July 2003: 7A.

Print.

1. Give the name of the author or authors of the article, first author's name inverted for alphabetizing. List the names of the authors in the order given in the article if more than one author is given.

2. Give the title of the newspaper article in double quotation marks (followed by a period typed inside the final quotation marks).

3. Italicize the title of the newspaper, omitting articles such as *The*. Do not type a period after the title of the newspaper.

4. If the city is not named in the title of the newspaper, give it in square brackets (not italicized) after the title along with the MLA-recommended abbreviation for the state, Canadian province, or country if the city is not well known or could be confused with another city. (See chapter 22 for abbreviations.) You need not specify the city of publication for well-known, nationally published newspapers such as *USA Today* or the *Wall Street Journal*.

5. Give the day, month, and year of publication (not separated by commas), followed by a comma and one space. Abbreviate all months except May, June, and July.

6. If several editions of a newspaper are printed each day, give the edition you are using (*natl. ed., city ed., late ed.*) because different editions contain different articles, and the same article might be on a different page in a different edition. Look for the edition on the front-page masthead near the title of the newspaper.

7. Give the section letter and page number (or page number and section letter) just as they are given on the newspaper pages (followed by a period).

8. If the article begins on one page and skips to another (e.g., it begins on page C3 and continues on C12), give the first page number, a plus sign, and a period: C3+.

9. End with the medium of publication and a period.

A Newspaper Article with No Author Given and Lettered Sections

"Mayor Faces Tough Problems." *Morning Call* [Allentown, PA]

3 Feb. 2003: A1+. Print.

"One in Three Born in 2000 Are Likely to Become Diabetic, CDC

    Estimates." *Los Angeles Times* 15 June 2003, final ed.: A36.

    Print.

1. If the author is not given, begin with the title and alphabetize the article by the first significant word of the title, excluding *A, An,* and *The.*

2. Type double quotation marks around the title of the article, and type a period inside the end quotation marks.

3. Italicize the title of the newspaper, omitting articles such as *The.* Do not type a period after the title of the newspaper.

4. If the city is not named in the title of the newspaper, give it in square brackets (not italicized) after the title along with the MLA-recommended abbreviation for the state, Canadian province, or country if the city is not well known or could be confused with another city. (See chapter 22 for abbreviations.) You need not specify the city of publication for well-known, nationally published newspapers such as *USA Today* or the *Wall Street Journal.*

5. Give the day, month, and year of publication (not separated by commas), followed by a comma and one space. Abbreviate all months except May, June, and July. (See chapter 22.)

6. If several editions of a newspaper are printed each day, give the edition you are using (*natl. ed., city ed., late ed.*) because different editions contain different articles, and the same article might be on a different page in a different edition. Look for the edition on the front-page masthead near the title of the newspaper.

7. After the edition, type a colon and one space. Then give the section letter and page number together as they appear on the pages.

8. If the article begins on one page and skips to another (e.g., it begins on page C3 and continues on C12), give the first page number, a plus sign, and a period: C3+.

9. The parenthetical citations for these entries would be ("Mayor Faces" A1) and ("One in Three" A36).

10. End with the medium of publication and a period.

A Daily *New York Times* Article (Lettered Sections)

On Monday through Saturday, the *New York Times* is divided into lettered sections, each paginated separately. The section letter and page number are given together on each page (A3, C6, D9). After the edition, type a colon and one space. Then give the section letter and page number together just as they appear on the page. End with the medium of publication.

Bennet, James. "Mideast Talks Make Progress despite Attacks."

    New York Times 28 June 2003, late ed.: A1+. Print.

A Saturday *New York Times* Article (No Sections or Lettered Sections)

Sometimes the Saturday edition of the *New York Times* is paginated continuously from the first page to the last. If there are no section numbers, just give the page number after the edition, a period, and the medium of publication.

Salamon, Julie. "Young Potter Fans See Hero Maturing along with

    Them." *New York Times* 22 Apr. 2003, late ed.: 12. Print.

If the Saturday edition is divided into lettered sections, each paginated separately, the section letter and page number will be given together on each page (B6, C8, D10). After the edition, type a colon and one space. Then give the section letter and page number together just as they appear on the page. End with the medium of publication.

Lichtblau, Eric, with Monica Davey. "Suspect in Plot on Bridge

    Drew Interest Earlier." *New York Times* 21 June 2003, late

    ed.: A1. Print.

A Sunday *New York Times* Article (Numbered Sections)

The Sunday *New York Times* contains numbered sections, each paginated separately. After the date, type the edition, the appropriate section (*sec.*) number and a colon, one space, and the page number. Type a plus sign (1+) after the page number if the article skips to another page in the paper. End with the medium of publication.

Rosenbaum, Ron. "The Crucial First Clue to *Henry V.*" *New York*

    Times 29 June 2003, late ed., sec. 8: 1+. Print.

An Unsigned Editorial

"Court Decision Will Have Serious Implications." Editorial. *Post*

    and Courier [Charleston, SC] 26 Apr. 2003: 10A+. Print.

1. Begin the entry with the title of the editorial, and alphabetize the editorial under the first significant word of the title, excluding *A, An,* and *The.* If the editorial is untitled, move to step 3.

2. Type double quotation marks around the title of the editorial, and type a period inside the end quotation marks.

3. After the title, type *Editorial* (not italicized or in quotation marks), followed by a period and one space.

4. Italicize the title of the newspaper, omitting articles such as *The.* Do not type a period after the title of the newspaper.

5. If the city is not named in the title of the newspaper, give it in square brackets (not italicized) after the title along with the MLA-recommended abbreviation for the state, Canadian province, or country if the city is not well known or could be confused with another city. (See chapter 22 for abbreviations.) You need not specify the city of publication for well-known, nationally published newspapers such as *USA Today* or the *Wall Street Journal.*

6. The newspaper cited above gives the page number before the section letter, so cite the page and section just as they appear on the page.

7. If the article begins on one page and skips to another (e.g., it begins on page 10A and continues on 12A), give the first page number and the section letter, and then type a plus sign and a period: 10A+.

8. The parenthetical citation for the above entry would be ("Court Decision" 10A).

9. End with the medium of publication and a period.

A Signed Opinion Piece

Safire, William. "Big Media's Silence." Opinion piece. *New York Times* 26 June 2003, late ed.: A32. Print.

A Letter to the Editor

Schmidt, Louise K. Letter. *Los Angeles Times* 24 Feb. 2003, final ed., sec. 1: 12. Print.

Citing Reviews from Journals, Magazines, and Newspapers

Annotated Citation for a Review of a Book Taken from a Newspaper

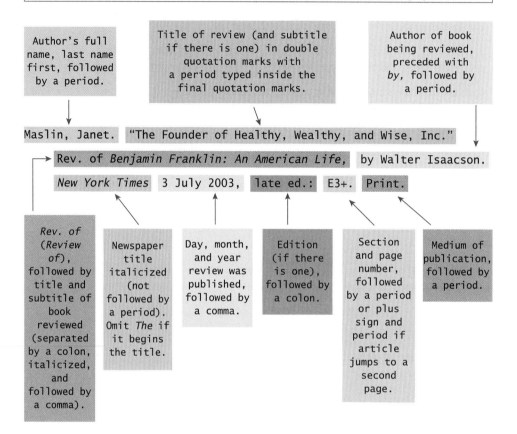

Author's full name, last name first, followed by a period.

Title of review (and subtitle if there is one) in double quotation marks with a period typed inside the final quotation marks.

Author of book being reviewed, preceded with *by,* followed by a period.

Maslin, Janet. "The Founder of Healthy, Wealthy, and Wise, Inc."

Rev. of *Benjamin Franklin: An American Life,* by Walter Isaacson.

New York Times 3 July 2003, late ed.: E3+. Print.

Rev. of (Review of), followed by title and subtitle of book reviewed (separated by a colon, italicized, and followed by a comma).

Newspaper title italicized (not followed by a period). Omit *The* if it begins the title.

Day, month, and year review was published, followed by a comma.

Edition (if there is one), followed by a colon.

Section and page number, followed by a period or plus sign and period if article jumps to a second page.

Medium of publication, followed by a period.

A Review of a Book Taken from a Newspaper

Maslin, Janet. "An Ultimately Sad Sack, Hopelessly Indefati-
gable." Rev. of *A Tragic Honesty: The Life and Works of
Richard Yates,* by Blake Bailey. *New York Times* 26 June
2003, late ed.: E1+. Print.

A Review of a Book Taken from the *New York Times Book Review*

Dowd, Maureen. Rev. of *Living History,* by Hillary Rodham Clinton. *New York Times Book Review* 29 June 2003: 1. Print.

A Review of a Book Taken from a Scholarly Journal

Whale, John. Rev. of *Romanticism, Economics, and the Question of Culture,* by Philip Connell. *Nineteenth-Century Literature* 57.2 (2003): 542-44. Print.

A Review of a Play Taken from a Newspaper

Weber, Bruce. "Siblings at Odds, A Stranger Uninvited." Rev. of *St. Scarlet,* by Julia Jordan. Dir. Chris Messina. Ontological Theater at St. Mark's Church, East Village, New York. *New York Times* 30 June 2003, late ed.: E8. Print.

A Review of a Ballet Taken from a Newspaper

Dunning, Jennifer. "A Romantic's Wry Musings on Love's Sweet Song." Rev. of *A Midsummer Night's Dream,* chor. George Balanchine. New York City Ballet. New York State Theater, New York. *New York Times* 26 June 2003, late ed.: E3. Print.

A Review of an Opera Taken from a Newspaper

Holland, Bernard. "Opera with Confetti and Leather." Rev. of *Damnation de Faust,* by Hector Berlioz. War Memorial Opera House, San Francisco. *New York Times* 26 June 2003, late ed.: E3. Print.

A Review of a Concert Taken from a Newspaper

Ratliff, Ben. "For Norah Jones, Nights Are Made for Sentiment and Slow Dancing." Concert review. *New York Times* 26 June 2003, late ed.: E1+. Print.

A Review of a Film (Movie) Taken from a Newspaper

Scott, A. O. "A Monotonic Cyborg Learns to Say 'Pantsuit.'"
    Rev. of *Terminator 3: Rise of the Machines,* dir. Jonathan
    Mostow. Writ. John Brancato and Michael Ferris. Perf.
    Arnold Schwarzenegger and Claire Danes. *New York Times*
    1 July 2003, late ed.: E10. Print.

A Review of a Film (Movie) Taken from a Popular Weekly or Biweekly Magazine

Travers, Peter. "The Hulk Reloaded: He's Mean and Green and
    Ready to Rip." Rev. of *Hulk,* dir. Ang Lee. Writ. James
    Schamus, John Turman, and Michael France. Perf. Eric Bana,
    Jennifer Connelly, Nick Nolte, and Sam Elliot. *Rolling
    Stone* 10 July 2003: 75. Print.

CHAPTER 11

Citing Miscellaneous Other Sources

A Pamphlet with an Author Given

Cite a pamphlet just as you would cite a book.

Smith, Bert Kruger. *Women Drinkers.* Austin: U of Texas, 1976.
    Print.

A Pamphlet with a Corporation or Organization Listed as Author

CH2M Hill. *Carolina Bays: A Natural Wastewater Treatment
    Program.* N.p.: United States Environmental Protection
    Agency, 1993. Print.

A Government Publication

Thomson, Michael, comp., and John Y. Cole, ed. Library of
    Congress. *Books Change Lives: 1993-1994 Reading Promotion
    Campaign.* Washington: GPO, 1995. Print.
United States. Subcommittee on Government Information and Regu-
    lation of the Committee on Governmental Affairs. *A Lesson
    of the Gulf War: National Security Requires Computer
    Security.* 102nd Cong., 1st sess. Senate Hearing 575.
    Washington: GPO, 1992. Print.

United States. Dept. of Health and Human Services. National

Institute on Aging. *Grow into Growing Older: Don't Take It*

Easy--Exercise! Washington: GPO, 1992. Print.

1. Give the author, editor (*ed.*), or compiler (*comp.*) if known.
2. If no author is listed, give the name of the federal (United States), state (Massachusetts), city (Boston), or local government responsible for the publication, followed by a period.
3. Next give the name of the agency (or agencies) that published the material. If several government agencies are listed on the publication, give the largest agency first, then the smaller agency (a period after each).
4. Give the title of the document and a period (both italicized).
5. Give the city, publisher, and year of publication (if known). Use the abbreviation *GPO* if the Government Printing Office is the publisher.
6. End with the medium of publication and a period.

An Unpublished Dissertation

Franson, Robert T. "Women in Shakespeare's History Plays."

Diss. U of Southern California, 1988. Print.

1. Give the author's name, inverted for alphabetizing.
2. Place the title in double quotation marks with a period inside the end quotation marks.
3. Type the abbreviation *Diss.*, and give the name of the degree-granting university, followed by a comma and one space. Then give the year the dissertation was completed and a period.
4. End with the medium of publication and a period.

An Unpublished Master's Thesis

Barker, Mary Katherine. "African Mythology in the Novels of

Toni Morrison." MA thesis Duke U, 2002. Print.

1. Give the author's name, inverted for alphabetizing.
2. Place the title in double quotation marks with a period inside the end quotation marks.
3. Type *MA thesis* (*Master of Arts*) or *MS thesis* (*Master of Science*) and give the name of the degree-granting university, followed by a comma and one space. Then give the year the thesis was completed and a period.
4. End with the medium of publication and a period.

A Published Dissertation

Gradius, Caroline P. *Biblical Imagery in the Novels of Herman*

   Melville. Diss. Wake Forest U, 1995. New York: UMI, 1996.

   Print.

1. Give the author's name, inverted for alphabetizing.
2. Italicize the title of a published dissertation and the period that follows.
3. Type the abbreviation *Diss.*, and give the name of the degree-granting university, followed by a comma and one space. Then give the year of completion and a period.
4. Give the city, publisher, and year of publication.
5. If University Microfilms International is the publisher, use the abbreviation *UMI*.
6. End with the medium of publication and a period.

An Abstract from *Dissertation Abstracts International*

Graham, Stephen A. "Mirror Imagery in the Poetry of Sylvia

   Plath." Diss. Duke U, 1993. *DAI* 54 (1993): 1269A. Print.

Currently in *Dissertation Abstracts International,* an *A* following the *D* at the beginning of an item number (DA 2219322) or used alone after an item or page number indicates a dissertation in the humanities or social sciences, a *B* indicates a dissertation in engineering or the sciences, and a *C* indicates a dissertation in a university located outside the United States. An item number follows the colon in place of the page number and is preceded by the word *item.* End with the medium of publication.

Add the word *Abstract* (not in italics or quotation marks) after the original publication information if you are citing an abstract (brief summary) of a work rather than a full-text version unless, as with materials taken from *Dissertation Abstracts International,* the title indicates that all materials are abstracts.

A Film

Gone with the Wind. Dir. Victor Fleming. Prod. David O.

   Selznick. Screenplay by Sidney Howard. Perf. Vivien Leigh

   and Clark Gable. MGM, 1939. Film.

Jordan, Neil, dir. *The End of the Affair.* Perf. Ralph Fiennes,

Julianne Moore, and Stephen Rea. Based on the novel by

Graham Greene. Columbia/Tristar, 2000. Film.

1. Give the title of the film (italicized).
2. Give the director (*Dir.*), the distributor (MGM, Paramount, etc.), and the year the film was released.
3. Give any other information that might be useful to your reader, such as producer (*Prod.*) and performers (*Perf.*), before the distributor. (See the list of MLA-recommended abbreviations in chapter 22.)
4. If you are primarily discussing the work of a particular person involved in the film (actor, actress, director, cinematographer, etc.), begin your entry with that person's name, followed by the abbreviation that describes the person's role in the film (e.g., Redford, Robert, dir.).
5. You may specify that a film is based on a novel or other literary work.
6. End with the format of presentation (*Film*).

A Videocassette, DVD, or Other Format

Titanic. Dir. James Cameron. Perf. Kate Winslet and Leonardo

DiCaprio. 1997. Paramount, 1998. Videocassette.

Runaway Bride. Dir. Garry Marshall. Perf. Julia Roberts and

Richard Gere. 1999. Paramount/Touchstone, 1999. DVD.

1. Give the title of the videocassette, DVD, laser disc, slide program, or filmstrip (italicized).
2. Give the director, performers, and any other useful information.
3. Give the date the film was originally released to theaters (if known).
4. Give the distributor, a comma, and the year that the videocassette, DVD, or other format was released.
5. End with the format (*Videocassette, DVD, Laser disc*), followed by a period.

A Television Program

"The Soul Hunter." *Babylon 5.* Science Fiction Channel. 15 June

2003. Television.

Burns, Ken, dir. "Gettysburg." *The Civil War.* PBS. WHMC,

Conway, SC. 22 May 1999. Television.

Madame Bovary. By Gustave Flaubert. Perf. Frances O'Connor and

Greg Wise. 2 episodes. *Masterpiece Theatre.* PBS. WHMC,

Conway, SC, 8 Feb.–13 Feb. 2000. Television.

1. Give the title of the episode (if available) in double quotation marks (e.g., "The Soul Hunter") with the period inside the closing marks.
2. Give the title of the program in italics (e.g., *Babylon 5*).
3. You may include any other information that might be useful to your reader—author of work being dramatized (By William Faulkner), director (*dir.*), directed by (*Dir.*), narrated by (*Narr.*), performer (*perf.*), performed by (*Perf.*), script written by (*Writ.*), adapted for television by (*Adapt.*), conductor (*cond.*), conducted by (*Cond.*).
4. If the abbreviation comes after the name, as it will when you begin the entry with a person's name (last name first), use the abbreviation beginning with the lowercase letter (e.g., Burns, Ken, dir.). If the abbreviation precedes the name, as it will when the person's name is placed after the title of the program, use the abbreviation beginning with the capital letter (e.g., Dir. Ken Burns).
5. Give the number of episodes in the program if relevant (e.g., 6 episodes).
6. If the program is part of a series, such as *Masterpiece Theatre,* put the title of the series in italics.
7. Give the network that broadcast the program, followed by a period (e.g., ABC, PBS, TNT, History Channel, Learning Channel).
8. If the program appeared on a local television station, give the call letters of the station, followed by a comma and one space. Then give the city of the station (e.g., WHMC, Conway, SC). Give the postal abbreviation for the state if the city is not well known or could be confused with another city. End with a comma and one space.
9. Next give the day, month, and year the program was broadcast.
10. End with the medium of reception (e.g., *Television*).
11. If you are citing the transcript of a program, do not end with *Television*. Instead, give the medium of publication (*Print*), followed by a period, and then type *Transcript* at the end of the entry (not in quotation marks or italics), followed by a period.

A Television Interview

Clinton, Hillary Rodham. Interview by Ted Koppel. *Nightline.*

ABC. WCIV, Charleston, SC, 5 June 2003. Television.

Updike, John. Interview. *Charlie Rose.* PBS. WHMC, Conway, SC,

12 Feb. 2003. Television.

1. Give the name of the person being interviewed, inverted for alphabetizing.
2. Give the title of the interview (if there is one) in double quotation marks with the period inside the final quotation marks.
3. If the interview has no title, type the word *Interview* (not italicized or in quotation marks) after the name of the person interviewed. Type *by,* and give the name of the interviewer (if known).
4. Give the title of the television show (italicized) and a period.
5. Give the network and a period.
6. If the program appeared on a local television station, give the call letters of the station, followed by a comma and one space. Then give the city of the station (e.g., WCIV, Charleston, SC). Give the postal abbreviation for the state if the city is not well known or could be confused with another city. (In the Clinton citation, Charleston, South Carolina, could be confused with Charleston, West Virginia.) End with a comma and one space.
7. Next, give the date the interview aired on the show and a period.
8. End with the medium of reception and a period.

A Transcript of a Television Interview

Miller, Arthur, Robert Falls, and Brian Dennehy. "An American

Classic: A Half-Century Anniversary." Interview by

Paul Solman. *NewsHour with Jim Lehrer.* PBS. 10 Feb. 1999.

Print. Transcript.

If you are citing the transcript of a television interview, follow the directions for a television interview, but do not end with *Television* (medium of reception). Instead, give the medium of publication (*Print*), followed by a period, and type *Transcript* at the end of the entry (not in quotation marks or italics) and a period.

A Radio Program

Brinker, Bob. *Moneytalk.* WRNN, Myrtle Beach, SC, 14 June 2003.

Radio.

1. Give the name of the host of the show (if there is one), the name inverted for alphabetizing. (In the prior citation, Bob Brinker is the host of a call-in radio show dealing with investment strategies.)
2. Give the title of the individual episode or segment (if there is one) in double quotation marks.
3. Give the name of the narrator (if there is one) preceded by the abbreviation *Narr.* (e.g., Narr. James Earl Jones) after the title of the episode. (Note: A host is the major focus of a show and would be speaking throughout the show, whereas a narrator might introduce the show, make some explanatory remarks during it, and make concluding remarks at the end.)
4. Give the title of the program (italicized) and a period.
5. Give the network (if known) (e.g., Natl. Public Radio, or NPR).
6. Give the call letters and city of the local station (separated by a comma and one space). Give the postal abbreviation for the state if the city is not well known or could be confused with another city. End with a comma and one space.
7. Next, give the day, month, and year the program was broadcast.
8. End with the medium of reception (*Radio*) and a period.

A Recording of a Classical Piece of Music

Leibowitz, René, cond. *Eroica.* By Ludwig van Beethoven. *The Nine Symphonies of Beethoven.* Royal Philharmonic Orchestra. RCA, n.d. LP.

Sutherland, Joan, perf. "Allelujah." *The Glory of Wolfgang Amadeus Mozart.* National Philharmonic Orchestra. Cond. Richard Bonynge. Decca, 1985. CD.

1. Give the composer (*comp.*), performer (*perf.*), or conductor (*cond.*), whichever is most important.
2. Italicize the title of a symphony or other long musical composition.
3. Type double quotation marks around a short musical composition or brief part of a longer musical composition.
4. Type *By,* and give the name of the composer of the music (if not given earlier or in the title of the CD, LP, audiotape, or audiocassette), followed by a period.
5. Give the title of the compact disc, record, audiocassette, or audiotape (italicized and followed by an italicized period).

6. Give the name of the orchestra that performed the musical composition, not italicized and not in quotation marks, followed by a period.

7. Identify the conductor (unless identified earlier), followed by a period.

8. Give the manufacturer (e.g., RCA, Capitol, Deutsche Grammophon), followed by a comma and one space.

9. Give the year of issue, or type *n.d.* if the date is unavailable. You may also give the date of the recording.

10. Identify the medium as a *CD* (compact disc), an *LP* (long-playing record), an *Audiotape* (reel-to-reel tape), or an *Audiocassette* (not italicized or in quotation marks).

A Popular Song

```
Springfield, Rick, comp. and perf. "Jessie's Girl." Working

     Class Dog. RCA, 1981. LP.

Pink Floyd, perf. "Another Brick in the Wall." Comp. Roger

     Waters. Pink Floyd: London 1994. Rec. 20 Oct. 1994.

     Red Line, 1996. CD.
```

1. Give the composer (*comp.*) or performer (*perf.*), whichever is most important, with the name inverted.

2. Place the title of the song in double quotation marks with a period before the end quotation marks.

3. Italicize the title of the compact disc, record, audiocassette, or audiotape.

4. Type *Rec.* (*Recorded on*), and give the date the material was recorded if you think the information would be useful to your reader.

5. Give the manufacturer (e.g., RCA, Capitol, Deutsche Grammophon), followed by a comma and one space.

6. Give the year of issue, or type *n.d.* if the date is unavailable.

7. Identify the medium as a *CD* (compact disc), an *LP* (long-playing record), *Audiotape* (reel-to-reel tape), or an *Audiocassette* (not italicized and not in quotation marks).

Song Lyrics from an LP Liner or Compact Disc Booklet

```
Knopfler, Mark. "Sultans of Swing." Liner. Dire Straits.

     Warner, 1978. LP.
```

Liner Notes or Booklet Essay
from a Compact Disc or a Record

DeCurtis, Anthony. "Eric Clapton: A Life at the Crossroads."

Booklet essay. *Crossroads*. By Eric Clapton. 4 Compact Disc

Edition. Polydor, 1988. CD.

1. Give the author of the liner notes or booklet (if available).
2. Give the title of the booklet, booklet essay, or liner notes in double quotation marks with a period inside the end quotation marks.
3. Give a description of the material—*Booklet, Booklet essay, Liner notes, Libretto*—capitalized (first word only), not italicized and not in quotation marks, and followed by a period.
4. Italicize the title of the compact disc, record, audiocassette, or audiotape.
5. Type *By,* and give the name of the performer or musical group.
6. Give the number of discs in a multiple-disc collection if you think the information would be useful.
7. Give the manufacturer (e.g., RCA, Capitol, Deutsche Grammophon), followed by a comma and one space.
8. Give the year of issue, or type *n.d.* if the date is unavailable.
9. Identify the medium as a *CD* (compact disc), an *LP* (long-playing record), an *Audiotape* (reel-to-reel tape), or an *Audiocassette* (not italicized or in quotation marks).

A Music Video

Henley, Don. "Taking You Home." *Inside Job*. Warner Bros., 2000.

Music video. Dir. Tom Krueger and Mary K. Place. VH1. 23

Apr. 2003. Television.

1. Give the name(s) of the performer(s) of the song.
2. Give the title of the song in double quotation marks.
3. Italicize the title of the CD, LP, or other medium and type a period, also italicized.
4. Give the manufacturer (record company), type a comma and one space, and give the date the CD, LP, or other medium was released.
5. Type *Music video* (not in quotation marks or italics) and a period.

6. Type the abbreviation *Dir.,* and give the name(s) of the director(s) of the video. (The director's name and other information needed for your citation will be given at the beginning and end of the video.)

7. Give the channel or network on which you watched the video.

8. Give the day, month, and year that you watched the video.

9. End with the medium of transmission (*Television*).

A Map

Alabama and Georgia. Map. Heathrow, FL: Amer. Automobile Assn.,

1995. Print.

1. Give the title of the map, italicized and followed by a period.

2. Type the word *Map* (not in quotation marks or italics) and a period.

3. Give the city (and state if needed), publisher, and year of publication.

4. End with the medium of publication.

An Advertisement in a Popular Monthly or Bimonthly Magazine

Impala LS Sport. Advertisement. *Better Homes and Gardens*

July 2003: 109. Print.

1. Give the name of the product being advertised (not italicized or in quotation marks), followed by a period.

2. Type the word *Advertisement* (not italicized or in quotation marks), followed by a period.

3. Give the title of the magazine (italicized and not followed by a period).

4. Give the month and year of publication, type a colon and one space, and give the page or pages on which the advertisement appeared.

5. End with the medium of publication.

An Advertisement in a Popular Weekly or Biweekly Magazine

Pontiac Grand Prix. Advertisement. *People* 30 June 2003: 88-89.

Print.

GAP Jeans. Advertisement. *Rolling Stone* 2 Mar. 2003: 27.

Print.

1. Give the name of the product being advertised (not italicized or in quotation marks), followed by a period.
2. Type the word *Advertisement* (not italicized or in quotation marks), followed by a period.
3. Give the title of the magazine (italicized) but no period.
4. Give the day, month, and year of publication; type a colon and a space; and give the page or pages on which the advertisement appeared, followed by a period.
5. End with the medium of publication and a period.

A Television Advertisement

Travelocity. Advertisement. WPDE, Florence, SC. 27 June 2003.

    Television.

1. Give the name of the product being advertised (not italicized or in quotation marks), followed by a period.
2. Type the word *Advertisement* (not italicized or in quotation marks), followed by a period.
3. Give the name of the station or network on which the advertisement aired (CNN, Science Fiction Channel), not italicized and followed by a period.
4. If the advertisement appeared on a local station, give the call letters and city (and state if needed) of the station, followed by a comma and one space.
5. Give the day, month, and year the advertisement was aired and a period.
6. End with the medium of transmission and a period.

A Cartoon or Comic Strip

Marlette, Doug. "Medicare Reform." Cartoon. *Sun News* [Myrtle

    Beach, SC] 25 June 2003: 10A. Print.

Browne, Chris. "Hagar the Horrible." Comic strip. *Sun News*

    [Myrtle Beach, SC] 27 June 2003: 8D. Print.

1. Give the name of the cartoonist (if available).
2. Give the title of the cartoon or comic strip (if available) in double quotation marks with a period typed inside the end quotation marks.
3. Type the words *Comic strip* or *Cartoon* (not in quotation marks or italicized), followed by a period.

4. Give the publication information for the newspaper or magazine.

5. End with the medium of publication and a period.

A Poster

The Harmful Effects of Steroids. Poster. Bakersfield, CA:

Algra, 1992. Print.

1. Give the title of the poster in italics, followed by a period.
2. Type *Poster* (not in quotation marks or italics) and a period.
3. Give the city of publication, publisher, and copyright date.
4. End with the medium of publication, followed by a period.

A Poster Published in a Monthly Magazine

Whales of the World. Poster. *National Geographic* Dec. 1976:

722A. Print.

1. Give the title of the poster (italicized and followed by a period).
2. Type the word *Poster* (not in quotation marks or italics) and a period.
3. Give the publication information for the magazine (title, date, page).
4. End with the medium of publication and a period.

A Speech, Lecture, or Presentation

Beard, John. "Metanarratives Be Damned: Teaching the Postmodern

Student." Back to the Future. College English Association

Conference. Charleston, SC. 7 Apr. 2000. Presentation.

Smith, Rachel T. "Using Assessment Strategies in the ESL

Classroom." South Atlantic Modern Language Association

Conference. Atlanta. 16 Nov. 1997. Presentation.

1. Give the speaker's name, last name first.
2. Give the title of the presentation in quotation marks with a period typed inside the final quotation marks.
3. Give the name of the meeting for that particular year (if known). (Each year's conference typically has a title.)

4. Give the name of the organization that sponsored the meeting.
5. Give the city in which the conference was held. Give the postal abbreviation for the state if the city is not well known or could be confused with another city (e.g., Charleston, SC; Charleston, WV).
6. Give the day, month, and year that the presentation was delivered, followed by a period.
7. End with the form of delivery—*Speech, Keynote address, Lecture, Address, Reading, Presentation*—not italicized and followed by a period.

A Published Interview

Piercy, Marge. "A Harsh Day's Light: An Interview with Marge

Piercy." By John Rodden. *Kenyon Review* ns 20.2 (1998):

132-43. Print.

Note that *ns* means *new series*.

A Personal Interview

Angelou, Maya. Personal interview. 15 Mar. 2010.

A Telephone Interview

Morrison, Toni. Telephone interview. 18 Apr. 2010.

An E-Mail Interview

Walker, Alice. E-mail interview. Web. 10 June 2010.

A Published Letter

Dickinson, Emily. "To Thomas Wentworth Higginson." 15 April

1862. *Selected Poems and Letters of Emily Dickinson*.

Ed. Robert N. Linscott. Garden City, NY: Anchor-Doubleday,

1959. 291-92. Print.

An Unpublished Letter

Walker, Alice. Letter to the author. 26 Apr. 2010. MS.

Note the medium of delivery: *MS* for a manuscript, *TS* for a typescript.

A Memo

Greene, Joshua. Memo to Francis Roberts. 12 Apr. 2010. TS.

Schwartz, Linda Smoak. Memo to faculty senators at Coastal
    Carolina Univ., Conway, SC. 26 Mar. 2010. TS.

Ennis, Jean. "Microsoft Word Workshop Rescheduled." Memo to
    faculty at Coastal Carolina Univ., Conway, SC. 15 Feb.
    2010. TS.

1. Give the name of the person who wrote the memo, inverted for alphabetizing.
2. If the memo has a specific title, enclose it in double quotation marks with a period typed inside the end quotation marks.
3. Type *Memo to*, and identify the recipient(s) of the memo (not italicized or in quotation marks), followed by a period and one space.
4. If appropriate, identify the university, company, or organization at which the memo was sent. Give the location (city) of the organization. If the city is not well known or could be confused with another city, give the postal abbreviation for the state.
5. Give the day, month, and year the memo was sent, followed by a period.
6. End with the medium of delivery (*TS* for a typescript, *MS* for a manuscript), followed by a period.

CHAPTER 12

Citing Internet, CD-ROM, and DVD-ROM Sources

Citing Internet Sources

The method of citing electronic sources is constantly changing as the materials available on the Internet change. The Modern Language Association regularly updates citation requirements, so you should be aware that citations you might see in your sources done even a year or two ago may be out of date by now. The guidelines in this text are based on MLA guidelines published in 2009.

Sometimes the Web page you are looking at will not have all the information you need to create your citation. You may have to go to the Web site's home page (the title page or first page of the site) or the site's search page to get some of the information you need, such as the name of the organization sponsoring the site or the name of the editor or Web master of the site. In addition, many sites have an "About Us" page that may give you the information you need for your citation.

If you think you might use information from a Web page, make sure you have all the information needed for your works-cited list recorded in your working bibliography before you move on to another page; otherwise, you may have to spend valuable time relocating the page later to get what you need.

Because the material on Web sites is constantly being updated, always download or print any material you think you might need to include in your works-cited list. The information may not be available or may have been altered the next time you visit the site.

Think of a **Web site** as a giant electronic book with numerous chapters (**Web pages** or **Web documents**). In a printed book you search the table of contents to find a chapter you need, or you search the index to find a page reference for a specific piece of information you are looking for. When searching the Internet, you use search engines (such as Yahoo!, Google, or AltaVista) to find either Web sites or Web pages related to your subject. Each Web site has a home page or search page that lists the various pages or documents within the site. Click on the name of the material you are looking for, and a hyperlink will take you to the Web page containing the material. If the search engine takes you to a page within the site, click on **Home** to find the home page of the site.

Just as you enclose the title of a short story, poem, or essay in double quotation marks when you are citing it from an anthology, you type double quotation marks around the title of the Web page you are citing. And just as you italicize the title of a book or literary anthology in your bibliographic citation, you italicize the title of the entire Web site you are citing.

General Guidelines for Citing Internet Sources

Include as much of the information listed here as you can find, but realize that you may not find everything for every electronic source. Give your reader enough information to be able to locate the information on the Internet.

1. Give the name of the author, editor (*ed.*), compiler (*comp.*), or translator (*trans.*) of the material on the Web page. Use the appropriate abbreviation after the name if the person is not an author (e.g., Smith, David T., ed.).

2. Type double quotation marks around the title of a Web page; an article from a journal, magazine, or newspaper; a short story; a short poem; an essay; a book chapter; a posting to a discussion list or Weblog (blog); or any other type of work usually formatted in double quotation marks. Type a period inside the final quotation marks.

3. Italicize the title of a book or play accessed online and the period after the title. Italicize the title of a scholarly journal, popular magazine, or newspaper; do not add a period after the title.

4. If you are citing an online book with both an author and an editor, compiler, or translator, give the author first (unless you are referring primarily to the work of the editor, compiler, or translator in your paper). Then give the title of the book (italicized) and the editor (*Ed.*), compiler (*Comp.*), or translator (*Trans.*) in the order given on the Web page, preceded by the appropriate abbreviation (Jamison, Jerome R. *Complete Stories.* Ed. Alison E. Wilmot.).

5. Give the city, publisher, and year of publication of the print version of a short story, essay, poem, play, novel, or book if the work has also been published in print form: Boston: Houghton, 2009.

6. Give the volume, issue, year of publication, and first and last page numbers of the print version of a scholarly journal article accessed online: 34.6 (2010): 34-49.

7. For a monthly or bimonthly magazine article accessed online, give the month, year, and first and last page numbers (Aug. 2010: 24-26) if there is a print version of the article.

8. For a weekly or biweekly magazine article accessed online, give the day, month, and year of publication and the first and last page numbers (5 Jan. 2010: 34-35.) if there is a print version.

9. If the total number of pages or paragraphs in the work is given rather than the specific page numbers, cite whatever is given, using the appropriate MLA-recommended abbreviations (e.g., 25 pp., 16 pars.).

10. If no page numbers or paragraph numbers are given for a journal or magazine article also available in print, use the abbreviation *n. pag.* to inform your reader that the information was not available.

11. If only the first page of the print version of a journal or popular magazine article is given for an article that is accessed online, and the article is obviously longer than one page, type the first page number, a hyphen, one space, and a period: 34.2 (2010): 246- .

12. Give the publication information for the print version of a newspaper article accessed online if that information is available. Give the day, month, and year of publication; a comma; the edition (*final ed., late ed., home ed.,* etc.); a colon and one space; and the section letter, followed by the page number of the article and a period: 5 Apr. 2010, home ed.: B7.

13. If the sections are numbered rather than lettered, type a comma after the day, month, and year of publication; give the edition (if known), followed by a comma; type *sec.* (*section*); and give the section number, followed by a colon, one space, the page number of the article, and a period: 5 Apr. 2010, final ed., sec. 5: 4.

14. If only the first page is given for a newspaper article available in print that is obviously longer than a single page, type a plus sign and a period after the page number: D4+.

15. If only the day, month, and year of publication; the section letter; and the page number of the article are given for an online newspaper article, cite the information available, followed by a period: 5 Apr. 2010: A7.

16. If no print publication information is given for an online newspaper article, give the author; the title of the article; the title of the online newspaper; the publisher; the day, month, and year of publication; the medium of access; the day, month, and year you accessed or printed the article; and a period.

17. Italicize the title of the Web site; online scholarly journal, popular magazine, or newspaper; library or personal subscription reference database; free reference database; scholarly project; professional Web site; personal Web site; or Weblog. If no title for the site is given, use a descriptive term such as *Home page* (not in quotation marks or italics) to identify the type of site you are referring to.

18. Give the name of the editor, Web master, or moderator of the site (if available). Check the site's home page or "About Us" page for this information if it is not given on the Web page.

19. Give the name of the sponsor or publisher of the site (or *N.p.* if unknown), not italicized and followed by a comma and space. The name of the sponsoring organization usually appears at the end of the Web page as well as on the home page and the "About Us" page.

20. Give the date the material was copyrighted, published online, or last updated, followed by a period.

21. Give the medium of publication (*Web*), followed by a period.

22. Give the date you accessed, downloaded, or printed the material from the site and a period: 25 Apr. 2010.

23. Give the URL (*uniform resource locator*). Include the URL in angle brackets (< >) followed by a period at the end of the entry if your instructor requires it or if you believe it will help your reader find the material more easily.

Here is a more concise list of the essential information you should give when documenting most Internet sources:

1. Author's name, last name first, followed by a period

2. Web page title in double quotation marks

3. Print version publication information (if given)

4. Web site or database name italicized

5. *Ed.* followed by name of editor or Web master

6. Name of sponsor or publisher of the site

7. Date of publication on the Web

8. Medium of publication (*Web*)

9. Day, month, and year of access

Including a URL

The MLA previously recommended that URLs of Web sources be included in citations. However, since URLs change often, can be specific to a particular means of access, and can be long and complicated, they are no longer considered useful or necessary for most works-cited entries. Readers today usually search the Web for the titles of works and names of authors rather than type URLs. Include a URL (after the date of access) only if you think that your readers would not be able to find the source without it or if your instructor requires it.

If you do include a URL (*uniform resource locator,* or electronic address), be scrupulously accurate when copying the URL into your citation. One incorrect space or typo will prevent you or anyone else from relocating the Web site. Reproduce capital and lowercase letters exactly as they appear on your screen or printout. Begin the URL with the access-mode identifier (e.g., *http, ftp, telnet*). Omit any characters that come before the access-mode identifier (e.g., *wysiwyg*).

`<wysiwyg://20/http://discoverer14.sirs.com>` should be cited as
`<http://discoverer14.sirs.com>`.

Breaking a URL by Typing One Space after a Slash Mark

Split the electronic address (URL) to two or more lines if necessary to avoid gaps in your bibliographic citation. In MLA-style documentation, a URL may be broken only by typing one space after a slash mark (/). Do not use a hyphen or any other method to break a URL because a single incorrect character typed into a URL will make it unusable for your reader.

The angle brackets typed before and after an electronic address inform your reader that any spaces typed into them should be ignored when the URL is used to find a Web page. The angle bracket typed at the end of the electronic address informs your reader that the period that ends the bibliographic citation is not a part of the URL.

<http://www.theatlantic.com/unbound/sage/ss2003-06-26.htm>.

You can break the URL above to two lines by typing one space after the following:

http://
.com/
unbound/
sage/

The hyphens that are already a part of the URL will also allow the URL to break to two lines at those points if they fall at the end of a line, but do not type any additional hyphens into a URL to break it. Do not type a space after a hyphen that falls at the end of a line in a URL.

Removing a Hyperlink in Microsoft Word

If your computer is converting the URLs you type to hyperlinks (usually appearing in a blue font), and you would like them to be formatted as regular text instead, go to the **Format** menu. Click on **AutoFormat**. Click on **Options**. Remove the check beside **Internet and network paths with hyperlinks**. Click on **OK**.

If you just want to convert a single hyperlink to plain text, place your cursor in the middle of the hyperlink, right-click your mouse, and left-click your mouse on **Remove Hyperlink**.

Creating Parenthetical Citations for Internet Sources

If a Web document has page numbers or paragraph numbers, use them in your parenthetical citations. Many Web documents, however, have neither page numbers nor numbered paragraphs. For those documents, you do not have to give a page or paragraph number in your parenthetical citation; just name the author or authors either in your sentence or in the parenthetical citation at the end of your sentence. You may also use the MLA abbreviation *n. pag.* to indicate that no pages were given.

Some instructors will ask you to turn in photocopies of all print materials and printouts of Web materials cited in your paper. An instructor who is checking your citations for accuracy may need you to identify the pages in the Web site printouts from which you quoted, paraphrased, or summarized information. In this case, follow your instructor's guidelines for giving printout page numbers in your parenthetical citations. MLA allows you to give additional information beyond the minimum requirements if you think such information will be useful to your reader or if your instructor requests it.

If the library or personal subscription database you are using offers the option of printing a PDF (Portable Document Format) version of the document using Adobe Reader, you can print the material exactly as it appears in the scholarly journal, popular magazine, newspaper, book, or other source. A PDF printout allows you to cite the exact pages of the original source in your parenthetical citations. (Information about downloading the latest version of Adobe Reader may be found at the *Adobe* Web site.)

When you opt for the PDF printout of the article, the journal title, the volume and issue numbers, the name of the subscription database, and the URL of the home page of the database used to access the article will not appear on your printout, so be sure you have copied all the information required for your works-cited entry into your working bibliography before leaving the database screen. Print a copy of the page containing the citation information, and attach it to your PDF printout so that you will be able to check the accuracy of the information in your citation when you are preparing the final draft of your works-cited page.

Listed below are some sample parenthetical citations for materials taken from a Web page. If the author's name is given in the lead-in to your quotation, paraphrase, or summary, do not repeat it in the parenthetical citation.

Page numbers given in document	(Chadwick 4)
Bottom of page 6 and top of page 7	(Barineau 6-7)
Web page with numbered paragraphs	(Roberts, par. 2)
Material from two numbered paragraphs	(Corrigan, pars. 2-3)
No page numbers or paragraphs given	(Wright) or (Wright n. pag.)
Professor requests printout page numbers	(Chadwick 2)
PDF printout page numbers available	(Winters 247)

Annotated Citation for a Web Page from a Print Source with an Author Given

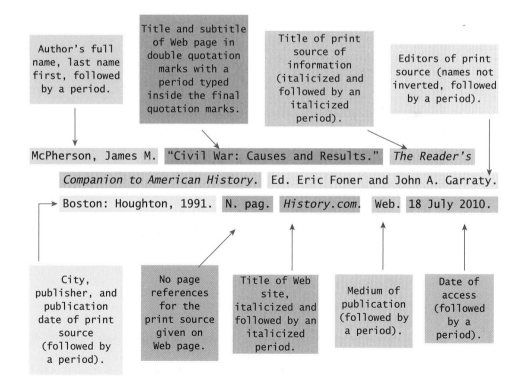

A Web Page with an Author Given

Gardner, Emily. "Hawaiian Monk Seals: Biology and Natural
    History." *Earthtrust.org.* Windward Environmental Center,
    Kailua, HI, 24 July 2010. Web. 22 Aug. 2010.

McAllister, Jim. "Nathaniel Hawthorne's Neighborhood." *Salem,
    Massachusetts: The City Guide: Salem Tales.* Salem Office
    of Tourism and Cultural Affairs, 23 July 2010. Web. 23
    July 2010.

Citing the Most Recent Update of a Web Page

The date a Web page was copyrighted or last updated is usually given at the end of the Web page. Give the day, month, and year the page was last updated if that information is available. For literary works or historical documents published on the Web, give the date of electronic publication. For an online encyclopedia or reference work, give the year of publication or most recent copyright date. If no date of copyright, electronic publication, or last revision is given, type *n.d.* (*no date*).

---

1. Give the author or authors of the material on the Web page, with the first author's name inverted. If only the initials of the author are given, check the home page, search page, or "About Us" page of the site to see if the full name is given there. If a name cannot be found, begin your citation with the title of the Web page.

2. Give the title of the Web page in double quotation marks with a period typed inside the final quotation marks.

3. Give the publication information for the print source of the information if it is given by the Web site.

4. Give the title of the entire Web site of which the Web page is a part (italicized and followed by an italicized period). You may need to check the site's home page for this information.

5. Give the publisher or sponsor of the site (or *N.p.* if unknown), followed by a comma.

6. Give the copyright date, date of posting, or date of the most recent update, followed by a period. This information is usually given at the end of the Web page. If no date can be found, use *n.d.*

7. Give the medium of publication, followed by a period.
8. Give the date you accessed, downloaded, or printed the Web page, followed by a period.

A Web Page with No Author Given

"Navigating the Night Sky: How to Tell What's What."

DiscoverySchool.com. Discovery Communications, 18 July 2010.

Web. 31 July 2010.

"Pyramids, Mummies, and Tombs: The Great Pyramid of Giza." *TLC.com.*

Discovery Communications, 18 July 2010. Web. 3 Aug. 2010.

1. Give the title of the Web page in double quotation marks with a period typed inside the final quotation marks.
2. Give the publication information for the print source of the information if it is given by the Web site.
3. Give the title of the entire Web site and a period (both italicized). Check the site's home page for this information.
4. Give the publisher or sponsor of the site (or *N.p., no publisher,* if unknown), followed by a comma.
5. Give the copyright date, date of posting, or date of the most recent update, followed by a period.
6. Give the medium of publication, followed by a period.
7. Give the date you accessed, downloaded, or printed the Web page, followed by a period.

A Web Page with No Author Given Taken from a Scholarly Project

"The *Amistad* Revolt." *Legal Information Institute (LII).* Ed.

Thomas R. Bruce and Peter W. Martin. Cornell Law School,

8 Mar. 1998. Web. 18 July 2010.

"William Gilmore Simms (1806-1870)." *Simms: A Literary Life.*

By John Caldwell Guilds. Fayetteville: U of Arkansas P,

1992. N. pag. *Two Hundred Years of Palmetto Poets.* Ed.

Daniel J. Ennis, Gregg Nystrom, and Heather Steere.

Coastal Carolina U, 2010. Web. 18 July 2010.

1. Give the title of the Web page in double quotation marks with a period typed inside the final quotation marks.

2. Give the publication information for the print source of the information (if given).

3. Give the title of the entire Web site of which the Web page is a part (italicized and followed by an italicized period). If the Web site name does not appear on the Web page, look for it on the site's home page or "About Us" page.

4. Type *Ed.* (*Edited by*), and give the editor or editors of the scholarly project (if available).

5. Give the name of the organization or university that sponsors the project (if available), not italicized and followed by a comma.

6. Give the copyright date, date of posting, or date of the most recent update (if available), followed by a period. This information is usually given at the end of the Web page.

7. Give the medium of publication, followed by a period.

8. Give the date you accessed, downloaded, or printed the Web page, followed by a period.

A Definition Taken from a Scholarly Project

"Mirror." *The Columbia Encyclopedia*. 6th ed. 2002.

> *Bartleby.com: Great Books Online*. Ed. Steven H. van
>
> Leeuwen. Bartleby.com, 2010. Web. 26 Apr. 2010.

1. Capitalize the term being defined, and put it in double quotation marks with a period typed inside the final quotation marks.

2. Following MLA guidelines for citing print sources, give the publication information for the print source of the definition (if it is given by the Web site).

3. Give the title of the scholarly project through which you accessed the definition (italicized and followed by an italicized period).

4. Type *Ed.* (*Edited by*), and give the editor or editors of the scholarly project (if available). Check the home page or "About Us" page for this information.

5. Give the name of the organization or university that sponsors the project, not italicized and followed by a comma. If unavailable, use *N.p.*

6. Give the copyright date, date of posting, or date the page containing the definition was most recently updated, followed by a period.

7. Give the medium of publication, followed by a period.

8. Give the date you accessed, downloaded, or printed the definition, followed by a period.

A Definition Taken from a Web Page

"Nebula." "Sky Watch: Astro Terms." *DiscoverySchool.com.*

   Discovery Communications, 18 July 2010. Web. 31 Aug. 2010.

1. Capitalize the term being defined, and put it in double quotation marks with a period typed inside the final quotation marks.

2. Give the title of the Web page on which the term is defined in double quotation marks with a period typed inside the final quotation marks.

3. Give the publication information for the print source of the information (if given).

4. Give the title of the Web site (italicized and followed by an italicized period). If the Web site name does not appear on the Web page, look for it on the site's home page or "About Us" page.

5. Give the publisher or sponsor of the site (or *N.p.* if unknown), followed by a comma.

6. Give the copyright date, date of posting, or date the page containing the definition was most recently updated, followed by a period.

7. Give the medium of publication, followed by a period.

8. Give the date you accessed, downloaded, or printed the definition, followed by a period.

A Table or Chart Taken from a Web Page

"Slave Population 1790-1860." Chart. *A Century of Population*

   Growth: From the First Census of the United States to the

   Twelfth, 1790-1900. Baltimore: Genealogical Publishing,

   1970. "Slavery." *History.com.* A&E Television Networks,

   2010. Web. 23 July 2010.

1. Give the title of the table or chart in double quotation marks with a period typed inside the final quotation marks.

2. If the table or chart has no title, create a title that describes the information contained in the table or chart (not in quotation marks, not italicized, followed by a period).

3. Type *Table* or *Chart* (and a period) to identify the type of material that you are citing.

4. Give the publication information for the print source of the material in the table or chart (if given).

5. Give the title of the Web page (if available) from which the table or chart was taken in double quotation marks with a period typed inside the final quotation marks.

6. Give the title of the entire Web site of which the Web page is a part, followed by a period (both italicized). If the Web site name does not appear on the Web page, look for it on the site's home page or "About Us" page.

7. Give the publisher or sponsor of the site (or *N.p.* if unknown), followed by a comma.

8. Give the copyright date, date of posting, or date of the most recent update, followed by a period.

9. Give the medium of publication, followed by a period.

10. Give the date you accessed, downloaded, or printed the Web page, followed by a period.

An Entire Web Site

American Presidents: Life Portraits. Natl. Cable Satellite
    Corp., 2007. Web. 22 July 2010.

American Writers II: The Twentieth Century. Natl.
    Cable Satellite Corp., 2010. Web. 27 Aug. 2010.

Encyclopaedia Britannica Online. Encyclopaedia Britannica,
    2010. Web. 2 Aug. 2010.

FranklinMint.com. The Franklin Mint, 2010. Web. 27 July 2010.

History.com. A&E Television Networks, 1 July 2010. Web. 3 Aug.
    2010.

New York Times. New York Times, 27 July 2010. Web. 27 July
    2010.

1. Give the title of the Web site (italicized and followed by an italicized period).

2. Give the version number for an encyclopedia if there is one (e.g., Vers. 2.1).

3. Give the name of the publisher or sponsoring organization or university (or *N.p.* if not available), not italicized, followed by a comma.
4. Give the copyright date or the date the site was last updated, followed by a period.
5. Give the medium of publication, followed by a period.
6. Give the date you accessed, downloaded, or printed material from the site and a period.

An Online Scholarly Database or Project

Bartleby.com: Great Books Online. Ed. Steven H. van Leeuwen.
    Bartleby.com, 2010. Web. 26 May 2010.

Electronic Text Center. Ed. David Seaman. Electronic Text Center,
    Alderman Lib., U of Virginia, 2010. Web. 2 July 2010.

The Perseus Digital Library. Ed. Gregory R. Crane. Tufts U,
    2010. Web. 18 July 2010.

Salem Witch Trials: Documentary Archive and Transcription
    Project. Ed. Benjamin C. Ray and Bernard Rosenthal. U of
    Virginia, 2010. Web. 18 July 2010.

Two Hundred Years of Palmetto Poets. Ed. Daniel J. Ennis, Gregg
    Nystrom, and Heather Steere. Coastal Carolina U, 2010.
    Web. 18 July 2010.

Victorian Women Writers Project. Ed. Perry Willett. Indiana U,
    10 Dec. 2009. Web. 26 May 2010.

Voice of the Shuttle: Web Site for Humanities Research. Ed.
    Alan Liu. Dept. of English, U of California, Santa
    Barbara, 6 Feb. 2009. Web. 19 July 2010.

Voices from the Gaps: Women Writers and Artists of Color. Ed.
    Toni McNaron and Carol Miller. U of Minnesota, 20 July
    2009. Web. 23 July 2010.

Women of the Romantic Period. Ed. Daniel Anderson and Morri
    Safran. U of Texas at Austin, 17 May 2010. Web. 19 July
    2010.

1. Give the title of the scholarly database or project (italicized and followed by an italicized period).
2. Type *Ed.* (*Edited by*), and give the name of the editor or editors of the scholarly project (names not inverted). Check the site's home page or "About Us" page for this information.
3. Give the name of the organization or university that sponsors the project (not italicized), followed by a comma. If unknown, use *N.p.*
4. Give the copyright date or date the site was last updated and a period.
5. Give the medium of publication, followed by a period.
6. Give the date you accessed, downloaded, or printed material from the project's site, followed by a period.

A Novel Published in Print Form and Online

Crosse, Victoria [Vivian Cory]. *The Woman Who Didn't.* London:

    Lane; Boston: Roberts, 1895. Transcribed, encoded, and

    proofed by Jessica Loving. *Victorian Women Writers*

    Project. Ed. Perry Willett. Indiana U. Web. 26 May 2010.

Eliot, George [Mary Ann Evans]. *The Mill on the Floss.* Ed.

    Charles W. Eliot. Vol. 9. New York: Collier, 1917. Harvard

    Classics Shelf of Fiction. *Bartleby.com: Great Books*

    Online. Ed. Steven H. van Leeuwen. Bartleby.com. Web. 29

    June 2010.

1. Give the author's name, last name first, followed by a period. If the author wrote under a pen name, you may give the author's real name in square brackets after the pen name (before the period).
2. Give the title of the work and a period (both italicized).
3. Give the editor (*Ed.*) or translator (*Trans.*) of the work (if given) in the order given on the Web page.
4. If you need to list a volume number, do so after the editor's name or the edition number and before the publication information.
5. Give the city, publisher, and date of publication for the printed version of the work, followed by a period.

6. If the work was part of a series (such as Harvard Classics Shelf of Fiction), give the title of the series (not italicized, not in quotation marks, followed by a period) after the publication information and before the title of the database. In a citation for a print publication, this series title goes after the medium of publication.

7. Give the name of the Web site or scholarly project that published the online version of the work (italicized and followed by a period).

8. Type *Ed.* (*Edited by*) and give the editor(s) of the site.

9. Give the name of the organization or university that sponsors the Web site or scholarly project (not italicized, followed by a period) and other supplementary information about the site or project.

10. Give the medium of publication, followed by a period.

11. Give the date you accessed, downloaded, or printed the work, followed by a period.

A Book with a Translator Published in Print Form and Online

Alighieri, Dante. *The Divine Comedy of Dante Alighieri: Hell,*

Purgatory, Paradise. Trans. Henry F. Cary. Ed. Charles W.

Eliot. Vol. 20. New York: Collier, 1909-14. The Harvard

Classics. *Bartleby.com: Great Books Online.* Ed. Steven H.

van Leeuwen. Bartleby.com. Web. 26 May 2010.

Give the print publication information as you would when citing a print book (see directions above). If the work is part of a series (such as The Harvard Classics), give the title of the series (not italicized or in quotation marks) after the date of print publication and before the title of the database.

An Introduction, Preface, Foreword or Afterword from an Online Book

McKay, David. Preface. *Leaves of Grass.* By Walt Whitman.

Philadelphia: McKay, 1900. *Bartleby.com: Great Books Online.*

Ed. Steven H. van Leeuwen. Bartleby.com. Web. 2 July 2010.

A Poetry Collection Available in Print and Online

Keats, John. *The Poetical Works of John Keats.* Ed. Francis
    Turner Palgrave. London: Macmillan, 1884. Golden Treasury
    Series. *Bartleby.com: Great Books Online.* Ed. Steven H.
    van Leeuwen. Bartleby.com. Web. 29 June 2010.

Whitman, Walt. *Leaves of Grass.* Philadelphia: McKay, 1900.
    Bartleby.com: Great Books Online. Ed. Steven H. van
    Leeuwen. Bartleby.com. Web. 26 May 2010.

A Play Available in Print and Online

O'Neill, Eugene. *Beyond the Horizon: A Play in Three Acts.*
    New York: Boni, 1920. *Bartleby.com: Great Books Online.*
    Ed. Steven H. van Leeuwen. Bartleby.com. Web. 2 July 2010.

Shakespeare, William. *Hamlet. The Works of William Shake-*
    speare. Ed. W[illiam] G[eorge] Clark and W[illiam] Aldis
    Wright. Globe ed. New York: Doubleday, n.d. *The Perseus*
    Digital Library. Ed. Gregory R. Crane. Tufts U. Web.
    18 July 2010.

1. Give the author's name, last name first, followed by a period.
2. Give the title of the play (italicized and followed by a period).
3. Give the editor (*Ed.*) or translator (*Trans.*) of the play (if given) in the order given on the Web page. Then list the edition number or name.
4. If there is one, give the title of the anthology or collection in which the play was originally published and a period (both italicized).
5. Type *Ed.*, and give the editor(s) of the anthology (followed by a period).
6. Give the city, publisher, and date of publication for the printed version of the work, followed by a period.
7. Give the name of the Web site or scholarly project that published the online version of the work and a period (both italicized).
8. Type *Ed.* and give the editor or editors of the site (if available).

9. Give the sponsor of the Web site or scholarly project and a period.

10. Give the medium of publication, followed by a period.

11. Give the date you accessed, downloaded, or printed the play, followed by a period.

A Translation of a Play Available in Print and Online

Sophocles. *Oedipus the King.* Trans. E[dward] H[ayes] Plumptre.

   Ed. Charles W[illiam] Eliot. New York: Collier, 1909-14.

   The Harvard Classics. Vol. 8. Pt. 5. *Bartleby.com: Great*

   Books Online. Ed. Steven H. van Leeuwen. Bartleby.com.

   Web. 26 May 2010.

1. Give the author's name, last name first, followed by a period.

2. Give the title of the play (italicized and followed by a period).

3. Give the editor (*Ed.*) or translator (*Trans.*) of the play (if given) in the order given on the Web page. Give the edition if there is one.

4. If there is one, give the title of the anthology or collection in which the play was originally published (italicized and followed by a period).

5. Type *Ed.* (*Edited by*), and give the editor or editors of the anthology (names not inverted, followed by a period).

6. Give the city, publisher, and date of publication for the printed version of the work, followed by a period.

7. If the work was part of a series, give the title of the series (not italicized or in quotation marks) after the publication information and before the title of the Web site or scholarly project. Add details such as the series volume and part numbers after the series title.

8. Give the name of the Web site or scholarly project that published the online version of the work (italicized and followed by a period).

9. Type *Ed.* and give the editor or editors of the site (if available).

10. Give the name of the organization that sponsors the Web site or scholarly project (if there is one), not italicized, followed by a period.

11. Give the medium of publication, followed by a period.

12. End with the date you accessed, downloaded, or printed the play and a period.

A Short Story Available in Print and Online

Melville, Herman. "Bartleby, the Scrivener: A Story of Wall-

Street." *Putnam's Monthly* Pt. 1: 2.11 (1853): 546-57;

Pt. 2: 2.12 (1853): 609-15. *Bartleby.com: Great Books Online.*

Ed. Steven H. van Leeuwen. Bartleby.com. Web. 29 June 2010.

Note that the short story cited above was published in two consecutive issues of *Putnam's Monthly*. Publication information is given on each issue in which the parts were published, with a semicolon separating the two parts.

A Poem Available in Print and Online

Allston, Washington. "The French Revolution." *The Sylphs of the*

Seasons, with Other Poems. Boston: Cummings, 1813. *Two*

Hundred Years of Palmetto Poets. Ed. Daniel J. Ennis,

Gregg Nystrom, and Heather Steere. Coastal Carolina U.

Web. 18 July 2010.

Citing Online Scholarly Journals

Annotated Citation for an Article with an Author Given from an Online Scholarly Journal

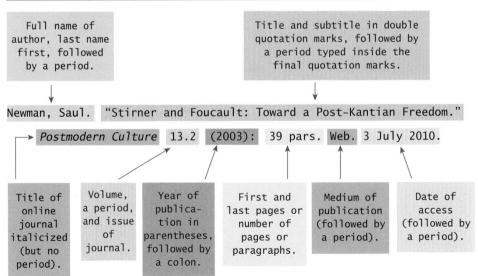

Full name of author, last name first, followed by a period.

Title and subtitle in double quotation marks, followed by a period typed inside the final quotation marks.

Newman, Saul. "Stirner and Foucault: Toward a Post-Kantian Freedom."

Postmodern Culture 13.2 (2003): 39 pars. Web. 3 July 2010.

Title of online journal italicized (but no period).

Volume, a period, and issue of journal.

Year of publication in parentheses, followed by a colon.

First and last pages or number of pages or paragraphs.

Medium of publication (followed by a period).

Date of access (followed by a period).

An Article with an Author Given
from an Online Scholarly Journal

Wagner, Geraldine. "Romancing Multiplicity: Female Subjectivity

    and the Body Divisible in Margaret Cavendish's *Blazing*

    World." *Early Modern Literary Studies* 9.1 (2003):

    59 pars. Web. 26 July 2010.

1. Give the author's name, last name first, followed by a period. If more than one author is given, cite the names in the order given on the title page with only the first author's name inverted.
2. Give the title and subtitle of the article in double quotation marks with a period typed inside the final quotation marks.
3. Give the title of the scholarly journal (italicized and not followed by a period). Omit the article *The* if it begins the title of a journal but not if it begins the title of an article in a journal.
4. Give the volume number, a period, and the issue number. Then type the year of publication in parentheses, a colon, and one space.
5. Give the first and last pages of the article or the total number of pages, paragraphs, or sections (if numbered), followed by a period. If no page numbers or paragraphs are given, use *n. pag.*
6. Give the medium of publication consulted, followed by a period.
7. End with the date you accessed, downloaded, or printed the article and a period.

A Book Review from an Online Scholarly Journal

Daems, Jim. Rev. of *Libertines and Radicals in Early Modern*

    London: Sexuality, Politics, and Literary Culture,

    1630-1685, by James Grantham Turner. *Early Modern Literary*

    Studies 9.1 (2003): 5 pars. Web. 26 July 2010.

Gwiazda, Piotr. "Modernism Old or New?" Rev. of *21st-Century*

    Modernism: The "New" Poetics, by Marjorie Perloff.

    Postmodern Culture 13.2 (2003): 9 pars. Web. 3 July

    2010.

1. Give the author's name, last name first, followed by a period. If more than one author is given, cite the names in the order given on the title page of the review with only the first author's name inverted.

2. Give the title and subtitle of the review in double quotation marks, followed by a period typed inside the final quotation marks. If the review is untitled, skip this step.

3. Type *Rev. of,* and give the title and subtitle of the work being reviewed (italicized), a comma, and the name of the author of the work being reviewed (not inverted), preceded with the word *by* and followed by a period.

4. Give the title of the scholarly journal (italicized and not followed by a period). Omit the article *The* if it begins the title of a journal but not if it begins the title of a review or article in a journal.

5. Give the volume number, a period, and the issue number. Then type one space, the year of publication (in parentheses), a colon, and a space.

6. Give the first and last pages of the review or the total number of pages, paragraphs, or sections (if numbered), followed by a period. If no page numbers or paragraphs are given, use *n. pag.*

7. Give the medium of publication (*Web*), followed by a period.

8. End with the date you accessed, downloaded, or printed the review (followed by a period).

Citing Online Popular Magazines

An Article with an Author Given from an Online Monthly or Bimonthly Magazine

Deuel, Nathan. "The Cruel Wit of Evelyn Waugh." *Atlantic*

    Online. Atlantic Monthly Group, April 2003. Web.

    17 July 2010.

Lawson, Willow. "Flavonoids: Antioxidants Help the Mind."

    Psychology Today. Sussex Publishers, July 2003. Web. 16

    July 2010.

1. Give the author's name, last name first, followed by a period. If there are more authors, cite the names in the order given on the title page, inverting only the first author's name.

2. Give the title and subtitle of the article in double quotation marks, followed by a period typed inside the final quotation marks.

3. Give the title of the online magazine and a period (both italicized). Omit *The* if it begins a magazine title but not if it begins a magazine article title.

4. Give the sponsor of the site (not italicized) and follow with a comma.

5. Give the month and year the article was published, followed by a period. For a bimonthly magazine, give both months (Jan.-Feb. 2010).

6. Do not give the volume and issue numbers for popular magazines even if that information is available.

7. Give the medium of publication, followed by a period.

8. End with the date you accessed, downloaded, or printed the article, followed by a period.

An Interview from an Online Monthly or Bimonthly Magazine

Bidart, Frank. "The Journey of a Maker." Interview by

Dan Chiasson. *Atlantic Unbound.* Atlantic Monthly Group,

July 2003. Web. 16 July 2010.

1. Give the name of the person being interviewed, last name first, followed by a period.

2. Give the title of the interview (if it has one) in double quotation marks, followed by a period typed inside the final quotation marks.

3. Type *Interview by,* and give the name(s) of the interviewer(s), followed by a period.

4. Give the title of the magazine (italicized and followed by a period).

5. Give the sponsor of the site (not italicized) and follow with a comma.

6. Give the month and year the article was published, followed by a period. For a bimonthly magazine, give both months (Jan.-Feb. 2010).

7. Do not give the volume and issue numbers for popular magazines even if that information is available.

8. Give the medium of publication, followed by a period.

9. End with the date you accessed, downloaded, or printed the article, followed by a period.

An Online Weekly or Biweekly Magazine Article

Gibbs, Nancy, with Mark Thompson. "A Soldier's Life: How the

War [in Iraq] Is Straining U.S. Soldiers--and Haunting

Those They Left at Home." *Time.* Time, 21 July 2003. Web.

16 July 2010.

Tyre, Peg. "Divorce: From Bad to Worse: In Tough Times, Split-

ting Couples Fight for Pennies." *Newsweek*. Newsweek, 21

July 2003. Web. 21 Oct. 2010.

1. Give the author's name, last name first, followed by a period. If there are more authors, cite the names in the order given on the title page, only inverting the first. Use *with* in place of *and* between the authors' names in the magazine: Gibbs, Nancy, with Mark Thompson.

2. Give the title and subtitle of the article in double quotation marks, followed by a period typed inside the final quotation marks. Follow MLA guidelines for capitalizing words in titles no matter how the title is formatted in the magazine.

3. Give the title of the magazine (italicized and followed by a period). Omit the article *The* if it begins the title of a magazine but not if it begins the title of an article in a magazine.

4. Give the publisher or sponsor of the site (not italicized) and a comma.

5. Give the day, month, and year the article was published and follow with a period.

6. Do not give the volume and issue numbers for a popular magazine even if that information is available. *(continued on page 165)*

Citing Online Newspaper Articles

Annotated Citation for an Article from an Online Newspaper

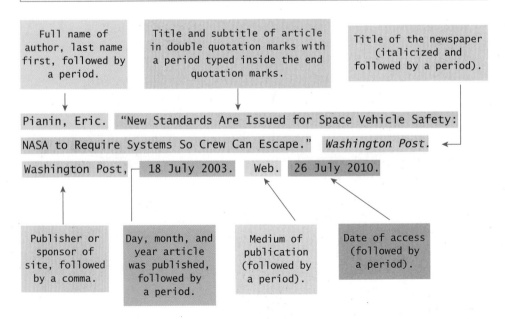

7. Give the medium of publication, followed by a period.
8. End with the date you accessed, downloaded, or printed the article, followed by a period.

An Article from an Online Newspaper

Bennet, James. "Palestinian Focus: The Internal Fight."

    New York Times. New York Times, 1 July 2003. Web.

    10 July 2010.

Greenhouse, Linda. "In a Momentous Term, Justices Remake the

    Law, and the Court." *New York Times*. New York Times,

    1 July 2003. Web. 10 July 2010.

Pianin, Eric, and R. Jeffrey Smith, with Kathy Sawyer. "Shuttle

    Flight's Chief Takes Responsibility on Decision: Official

    Says She Played Down Foam Strike's Importance but Relied

    on Boeing Engineers' Assurances." *Washington Post*.

    Washington Post, 23 July 2003. Web. 26 July 2010.

1. Give the author's name, last name first, followed by a period. If there are more authors, cite the names in the order given on the title page, inverting only the first author's name.
2. If no author is given, begin the entry with the title of the article and alphabetize the entry in your works-cited list by the first significant word of the title, excluding *A, And,* and *The.*
3. Give the title and subtitle of the article in double quotation marks, followed by a period typed inside the final quotation marks. Follow MLA guidelines for capitalizing words in titles no matter how the title is formatted in the newspaper.
4. Give the title of the online newspaper (italicized and followed by a period). Omit the article *The* at the beginning of the title of a newspaper but not at the beginning of an article in a newspaper.
5. Give the sponsor of the site (not italicized) and follow with a comma.
6. Give the day, month, and year of electronic publication, followed by a period.
7. Give the medium of publication, followed by a period.
8. End with the date you accessed, downloaded, or printed the article (followed by a period).

An Editorial with No Author Given from an Online Newspaper

"A Needed Human Rights Law." Editorial. *New York Times.* New

    York Times, 2 June 2003. Web. 13 June 2010.

An Opinion Piece with an Author Given from an Online Newspaper

Herbert, Bob. "The Reverse Robin Hood." Opinion piece. *New York*

    Times. New York Times, 2 June 2003. Web. 3 June 2010.

Safire, William. " 'You Lied to Us.' " Opinion piece. *New York*

    Times. New York Times, 2 June 2003. Web. 3 June 2010.

A Book Review from an Online Newspaper

Maslin, Janet. "The Founder of Healthy, Wealthy, and Wise,

    Inc." Rev. of, *Benjamin Franklin: An American Life,* by

    Walter Isaacson. *New York Times.* New York Times, 3 July

    2003. Web. 13 July 2010.

A Film Review from an Online Newspaper

Caro, Mark. Rev. of *Charlie's Angels: Full Throttle,*

    dir. McG [Joseph McGinty Nichol]. Perf. Cameron Diaz,

    Lucy Liu, Drew Barrymore, Bernie Mac, and Demi Moore.

    Chicago Tribune. Chicago Tribune, 25 June 2003. Web. 27

    July 2010.

Holden, Stephen. "Fathers, Sons, and Grandsons, in the Script

    and Real Life." Rev. of *It Runs in the Family,* dir. Fred

    Schepisi. Perf. Kirk Douglas, Michael Douglas, Cameron

    Douglas, and Diana Douglas. *New York Times.* New York

    Times, 25 Apr. 2003. Web. 25 Apr. 2010.

A Play Review from an Online Newspaper

Brantley, Ben. "New Momma Takes Charge." Rev. of *Gypsy,* dir.
Sam Mendes. Perf. Bernadette Peters. Shubert Theater,
New York. *New York Times.* New York Times, 2 May 2003.
Web. 2 May 2010.

Brantley, Ben. "Twain's Tale, with Music for the Ear and Eye."
Rev. of *Big River: The Adventures of Huckleberry Finn,*
dir. and chor. Jeff Calhoun. Music and lyrics by Roger
Miller. Adapt. William Hauptman. Perf. Tyrone Giordano,
Michael McElroy, Daniel Jenkins, and Michael Arden. Based
on *The Adventures of Huckleberry Finn,* by Mark Twain.
American Airlines Theater, New York. *New York Times.* New
York Times, 25 July 2003. Web. 10 July 2010.

A Ballet Review from an Online Newspaper

Kisselgoff, Anna. "Swans in an Up-to-Date Lake." Rev. of *Swan
Lake,* chor. Peter Martins. New York City Ballet. New York
State Theater, New York. *New York Times.* New York Times,
5 May 2003. Web. 15 May 2010.

An Art Show Review from an Online Newspaper

O'Sullivan, Michael. "Lesley Dill, in So Many Words." Rev. of
"Lesley Dill: A Ten Year Survey," by Lesley Dill. National
Museum of Women in the Arts, Washington. *Washington Post.*
Washington Post, 25 July 2003. Web. 26 July 2010.

A Classical Music Concert Review
from an Online Newspaper

Ginell, Richard S. "The Philharmonic's Rocking, Socking Night."
Rev. of a concert by the Los Angeles Philharmonic, cond.

Esa-Pekka Salonen. Hollywood Bowl. *Los Angeles Times.* Los

Angeles Times, 24 July 2010. Web. 26 July 2010.

A Concert or Festival Review from an Online Newspaper

Lewis, Randy. "Strumming a Cynical Chord: Steely Dan Starts

Its Summer Tour of *Everything Must Go* in All Its Jaded

Glory." Rev. of Steely Dan concert. *Los Angeles Times.*

Los Angeles Times, 25 July 2003. Web. 26 July 2010.

Pareles, Jon. "Lollapalooza Hits a Commercial Note." Rev. of Lol-

lapalooza Festival. PNC Bank Arts Theater, New York. *New*

York Times. New York Times, 25 July 2003. Web. 25 July 2010.

Citing Other Miscellaneous Internet Sources

An E-Mail Message

McIntyre, Debbie. "Party Details and Directions to My New

House." Message to Julia Tucker. 28 May 2010. E-mail.

1. Give the name of the writer of the electronic mail, last name first, followed by a period.
2. Give the title of the message (taken from the subject line) in double quotation marks with a period typed inside the final quotation marks.
3. Type *Message to the author* or *Message to* (name of recipient), followed by a period.
4. Give the day, month, and year of the message, followed by a period.
5. End with the medium of delivery (*E-mail*).

An Online Posting to an E-Mail Discussion Group, Listserv, or Blog (Weblog)

McCarty, Willard. "Happy Sweet Sixteen." Online posting.

Humanist Discussion Group. 7 May 2010. Web. 27 Aug. 2010.

<http://lists.village.virginia.edu/lists_archive/

Humanist/v17/0000.html>.

Hartnett, Sam. "Rick Springfield Interview in Local Paper."

    Online posting. *Rick Rocks The Planet*. Rick Rocks the

    Planet, 22 Aug. 2010. Web. 25 Aug. 2010.

1. Give the author's name, last name first, followed by a period.
2. Give the title of the document taken from the subject line of the posting (in double quotation marks with a period typed inside the final quotation marks). Follow MLA guidelines for capitalizing words in titles.
3. After the title, type *Online posting* (not in quotation marks or italics), followed by a period.
4. If relevant, give the name of the discussion group, listserv, or blog (not italicized or in quotation marks), followed by a period.
5. Give the title of the Web site for the discussion group, listserv, or blog, italicized and followed by a period.
6. Give the sponsor of the site (if relevant), followed by a comma.
7. Give the day, month, and year the material was posted online (followed by a period).
8. Give the medium of publication (*Web*), followed by a period.
9. Give the day, month, and year you accessed or printed the material (followed by a period).
10. Give the URL in angle brackets followed by a period if your instructor requires it or if you think it will help readers find the material.
11. If possible, cite an archived version of the posting taken from the group's Web site, which will make it easier for your readers to find your source if they should wish to do so.

A Forwarded Online Posting

Smiley, Kate. "Rick's Concert at Myrtle Beach House of Blues

    Rescheduled." 20 Aug. 2010. Fwd. by Mark Sanders. Online

    posting. *Rick Springfield East Coast Fan Club*. Rick Spring-

    field East Coast Fan Club, 23 Aug. 2010. Web. 25 Aug. 2010.

1. Give the name of the author of the original posting, last name first, followed by a period.
2. Give the title of the document taken from the subject line of the posting (in double quotation marks with a period typed inside the final quotation marks). Follow MLA guidelines for capitalizing words in titles.

3. Give the day, month, and year when the original message was posted, followed by a period.

4. Type *Fwd. by* (*Forwarded by*), and give the name of the person who forwarded the message (followed by a period).

5. Type *Online posting* (not in quotation marks and not italicized), followed by a period.

6. If relevant, give the name of the discussion group, listserv, news group, or blog (not italicized or in quotation marks), followed by a period.

7. Give the title of the Web site (italicized), followed by a period.

8. Give the sponsor of the site, followed by a comma.

9. Give the day, month, and year that the message was forwarded, followed by a period.

10. Give the medium of publication(*Web*), followed by a period.

11. Give the day, month, and year when you accessed or printed the material, followed by a period.

12. Give the URL in angle brackets followed by a period if your instructor requires it or if you think it will help readers find the material.

An Online Posting to a News Group

Briggs, Dave. "Online Literary Community." Online posting.

9 July 2010. Web. 27 Aug. 2010. <news:alt.literature>.

1. Give the author's name, last name first, followed by a period.

2. Give the title of the document taken from the subject line of the posting (in double quotation marks with a period typed inside the final quotation marks). Follow MLA guidelines for capitalizing words in titles.

3. After the title, type *Online posting* (not in quotation marks and not italicized), followed by a period.

4. Give the day, month, and year when the material was posted to the news group (followed by a period).

5. Give the medium of publication (*Web*), followed by a period.

6. Give the day, month, and year when you accessed or printed the material (followed by a period).

7. Type *news* followed by a colon, no space, and the name of the news group (all within angle brackets, followed by a period).

A Review of a CD Taken from a Discussion Group or Fan Web Site

Nicholson, Angie. "*Sahara Snow:* 10 out of 10." Rev. of *Sahara*

    Snow, perf. Rick Springfield, Tim Pierce, and Bob

    Marlette. *Rick Rocks the Planet.* Rick Rocks the Planet,

    27 Aug. 2010. Web. 31 Aug. 2010.

1. Give the author of the review, last name first, and a period.
2. Give the title of the review (in double quotation marks with a period typed inside the final quotation marks). Follow MLA guidelines for capitalizing words in titles.
3. Type *Rev. of* and give the title of the CD (italicized and followed by a comma and one space).
4. Type *perf.* (*performed by*) and give the names of the performer or performers, followed by a period.
5. Give the name of the online discussion group or fan Web site (Web site italicized), followed by a period.
6. Give the name of the sponsor of the site, followed by a comma.
7. Give the date when the review was posted to the site.
8. Give the medium of publication (*Web*), followed by a period.
9. Give the date when you accessed or printed the review (and a period).
10. Give the URL of the home page of the discussion group or fan Web site in angle brackets followed by a period if your instructor requires it or if you think it will help readers find the material.

A Biographical Sketch of an Artist Taken from the Artist's Web Site

Springfield, Rick. "A Biography (of Sorts): Are You Sitting

    Comfortably?" *Rick Springfield.com.* Rick Springfield, 27

    Aug. 2010. Web. 31 Aug. 2010.

Yoder, Tom. "Tom's Journey, Courtesy of the Man Himself."

    The Official Tom Yoder Web Site. Tom Yoder, 25 Aug. 2010.

    Web. 30 Aug. 2010.

1. Give the name of the author of the biographical sketch, last name first, followed by a period.

2. Give the title of the biographical sketch (in double quotation marks with a period typed inside the final quotation marks). Follow MLA guidelines for capitalizing words in titles.

3. Give the name of the artist's Web site (italicized and followed by an italicized period).

4. Give the sponsor of the site, followed by a comma.

5. Give the date when the sketch was posted, followed by a period.

6. Give the medium of publication, followed by a period.

7. Give the date when you accessed or printed the biographical sketch (followed by a period).

A Home Page for a Business or Corporation

Home page. *Lattice Semiconductor Corporation.* Lattice Semicon-
     ductor Corporation, 27 July 2010. Web. 31 July 2010.

1. Type *Home page* (not in quotation marks or italics). The home page is the title page or first page of a Web site from which you access (through hypertext links) the other pages on the site.

2. Give the title of the corporate Web site (italicized and followed by an italicized period).

3. Give the sponsor of the site, followed by a comma.

4. Give the date when the home page was copyrighted or last updated, followed by a period.

5. Give the medium of publication, followed by a period.

6. Give the date when you accessed or printed material from the home page, followed by a period.

An Annual Report for a Business or Corporation

Lattice Semiconductor Corporation 2002 Annual Report:
     Evolution, Adaptation, and Differentiation. Lattice
     Semiconductor Corporation. Lattice Semiconductor
     Corporation, 14 Feb. 2003. Web. 31 July 2010.

1. Give the title of the annual report as it appears on the title page of the report (italicized and followed by an italicized period).

2. Give the title of the corporation's Web site, italicized and followed by an italicized period.
3. Give the name of the sponsor of the site, followed by a comma.
4. Give the date when the report was posted, followed by a period.
5. Give the medium of publication, followed by a period.
6. End with the date when you accessed the site, followed by a period.

A Home Page for a Government Site

Home page. *Office of Elementary and Secondary Education.* Office

of Elementary and Secondary Education, 24 Jan. 2010. Web.

13 July 2010.

1. Type *Home page* (not in quotation marks or italicized, followed by a period).
2. Give the name of the government agency Web site, italicized and followed by an italicized period.
3. Give the sponsor of the site, followed by a comma.
4. Give the date when the home page was copyrighted or last updated, followed by a period.
5. Give the medium of publication, followed by a period.
6. Give the date when you accessed or printed material from the home page, followed by a period.

A Home Page for a University

Home page. *Coastal Carolina University.* Coastal Carolina

University, 18 July 2010. Web. 31 July 2010.

Home page. *Georgia Institute of Technology.* Georgia Institute

of Technology, 24 July 2010. Web. 30 July 2010.

1. Type *Home Page* (not in quotation marks or italics) and a period.
2. Give the name of the university Web site and a period (both italicized).
3. Give the sponsor of the site, followed by a comma.
4. Give the date when the home page was copyrighted or last updated, followed by a period.
5. Give the medium of publication, followed by a period.

6. Give the date when you accessed or printed material from the home page, followed by a period.

A Home Page for a College, School, or Division within a University

Home page. *School of Literature, Communication, and Culture.*

School of Literature, Communication, and Culture, Georgia

Institute of Technology, 24 July 2010. Web. 31 July 2010.

Home page. *Thomas W. and Robin W. Edwards College of Humanities*

and Fine Arts. Thomas W. and Robin W. Edwards College of

Humanities and Fine Arts, Coastal Carolina U, 24 July

2010. Web. 30 July 2010.

1. Type *Home page* (not in quotation marks or italics, followed by a period).
2. Give the name of the Web site of the school, college, or division, italicized and followed by an italicized period.
3. Give the name of the sponsor of the site, followed by a comma.
4. Give the date when the home page was copyrighted or last updated, followed by a period.
5. Give the medium of publication, followed by a period.
6. Give the date when you accessed or printed material from the home page (followed by a period).

A Home Page for an Academic Department at a University

Dept. home page. Dept. of Marine Science. *Coastal Carolina*

University. Dept. of Marine Science, Coastal Carolina U,

2010. Web. 22 July 2010.

1. Type *Dept. home page* (not italicized or in quotation marks, followed by a period).
2. Give the name of the department (not italicized or in quotation marks, followed by a period).
3. Give the name of the university Web site (italicized and followed by an italicized period).

4. Give the name of the sponsor of the site, followed by a comma.
5. Give the date when the home page was copyrighted or last updated, followed by a period.
6. Give the medium of publication, followed by a period.
7. Give the date when you accessed or printed material from the home page (followed by a period).

A Home Page for a Course at a University

Young, Rob. Course home page. Marine Science 375: The Biology

of Marine Mammals. Jan. 2010-May 2010. Dept. of Marine

Science. *Coastal Carolina University*. Dept. of Marine

Science, Coastal Carolina U, 23 Apr. 2010. Web. 1 May 2010.

1. Give the name of the instructor or professor, last name first, followed by a period. If more than one person is teaching the course, give all the names, inverting only the first name listed.
2. Type *Course home page* (not in quotation marks, not italicized, followed by a period).
3. Give the title of the course (not in quotation marks or italicized, followed by a period). Follow MLA-recommended guidelines for capitalizing words in titles.
4. Give the month and year when the course began, a hyphen, and the month and year the course ended or will end, followed by a period.
5. Give the name of the department in which the course is or was taught (not italicized or in quotation marks, followed by a period).
6. Give the name of the university Web site (italicized and followed by an italicized period).
7. Give the sponsor of the site, followed by a comma.
8. Give the date when material on the home page was posted or updated (followed by a period).
9. Give the medium of publication, followed by a period.
10. Give the the the date when you accessed the home page, followed by a period.

A Handout Taken from a Professor's University Home Page

Ellis, Scott. "Handout: Close Reading a Poem." Teaching page.

English 101: Writing the Community/Writing Ourselves.

School of Literature, Communication, and Culture. *Georgia Institute of Technology.* School of Literature, Communication, and Culture, Georgia Institute of Technology, 24 July 2010. Web. 30 July 2010.

A Journal Article Reprinted on a Professor's University Home Page

Ewert, Jeanne. "Deep and Dark Waters: Raymond Chandler Revisits the Fin-de-Siècle." *Genre* 27.3 (1994): 255-74. Jeanne Ewert's home page. *Georgia Institute of Technology.* School of Literature, Communication, and Culture, Georgia Institute of Technology, 2 Sept. 2009. Web. 3 Mar. 2010.

A Personal Site

Rasnake, David K., ed. *The William Wordsworth Page.* David K. Rasnake, 19 July 2010. Web. 22 July 2010.

Yoder, Tom. *The Official Tom Yoder Web Site.* Tom Yoder, 24 July 2010. Web. 30 July 2010.

1. Give the name of the person who created the site, last name first, followed by a period.
2. Give the title of the site in italics and followed by a period.
3. Give the sponsor of the site, followed by a comma.
4. Give the date when the site was last updated, followed by a period.
5. Give the medium of publication, followed by a period.
6. Give the date when you accessed, downloaded, or printed material from the Web site (followed by a period).

An Online Government Publication

United States. Dept. of Education. Office for Civil Rights. *Sex Discrimination: Overview of the Law. Department of Education.* 12 Feb. 2010. Web. 3 July 2010.

```
United States. Food and Drug Administration. The Bioterrorism

    Act of 2002. Food and Drug Administration. 27 May 2010.

    Web. 3 July 2010.
```

1. Give the author, editor (*ed.*), or compiler (*comp.*) of the material (if available).
2. If no author is listed, give the name of the federal (United States), state (California), city (San Francisco), or local government responsible for the publication.
3. Next give the name of the agency (or agencies) that published the material. If several government agencies are listed, give the largest agency first; then give the smaller agencies, from largest to smallest.
4. Give the title of the document (italicized and followed by a period). If you are citing a historical document, act, or law, do not italicize the title or place it in quotation marks, but do type a period after it.
5. Give the title of the Web site and a period (both italicized).
6. Give the date of copyright or last update, followed by a period.
7. Give the medium of publication, followed by a period.
8. Give the date when you accessed, downloaded, or printed the document (followed by a period).

An Online Cartoon or Comic Strip

```
Stossel, Sage. "Zen and the Art of College Admissions."

    Cartoon. Atlantic Unbound. Atlantic Monthly Group,

    26 June 2003. Web. 2 July 2010.
```

1. Give the name of the cartoonist (if known).
2. Give the title of the cartoon (if known) or comic strip in double quotation marks with a period typed inside the final quotation marks.
3. Type *Cartoon* or *Comic strip* (not in quotation marks or italicized and followed by a period). If no cartoonist or title is known, begin the entry with *Cartoon* or *Comic strip*.
4. Give the title of the online magazine or newspaper (italicized and followed by an italicized period).
5. Give the sponsor or publisher of the site, followed by a comma.
6. Give the day, month, and year that the cartoon was published, followed by a period.

7. Give the medium of publication, followed by a period.

8. Give the date that you accessed or printed the cartoon or comic strip (followed by a period).

An Online Illustration

"The June 10, 1692, Hanging of Bridget Bishop." Illustration. *Famous*

American Trials: Salem Witchcraft Trials 1692. Ed. Douglas O.

Linder. UMKC School of Law, June 2010. Web. 2 July 2010.

1. Give the title of the illustration in double quotation marks with a period typed inside the final quotation marks.

2. Type the word *Illustration*, followed by a period.

3. Give the title of the Web site and a period (both italicized).

4. Type *Ed.* (*Edited by*), and give the editor or Web master (if known), followed by a period.

5. Give the sponsor or publisher of the site, followed by a comma.

6. Give the date when the Web site was last updated, followed by a period.

7. Give the medium of publication, followed by a period.

8. Give the date when you accessed or printed the illustration (followed by a period).

An Online Photograph

McAllister, Jim. "House of the Seven Gables." Photograph.

Salem, Massachusetts: The City Guide: Salem Tales.

Ed. Jim McAllister. Salem Office of Tourism and Cultural

Affairs, 6 June 2010. Web. 28 June 2010.

1. Give the name of the photographer (if available).

2. Give the title of the photograph in double quotation marks with a period typed inside the final quotation marks.

3. Type the word *Photograph* (not in quotation marks or italics), followed by a period.

4. Give the name of the Web site and a period (both italicized).

5. Type *Ed.* (*Edited by*), and give the editor or Web master (if known), followed by a period.

6. Give the sponsor of the site, followed by a comma.

7. Give the date the site was last updated, followed by a period.

8. Give the medium of publication, followed by a period.

9. Give the date when you accessed or printed the photograph (followed by a period).

An Online Map

"Salem in 1692: Town and Village." Map. *Famous American Trials:*

   Salem Witchcraft Trials 1692. Ed. Douglas O. Linder. UMKC

   School of Law, 2 July 2010. Web. 15 July 2010.

1. Give the title of the map in double quotation marks with a period typed inside the final quotation marks.

2. Type the word *Map* (not in quotation marks or italics), followed by a period.

3. Give the title of the Web site and a period (both italicized).

4. Type *Ed.* (*Edited by*), and give the editor or Web master (if known), followed by a period.

5. Give the sponsor of the site, followed by a comma.

6. Give the date when the Web site was last updated, followed by a period.

7. Give the medium of publication, followed by a period.

8. Give the date when you accessed or printed the map (followed by a period).

An Online Sound Recording or Sound Clip

Boose, Linda, Hugh Richmond, and Katherine Rowe. "Shakespeare

   in Performance: *Othello* and *The Taming of the Shrew.*"

   Sound recording. *What's the Word?* 1999. *Modern Language*

   Association. MLA, 5 June 2010. Web. 15 June 2010.

1. Give the name of the performer, the person or persons narrating the sound recording, or the participants in the recorded discussion. If more than one person is listed, only invert the name of the first.

2. Give the title of the sound recording or sound clip in double quotation marks with a period typed inside the final quotation marks. Note that in the citation above, the titles of Shakespeare's plays are italicized.

3. Type *Sound recording* or *Sound clip* (not in quotation marks or italics), followed by a period.

4. Give the title of the program of which the sound recording is a part or episode (italicized and followed by an italicized period).

5. Give the date when the program was recorded or broadcast (if known).

6. Give the title of the Web site through which you accessed the material (italicized and followed by an italicized period).

7. Give the organization or university sponsoring the site (not in quotation marks, not italicized, followed by a comma).

8. Give the date when the Web site was last updated, followed by a period.

9. Give the medium of publication, followed by a period.

10. Give the date when you accessed or listened to the recording or clip (followed by a period).

An Online Music Video

Dion, Celine. "Have You Ever Been in Love?" *A New Day Has Come.*

Sony, 2002. Music video. Web. 27 July 2010. <http://

entertainment.msn.com/album/Default.aspx?album=634307>.

1. Give the name of the performer, last name first, followed by a period.

2. Give the title of the song performed in the video in double quotation marks with a period typed inside the final quotation marks.

3. Give the title of the CD on which the song was recorded (italicized and followed by an italicized period).

4. Give the distributor of the CD, followed by a comma, one space, and the year the CD was released.

5. Type *Music video* (not in quotation marks, not italicized, followed by a period).

6. Give the medium of transmission (*Web*), followed by a period.

7. Give the date you accessed or watched the online music video (followed by a period).

8. Give the electronic address of the video in angle brackets, followed by a period.

An Online Video Clip

Dion, Celine. "Celine: Through the Eyes of the World." Sony

　　　Pictures, 2010. Video clip. *Music.msn.com.* Web. 27 July

　　　2010.

1. Give the name of the performer or narrator of the video clip, last name first, followed by a period.
2. Give the title of the video clip in double quotation marks with a period typed inside the final quotation marks.
3. Type the name of the distributor, a comma, and the year of release.
4. Type *Video clip,* not in quotation marks or italics, and a period.
5. Type the name of the Web site and a period (both italicized).
6. Give the medium of reception (*Web*), followed by a period.
7. Give the date when you accessed or watched the online video clip (followed by a period).

An Online Sound Clip from a Music CD

Dion, Celine. "I'm Alive." Sound clip. *A New Day Has Come.*

　　　Sony, 2002. *Music.msn.com.* Web. 27 July 2010.

1. Give the name of the performer, last name first, followed by a period.
2. Give the title of the song from which the clip was taken in double quotation marks with a period typed inside the final quotation marks.
3. Type *Sound clip* (not in quotation marks or italics), followed by a period.
4. Give the title of the CD on which the song was recorded (italicized and followed by an italicized period).
5. Give the name of the distributor of the CD, followed by a comma, one space, and the year the CD was released.
6. Give the name of the Web site and a period (both italicized).
7. Give the medium of reception (*Web*), followed by a period.
8. Give the date when you accessed or listened to the sound clip (followed by a period).

A Live Radio Program Accessed Online

Brinker, Bob. *Moneytalk with Bob Brinker.* KGO, San Francisco,

27 July 2010. *KGONewstalkAM810.* Web. 27 July 2010.

Edwards, Bob. *Morning Edition.* Natl. Public Radio. 27 July

2010. *National Public Radio.* Web. 27 July 2010.

1. Give the name of the host of the show (if there is one). If the show had a narrator (*narr.*) or performer (*perf.*) rather than a host, follow the name with the appropriate abbreviation (e.g., Sutherland, Donald, narr.).
2. Give the title of the individual episode (if there is one) in double quotation marks with a period typed inside the final quotation marks.
3. Give the title of the radio program (italicized and followed by a period).
4. Give the network and/or call letters and city of the local station on which the show was broadcast online. Give the postal abbreviation for the state if the city is not well known or could be confused with another city. If you give the city (and state), follow with a comma. If you only list the network, follow it with a period.
5. Give the day, month, and year when the program was broadcast online (followed by a period).
6. Give the Web site from which you accessed the radio program, italicized and followed by an italicized period.
7. Give the medium of reception (*Web*), followed by a period.
8. Give the day, month, and year that you listened to the broadcast online, followed by a period.

A Radio Program Accessed from an Online Archive

Edwards, Bob. "The Balfour Declaration and the British

Mandate." Pt. 2 of The Mideast: A Century of Conflict.

7 parts. Reported by Mike Schuster. *Morning Edition.*

Natl. Public Radio. 1 Oct. 2002. *National Public Radio.*

Web. 4 July 2010.

Edwards, Bob. "Lucinda Williams: *World without Tears:* Getting

the Last Word in Her Songs of Heartbreak." With Lucinda

Williams. *Morning Edition.* Natl. Public Radio. 3 July

2003. *National Public Radio.* Web. 27 July 2010.

1. Give the name of the host of the show (if there is one). If the show had a narrator (*narr.*) or performer (*perf.*) rather than a host, follow the name with the appropriate abbreviation (e.g., Smith, Robert T., narr.).

2. Give the title of the individual episode in double quotation marks (if available).

3. Type *With,* and give the names of any guests appearing on the show (names not inverted), followed by a period. Credit other persons involved with the show as appropriate.

4. Give the title of the radio program (italicized and followed by a period).

5. If the episode was a part of a series on a particular topic, type *Pt.,* the number of the episode, *of,* and the name of the series, followed by a period. Do not italicize or type quotation marks around the title of the series.

6. Give the network that broadcast the radio program (if available), not italicized and followed by a period.

7. Give the day, month, and year that the program was originally broadcast, followed by a period.

8. Give the name of the Web site from which the program was accessed (italicized and followed by an italicized period).

9. Give the medium of reception (*Web*), followed by a period.

10. Give the date that you accessed or listened to the archived broadcast of the program (followed by a period).

A Transcript of a Radio Program Accessed from an Online Archive

Edwards, Bob. "Lucinda Williams: *World without Tears:* Getting

    the Last Word in Her Songs of Heartbreak." With Lucinda

    Williams. *Morning Edition.* Natl. Public Radio. 3 July 2003.

    National Public Radio. Web. 27 July 2010. Transcript.

Edwards, Bob. "The 1967 Six Day War." Pt. 4 of The Mideast:

    A Century of Conflict. 7 parts. Reported by Mike Schuster.

    Morning Edition. Natl. Public Radio. 3 Oct. 2002.

    National Public Radio. Web. 4 July 2010. Transcript.

1. Give the name of the show host (if there is one). If there was a narrator (*narr.*) or performer (*perf.*) rather than a host, follow the name with the needed abbreviation (e.g., Rickman, Alan, narr.).

2. Give the title of the individual episode in double quotation marks (if available) with a period inside the end marks.

3. Type *With,* and give the names of any guests appearing on the show (names not inverted), followed by a period. Credit other persons involved with the show as appropriate.

4. If the episode was a part of a series, type *Pt.,* the number of the episode, *of,* and the name of the series, followed by a period. Do not italicize or type quotation marks around the title of the series.

5. Give the title of the program (italicized and followed by a period).

6. Give the name of the network that broadcast the radio program (if available), not italicized and followed by a period.

7. Give the day, month, and year that the program was broadcast, followed by a period.

8. Give the name of the Web site from which the transcript of the program was accessed (italicized and followed by a period).

9. Give the medium of publication (*Web*), followed by a period.

10. Give the day, month, and year that you accessed the Web site, followed by a period.

11. Type *Transcript* (neither italicized nor in quotation marks), followed by a period.

An Online Film Trailer

Charlie's Angels: Full Throttle. Dir. McG [Joseph McGinty

 Nichol]. Perf. Cameron Diaz, Drew Barrymore, Lucy Liu,

 Bernie Mac, and Demi Moore. Film trailer. Columbia,

 2003. *Movies.msn.com.* Web. 26 July 2010.

1. Give the title and subtitle of the film (italicized and followed by a period).

2. Type *Dir.* (*Directed by*), and give the name of the director, followed by a period.

3. Type *Perf.* (*Performed by*), and give the principal performers in the film (names not inverted), followed by a period.

4. Type *Film trailer* (not in quotation marks, not italicized), followed by a period.

5. Give the distributor of the film, followed by a comma, one space, and the year the film was released.

6. Give the title of the Web site (italicized), followed by a period.

7. Give the medium of reception (*Web*), followed by a period.

8. Give the date that you accessed or watched the trailer on the Web (followed by a period).

An Online Advertisement

Jane Austen's Elinor from *Sense and Sensibility* (Porcelain).

  Advertisement. N.d. *FranklinMint.com.* Web. 27 July 2010.

1. Give the name of the item being advertised (not in quotation marks, not italicized, followed by a period).
2. Type *Advertisement* (not in quotation marks or italics) and a period.
3. Give the date the advertisement was posted (or type *n.d.* if no date).
4. Give the title of the Web site (italicized), followed by a period.
5. Give the medium of publication, followed by a period.
6. Give the date when you viewed or printed out the advertisement (followed by a period).

Downloaded Computer Software

Adobe Reader. Vers. 9.0. *Adobe.com/reader.* Web. 19 May 2010.

1. Give the name of the software (italicized and followed by a period).
2. Give the version of the software (if available), followed by a period.
3. Give the Web site from which you downloaded the software (italicized), followed by a period.
4. Give the medium of publication, followed by a period.
5. Give the date that you downloaded the software (followed by a period).

Citing Materials from a CD-ROM or DVD-ROM

Material with an Author Given from a CD-ROM or DVD-ROM

Hillenbrand, William. "Weariness and Resolve: The Federal

  Offensives of 1862." Narr. David Inglehart. Music by

  Dennis Kennedy. *Fateful Lightning: A Narrative History*

  of the Civil War. Northfield, MA: Troubadour

  Interactive, 1995. CD-ROM.

1. Give the name of the author, editor (*ed.*), compiler (*comp.*), or translator (*trans.*) of the material on the CD-ROM or DVD-ROM. Use the appropriate abbreviation after the name if the person was not an author (e.g., Smith, David T., ed.). Invert the name of the first person listed.

2. If no author, editor, compiler, or translator is given, begin the entry with the title of the material in double quotation marks with a period typed inside the final quotation marks.

3. If other contributors are listed (narrator, compiler), type the appropriate abbreviation and give the contributor(s) name(s) after the title: Narr. David Inglehart.

4. Give the title of the CD-ROM or DVD-ROM (italicized and followed by an italicized period).

5. Give the city of publication and the postal abbreviation for the state if the city is not well known or could be confused with another city (followed by a colon and one space).

6. Give the publisher of the CD-ROM or DVD-ROM, followed by a comma and one space.

7. Give the year of publication or most recent copyright date, followed by a period.

8. Give the medium of publication (*CD-ROM* or *DVD-ROM*), followed by a period.

Material with No Author Given from a CD-ROM or DVD-ROM

"The Treasures of the Tomb Complex of Qin Shi Huang Di, the
First Emperor of China." *The First Emperor of China*. Project dir. Ching-chih Chen. New York: Voyager, 1994. CD-ROM.

A Scholarly Journal Article from a Textbook's Supplementary CD-ROM or DVD-ROM

Billingslea, Oliver. "Fathers and Sons: The Spiritual Quest
in Faulkner's 'Barn Burning.'" *Mississippi Quarterly* 44.3
(1991): n. pag. *The Craft of Literature*. CD-ROM for
Literature: An Introduction to Fiction, Poetry, and Drama.
Ed. X. J. Kennedy and Dana Gioia. 8th ed. Interactive ed.
New York: Longman, 2002. CD-ROM.

1. Give the author or authors of the scholarly journal article. Invert the name of the first author listed.

2. Type double quotation marks around the title of the journal article with a period typed inside the final quotation marks.

3. Type single quotation marks around the title of a short story, poem, or essay appearing within the title of the article.

4. Check the "Acknowledgments" section of the DVD-ROM or CD-ROM to learn where the journal article was originally published.

5. Give the title of the scholarly journal (italicized and not followed by a period).

6. Give the volume and issue number, separated by a period; the year of publication in parentheses, followed by a colon; and the first and last pages of the article as published in the journal (followed by a period). If no page numbers are given, type *n. pag.* after the year of publication.

7. Give the title of the CD-ROM or DVD-ROM (italicized and followed by an italicized period).

8. Type *CD-ROM* or *DVD-ROM for,* and give the title of the textbook for which the CD-ROM or DVD-ROM is a supplement (italicized and followed by an italicized period).

9. Type the abbreviation *Ed.* (*Edited by*), and give the name(s) of the editor(s) of the anthology (followed by a period). If two editors are listed, do not type a comma after the first editor's name (Ed. X. J. Kennedy and Dana Gioia.).

10. If the anthology is not a first edition, specify the edition number using the suggested MLA abbreviation (*2nd ed., Rev. ed.*) as listed in chapter 22. If this is a specialized edition of a text, such as an interactive edition (one that comes with a CD-ROM or DVD-ROM and Web links), specify the type of edition.

11. Give the city of publication, the publisher, and the date of publication or most recent copyright date of the CD-ROM or DVD-ROM, followed by a period.

12. Give the medium of publication (*CD-ROM* or *DVD-ROM*), followed by a period.

A Biographical Sketch of an Author from a Textbook's Supplementary CD-ROM or DVD-ROM

"William Shakespeare (1564-1616)." *The Craft of Literature.*

    CD-ROM for *Literature: An Introduction to Fiction, Poetry,*

and Drama. Ed. X. J. Kennedy and Dana Gioia. 8th ed.
Interactive ed. New York: Longman, 2002. CD-ROM.

A Critical Overview of an Author from a Textbook's Supplementary CD-ROM or DVD-ROM

"Flannery O'Connor: Critical Overview." *The Craft of Litera-*
ture. CD-ROM for *Literature: An Introduction to Fiction,*
Poetry, and Drama. Ed. X. J. Kennedy and Dana Gioia.
8th ed. Interactive ed. New York: Longman, 2002. CD-ROM.

A Video Clip from a Textbook's Supplementary CD-ROM or DVD-ROM

Shakespeare Workshop: The Tortured Mind. Princeton: Films for
the Humanities and Sciences, n.d. Video clip no. 2748.
Lit21: Literature in the 21st Century. CD-ROM for
Literature: Reading, Reacting, Writing. Ed. Laurie
G. Kirszner and Stephen R. Mandell. 5th ed. Interactive
ed. Boston: Wadsworth-Thomson, 2004. CD-ROM.

An Audio Clip from a Textbook's Supplementary CD-ROM or DVD-ROM

Piercy, Marge. "The Friend." Read by Marge Piercy. *Circles on the*
Water: Selected Poems of Marge Piercy. [New York]: Knopf,
1982. Audio clip. *Lit21: Literature in the 21st Century*.
CD-ROM for *Literature: Reading, Reacting, Writing*. Ed.
Laurie G. Kirszner and Stephen R. Mandell. 5th ed.
Interactive ed. Boston: Wadsworth-Thomson. 2004. CD-ROM.

CHAPTER 13

Citing Materials from Reference Databases and Books

Citing Personal Subscription Databases

Info Trac College Edition is a personal subscription database that your instructor can order for use with this and other texts published by Wadsworth-Cengage. *InfoTrac College Edition* gives you access to millions of full-text articles from scholarly journals, magazines, and the *New York Times*. Cite an article accessed through this or any other personal subscription database as you would an article accessed through a Web site, but substitute the name of the database (italicized) for the name of the Web site.

Annotated Citation for a Scholarly Journal Article from a Personal Subscription Database

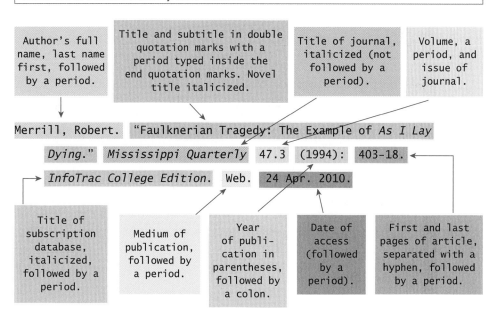

189

A Scholarly Journal Article
from a Personal Subscription Database

Muldoon, Paul. "The End of the Poem: 'The Mountain' by

Robert Frost." *American Poetry Review* 30.1 (2001): 41-46.

InfoTrac College Edition. Web. 24 Aug. 2010.

Edenfield, Olivia Carr. "'Endure and Then Endure': Rosa

Coldfield's Search for a Role in William Faulkner's

Absalom! Absalom!" *Southern Literary Journal* 32.1

(1999): 57-68. *InfoTrac College Edition.* Web.

10 July 2010.

1. Give the author's full name (inverted for alphabetizing). If there are two or more authors, invert only the name of the first author.

2. Give the title of the article in double quotation marks with a period typed inside the final quotation marks.

3. Give the title of the journal (italicized, not followed by a period). Omit the article *The* if it begins the title of a journal but not if it begins the title of an article in a journal.

4. Give the volume number, a period, the issue number, one space, and the year of publication in parentheses. Then follow with a colon, one space, and the first and last page numbers of the article, separated by a hyphen: 45.4 (2003): 245-52.

5. If the database gives only the first page number of a journal article that is clearly longer than a single page, type the first page number, a hyphen, one space, and a period: 52.4 (2003): 342- .

6. If the database gives the first page number and the total number of pages in the article, as in 45(17), which means that the article begins on page 45 and is seventeen pages long, figure out what the last page number of the article would be and cite it: 66.7 (2003): 45-61.

7. If the database gives you the option of printing the article as a PDF file, you can print the pages of the article exactly as they appear in the

print journal. Because the page numbers that appeared when the article was originally published will appear on the PDF printout, use those page numbers in your parenthetical citations.

8. Use the abbreviation *n. pag.* if no page references are given by the database: 32.4 (2003): n. pag.

9. Give the name of the database (*InfoTrac College Edition*), italicized and followed by a period and one space.

10. Give the medium of publication (*Web*), followed by a period.

11. Give the date when you accessed or printed the material (followed by a period).

Citing Online Library Subscription Databases

Your university library pays a fee to allow students and faculty access to a number of online subscription reference databases. Check your library's Web site for access to and information about these databases. For example, *InfoTrac OneFile, Expanded Academic ASAP, Health Reference Center Academic,* and *General BusinessFile ASAP* are InfoTrac databases offered to libraries for a subscription fee by Gale Group, a division of Cengage Learning. *Academic Search Elite, MasterFile Premier, ContentSelect,* and *MagillOnLiterature* are just a few of the EBSCOhost databases offered to libraries for a subscription fee by EBSCOhost Information Services. *LexisNexis Academic Universe,* offered to libraries by LexisNexis, indexes materials in the following areas: *Reference* (a world almanac, biographies of well-known people, famous quotations, polls, surveys, and profiles of states and countries); *News* (articles from newspapers, scholarly journals, and popular magazines); *Business* (company news and financial information); *Medical* (information about health issues and medical research); *Legal Research* (state, federal, and international law; case law; information relating to patents; and legal career information).

Annotated Citation for a Scholarly Journal Article from *InfoTrac OneFile*

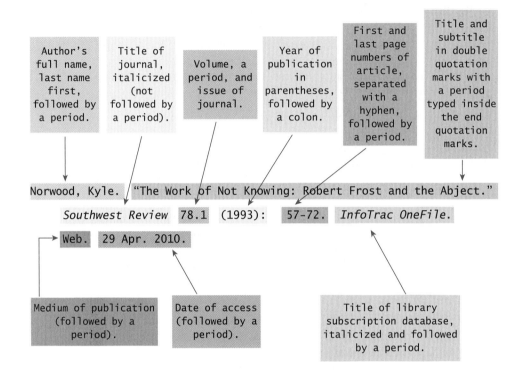

A Scholarly Journal Article from *InfoTrac OneFile*

Fennell, Lee Anne. "Unquiet Ghosts: Memory and Determinism
      in Faulkner." *Southern Literary Journal* 31.2 (1999):
      35- . *InfoTrac OneFile.* Web. 9 May 2010.

Anderson, Craig A., and Brad J. Bushman. "The Effects of
      Media Violence on Society." *Science* 295.5564 (2002):
      2377-78. *InfoTrac OneFile.* Web. 12 July 2010.

1. Give the author's full name (inverted for alphabetizing). If there are two
   or more authors, invert only the name of the first author listed.
2. Give the title of the article in double quotation marks with a period
   typed inside the final quotation marks.

3. Give the title of the journal (italicized, not followed by a period). Omit the article *The* if it begins the title of a journal but not if it begins the title of an article in a journal.

4. For a scholarly journal article, give the volume number, a period, the issue number, one space, and the year of publication in parentheses. Then follow with a colon, one space, and the first and last page numbers of the article, separated by a hyphen: 45.4 (2010): 245-52.

5. If the database gives only the first page number of a journal article that is clearly longer than a single page, give the first page number, a hyphen, one space, and a period: 52.4 (2010): 342- .

6. If the database gives the first page number and the total number of pages in the article, as in 45(17), which means that the article begins on page 45 and is seventeen pages long, figure out what the last page number of the article would be and cite it: 66.7 (2010): 45-61.

7. If the database gives you the option of printing the article as a PDF file, you can print the pages of the article exactly as they appear in the journal. Because the page numbers that appeared when the article was originally published will appear on the PDF printout, use those page numbers in your parenthetical citations.

8. Use the abbreviation *n. pag.* if no page references are given by the database: 32.4 (2010): n. pag.

9. Give the name of the database (*InfoTrac OneFile*), italicized and followed by a period and one space.

10. Give the medium of publication (*Web*), followed by a period.

11. Give the date when you accessed or printed the material (followed by a period).

12. MLA style no longer requires the listing of the name of the subscription service that provides access to the database, the name and location of the library providing the access, or the URL of the database.

A Monthly Magazine Article from *InfoTrac OneFile*

Stanten, Michelle. "Weight Loss in a Bottle: The Feds Take Aim at Bogus Claims." *Prevention* May 2003: 83-84. *InfoTrac OneFile.* Web. 5 July 2010.

1. Give the author's full name (inverted for alphabetizing). If there are two or more authors, invert only the name of the first author listed.

2. Give the title of the article in double quotation marks with a period typed inside the final quotation marks.

3. Give the title of the magazine (italicized, not followed by a period).

4. Give the month (abbreviated except for May, June, and July) and year of publication, type a colon and one space, and give the first and last page numbers of the article, separated by a hyphen. Do not give the volume and issue numbers for a monthly or bimonthly magazine even if they are available. (*continued on page 195*)

How to Tell the Difference between a Scholarly Journal and a Popular Magazine

Scholarly journal articles tend to be relatively long, whereas popular magazine articles are rarely more than a few pages in length. If you are looking at a copy of the publication, scholarly journals tend to be rather plain looking with a great deal of text and few if any pictures or illustrations. They are written by experts with the expectation that the articles will be read by students or other scholars doing research or keeping up with the latest advancements in their fields of expertise. Scholarly journal articles often end with a list of works cited or consulted; a popular magazine article does not usually include a bibliography. Popular magazines often have as many pictures and advertisements as pages of text and are written for general readers, not experts or scholars. Although some scholarly journals are published weekly or monthly, the majority are published four times per year (quarterly). Popular magazines tend to be published much more frequently than scholarly journals (weekly, biweekly, monthly, or bimonthly).

If you can find a copy of the periodical in your library, the front matter of any issue will tell you how frequently the journal or magazine is published, but bear in mind that some scholarly journals are published weekly, so frequency of publication does not always tell you whether you are citing a journal or a popular magazine.

For more information on a publication, search your library's online catalog by using the title of the journal or magazine.

You can also check for information about a journal or magazine in a directory such as *Magazines for Libraries* (Z6941/.M23), *Standard Periodical Directory* (Z6951/.S78), or *Ulrich's International Periodicals Directory* (Z6941/.U5).

If you are still not certain what type of publication you are citing, ask a librarian or your professor to help you.

5. If the database gives only the first page number of a magazine article that is clearly longer than a single page, give the first page number, a hyphen, one space, and a period: Apr. 2010: 42- .

6. If the database gives the first page number and the total number of pages in the article, as in 42(3), which means that the article begins on page 42 and is three pages long, figure out what the last page number of the article would be and cite it: Apr. 2010: 42-44.

7. If the database gives you the option of printing the article as a PDF file, you can print the pages of the article exactly as they appear in the magazine. Because the page numbers that appeared when the article was originally published will appear on the printout, use those page numbers in your parenthetical citations.

8. Use the abbreviation *n. pag.* if no page references are given by the database: Apr. 2010: n. pag.

9. Give the name of the database (*InfoTrac OneFile*), italicized and followed by a period and one space.

10. Give the medium of publication, followed by a period.

11. Give the date you accessed or printed the material (followed by a period).

12. MLA style no longer requires the listing of the name of the subscription service that provides access to the database, the name and location of the library providing the access, or the URL of the database.

A Monthly Magazine Article with No Author Given from *InfoTrac OneFile*

"New Risk Factor: Snoring: Sawing Logs Raises Blood Sugar."

 Prevention Aug. 2002: 146. *InfoTrac OneFile*. Web.

 5 July 2010.

1. If no author is given, begin your entry with the title of the article in double quotation marks with a period typed inside the final quotation marks. Note that the above article has two subtitles and that both are given.

2. Give the title of the magazine (italicized, not followed by a period).

3. Give the month (abbreviated except for May, June, and July) and year of publication, type a colon and one space, and give the first and last page numbers of the article, separated by a hyphen. Do not give the volume and issue numbers for a monthly or bimonthly magazine even if they are available.

4. If the database gives only the first page number of a magazine article that is clearly longer than a single page, give the first page number followed by a hyphen, one space, and a period: Apr. 2010: 42- .

5. If the database gives the first page number and the total number of pages in the article, as in 42(3), which means that the article begins on page 42 and is three pages long, figure out what the last page number of the article would be and cite it: Apr. 2010: 42-44.

6. If the database gives you the option of printing the article as a PDF file, you can print the pages of the article exactly as they appear in the magazine. Because the page numbers that appeared when the article was originally published will appear on the PDF printout, use those page numbers in your parenthetical citations.

7. Use the abbreviation *n. pag.* if no page references are given by the database: Apr. 2010: n. pag.

8. Give the name of the database (*InfoTrac OneFile*), italicized and followed by a period and one space.

9. Give the medium of publication, followed by a period.

10. Give the date when you accessed or printed the material (followed by a period).

11. MLA style no longer requires the listing of the name of the subscription service that provides access to the database, the name and location of the library providing the access, or the URL of the database.

A Weekly Magazine Article from *InfoTrac OneFile*

Spake, Amanda. "The Science of Slimming." *U.S. News and World Report* 16 June 2003: 34-38. *InfoTrac OneFile*. Web. 2 May 2010.

Sancton, Thomas, and Scott Macleod. "The Final Hours: The Deaths of Princess Diana and Dodi Fayed." *Time* 16 Feb. 1998: 74-79. *InfoTrac OneFile*. Web. 2 May 2010.

1. Give the author's full name (inverted for alphabetizing). If there are two or more authors, invert only the name of the first author.

2. Give the title of the article in double quotation marks with a period typed inside the final quotation marks.

3. Give the title of the magazine (italicized, not followed by a period).

4. Give the day, month, and year of publication; type a colon and one space; and give the first and last page numbers of the article.

5. If the database gives only the first page number of a magazine article clearly longer than one page, give the first page number followed by a hyphen, one space, and a period: 15 Apr. 2010: 44- .

6. If the database gives the first page number of the article and the total number of pages in the article, as in 67(3), which means that the article begins on page 67 and is three pages long, figure out what the last page number of the article would be and cite it: 12 Jan. 2010: 67-69.

7. If the database gives you the option of printing the article as a PDF file, you can print the pages of the article exactly as they appear in the magazine. Because the page numbers that appeared when the article was originally published will appear on the PDF printout, use those page numbers in your parenthetical citations.

8. Use the abbreviation *n. pag.* if no page references are given by the database: 12 Jan. 2010: n. pag.

9. Give the name of the database (*InfoTrac OneFile*), italicized and followed by a period and one space.

10. Give the medium of publication, followed by a period.

11. Give the date when you accessed or printed the material (followed by a period).

12. MLA style no longer requires the listing of the name of the subscription service that provides access to the database, the name and location of the library providing the access, or the URL of the database.

A Scholarly Journal Article from *Expanded Academic ASAP*

Hall, Christine C. Iijima, and Matthew J. Crum. "Women and

'Bodyisms' in Television Beer Commercials."

Sex Roles: A Journal of Research 31.5-6 (1994):

329-37. *Expanded Academic ASAP.* Web. 11 Apr. 2010.

1. Give the author's full name (inverted for alphabetizing). If there are two or more authors, invert only the name of the first author listed.

2. Give the title of the article in double quotation marks with a period typed inside the final quotation marks.

3. Give the title of the journal (italicized, not followed by a period). Omit the article *The* if it begins the title of a journal but not if it begins the title of an article in a journal.

4. For a scholarly journal article, give the volume number, a period, the issue number, one space, and the year of publication in parentheses. Then follow with a colon, one space, and the first and last page numbers of the article, separated by a hyphen: 45.4 (2003): 245-52. For a double issue, give the numbers for both issues, separated by a hyphen.

5. If the database gives only the first page number of a journal article that is clearly longer than a single page, give the first page number followed by a hyphen, one space, and a period: 52.4 (2003): 342- .

6. If the database gives the first page number and the total number of pages in the article, as in 45(17), which means that the article begins on page 45 and is seventeen pages long, figure out what the last page number of the article would be and cite it: 66.7 (2003): 45-61.

7. If the database gives you the option of printing the article as a PDF file, you can print the pages of the article exactly as they appear in the journal. Because the page numbers that appeared when the article was originally published will appear on the PDF printout, use those page numbers in your parenthetical citations.

8. Use the abbreviation *n. pag.* if no page references are given by the database: 66.7 (2003): n. pag.

9. Give the name of the database (*Expanded Academic ASAP*), italicized and followed by a period and one space.

10. Give the medium of publication, followed by a period.

11. Give the date when you accessed or printed the material (followed by a period).

12. MLA style no requires the listing of the name of the subscription service that provides access to the database, the name and location of the library providing the access, or the URL of the database.

A Scholarly Journal Article
from *Health Reference Center Academic*

Rooks, Daniel S., and Jeffrey N. Katz. "Managing Fibromyalgia: The Role of Exercise: Graduated Exercise Can Improve Functioning and Increase Well-Being." *Journal of Musculoskeletal Medicine* 19.11 (2002): 439-45. *Health Reference Center Academic.* Web. 12 July 2010.

A Monthly Magazine Article
from *Health Reference Center Academic*

Foston, Nikitta A. "How to Deal with Chronic Pain." *Ebony* July

2003: 52-55. *Health Reference Center Academic*. Web. 12

July 2010.

A Definition from a Dictionary
from *Health Reference Center Academic*

"Body Image." *Mosby's Medical, Nursing, and Allied Health

Dictionary*. 1998 ed. *Health Reference Center Academic*.

Web. 17 Apr. 2010.

An Article from an Encyclopedia
from *Health and Wellness Resource Center*

"Allergic Rhinitis." *Gale Encyclopedia of Medicine*. Ed.

Jacqueline L. Longe. 2nd ed. Farmington Hills, MI: Gale,

2001. *Health and Wellness Resource Center*. Web. 7 July 2010.

A Scholarly Journal Article
from *Health and Wellness Resource Center*

Furnham, Adrian, Nicola Badmin, and Ian Sneade. "Body Image

Dissatisfaction: Gender Differences in Eating Attitudes,

Self-Esteem, and Reasons for Exercise." *Journal of Psy-

chology* 136.6 (2002): 581-96. *Health and Wellness Resource

Center*. Web. 7 July 2010.

An Overview of an Author from *Dictionary of Literary*
Biography Taken from *Literature Resource Center*

Skei, Hans H. "William Faulkner." *American Short-Story Writers,

1910-1945*. Ed. Bobby Ellen Kimbel. Vol. 102 of *Dictionary of

Literary Biography*. [Detroit]: Bruccoli-Gale, 1991. 75-102.

2nd ser. *Literature Resource Center*. Web. 12 July 2010.

A Scholarly Journal Article from *Literature Resource Center*

Davis, William V. "Another Flower for Faulkner's Bouquet: Theme
    and Structure in 'A Rose for Emily.'" *Notes on Mississippi
    Writers* 7.2 (1974): 34-38. *Literature Resource Center.*
    Web. 12 July 2010.

Note that the title of William Faulkner's short story "A Rose for Emily" is formatted in single quotation marks in the title of the journal article. Type the period inside both the single and the double quotation marks at the end of the title of the article.

An Overview of a Novel from a Reference Book Taken from *Literature Resource Center*

Wagner, Linda W. "*The Sound and the Fury:* Overview." By William
    Faulkner. *Reference Guide to American Literature.* Ed. Jim
    Kamp. 3rd ed. [Detroit]: St. James, 1994. N. pag. *Litera-
    ture Resource Center.* Web. 12 July 2010.

Note that the title of William Faulkner's novel *The Sound and the Fury* is italicized in the title of the journal article.

A Scholarly Journal Article from *Contemporary Literary Criticism – Select*

Castille, Philip Dubuisson. "Dilsey's Easter Conversion
    in Faulkner's *The Sound and the Fury.*" *Studies in
    the Novel* 24.4 (1992): 423-33. *Contemporary Literary
    Criticism-Select.* Web. 12 July 2010.

Note that the title of William Faulkner's novel *The Sound and the Fury* is italicized in the title of the journal article.

An Excerpt from an Essay in an Essay Collection Taken from *Contemporary Literary Criticism – Select*

Perluck, Herbert A. "'The Bear': An Unromantic Reading." *Religious Perspectives in Faulkner's Fiction: Yoknapatawpha and Beyond.* Ed. J. Robert Barth. [South Bend, IN]: U of Notre Dame P, 1972. 173-201. *Contemporary Literary Criticism–Select.* Web. 12 July 2010.

1. Note that the title of William Faulkner's short story "The Bear" is formatted in single quotation marks in the title of the journal article.
2. Note that the colon between the title and subtitle of the journal article is typed outside, not inside, the end single quotation mark.

An Untitled Interview from an Essay Collection from *DISCovering Authors*

Greene, Graham. Interview by Martin Shuttleworth and Simon Raven. *Graham Greene: A Collection of Critical Essays.* Ed. Samuel Hynes. [Englewood Cliffs, NJ]: Prentice, 1973. 154-67. *Discovering Collection: DISCovering Authors.* Web. 15 June 2010.

1. Give the name of the person being interviewed, last name first.
2. If the interview has a title, give it after the name of the person being interviewed in double quotation marks with a period typed inside the final quotation marks. After the title, type *Interview by* and give the name or names of the persons who conducted the interview.
3. If the interview is untitled, type *Interview by* and give the name or names of the persons who conducted the interview.
4. Give the title and subtitle of the essay collection, italicized and followed by a period.
5. Type *Ed.* (*Edited by*), and give the name of the editor or editors of the collection, followed by a period.
6. Give the city, publisher, and date of publication for the collection, followed by a period. In the above entry, the city of publication is given in square brackets because it was taken from a source other than the

database cited. The state of publication is given because student readers might not know the state in which Englewood Cliffs is located.

7. Give the first and last page numbers of the interview as published in the essay collection.

8. Use the abbreviation *n. pag.* if no page references are given: City: publisher, year. N. pag.

9. Give the title and subtitle of the reference database (*Discovering Collection: DISCovering Authors*), italicized and followed by a period and one space.

10. Give the medium of publication, followed by a period.

11. Give the date when you accessed or printed the material (followed by a period).

12. MLA style no longer requires the listing of the name of the subscription service that provides access to the database, the name and location of the library providing the access, or the URL of the database.

An Article from a Popular Weekly or Biweekly Magazine from *DISCovering Authors*

Waugh, Evelyn. "Felix Culpa?" *Commonweal* 16 July 1948: 322-25.

  Discovering Collection: DISCovering Authors. Web. 15 June

  2010.

The *Commonweal* is a popular biweekly magazine. Omit the article *The* when it begins the title of a journal, popular magazine, or newspaper, but do not omit *The* from the titles of the articles published in periodicals.

An Article from *Dictionary of Literary Biography* Taken from *DISCovering Authors*

Macdonald, Andrew, and Gina Macdonald. "Graham Greene."

  British Mystery Writers, 1920-1939. Ed. Bernard

  Benstock and Thomas F. Staley. Vol. 77 of *Dictionary*

  of Literary Biography. Detroit: Gale, 1988. 134-52.

  Discovering Collection: DISCovering Authors. Web.

  15 June 2010.

Cite the article just as you would cite an article from the print version of one of the volumes in *Dictionary of Literary Biography*. See the model citation on page 217. Then give the publication information for the database you used to access the article.

A Plot Summary of a Novel from a Book Taken from *DISCovering Authors*

[Harris, Laurie Lanzen.] *"The End of the Affair,* by Graham (Henry) Greene: Plot Summary." *Characters in Twentieth-Century Literature.* [Detroit]: Gale, 1990. N. pag. *DisScovering Collection: DISCovering Authors.* Web. 15 June 2010.

A Scholarly Journal Article from *Biography Resource Center*

Rose, Phyllis. " 'Getting and Spending': Nostalgia for the Old Way of Reading Poetry." *American Scholar* 70.4 (2001): 79-86. *Biography Resource Center.* Web. 10 July 2010.

A Weekly Popular Magazine Article from *Biography Resource Center*

Gates, David. "Back to the Ted and Sylvia Show: How Can We Miss Them When They Won't Go Away?" *Newsweek* 17 Apr. 2000: 68. *Biography Resource Center.* Web. 10 July 2010.

A Biographical Sketch with No Author Given from an Edited Collection from *Biography Resource Center*

"Sylvia Plath." *Feminist Writers.* [Ed. Pamela Kester-Shelton.] [Detroit]: St. James, 1996. N. pag. *Biography Resource Center.* Web. 10 July 2010.

In the above entry, the editor and city of publication for *Feminist Writers* were not given by *Biography Resource Center*. That information was taken from the Library of Congress online catalog entry for the book, found at <http://catalog.loc.gov>. Type square brackets around any information taken from a source other than the database you are citing. The abbreviation *N. pag.* informs the reader of the citation that the pages of the biographical sketch about Sylvia Plath were not supplied by the database.

A Biographical Sketch with No Author Given from a Reference Book from *Biography Resource Center*

"William Wordsworth." *Writers of the Romantic Period,*

1789-1832. Vol. 3 of *Concise Dictionary of British*

Literary Biography. [Detroit]: Gale, 1992. N. pag.

Biography Resource Center. Web. 10 July 2010.

A Scholarly Journal Article from *Academic Search Elite*

Smith, Greg. "Whitman, Springsteen, and the American Working

Class." *Midwest Quarterly* 41.3 (2000): 302-20. *Academic*

Search Elite. Web. 13 Apr. 2010.

A Film (Movie) Review from a Weekly Magazine from *Academic Search Elite*

McGuigan, Cathleen. "A Fiennes Romance This Is." Rev. of *The*

End of the Affair. Dir. Neil Jordan. Perf. Ralph Fiennes,

Julianne Moore, and Stephen Rea. Based on *The End of the*

Affair, by Graham Greene. *Newsweek* 12 June 1999: 82. *Acad-*

emic Search Elite. Web. 13 Apr. 2010.

An Article from a Scholarly Journal from *ContentSelect: General Interest*

Beer, Siegfried. "*The Third Man.*" *History Today* 51.5 (2001):

45-51. *ContentSelect: General Interest.* Web. 13 Apr. 2010.

1. Note that the title of the film *The Third Man* is both italicized and in double quotation marks because the title refers to an analysis of the film, not to a copy of the film itself.
2. This article is an analysis of the historical and biographical elements to be found in this classic film. It is a critical analysis rather than a review of the film. Use the review format to cite a review of a film.

A Scholarly Journal Article from *MasterFILE Premier*

Johnson, David. "You've Never Seen Anything Like It." *Theatre Crafts International (TCI): The Business of Entertainment Technology and Design* 32.10 (1998): 56-66. *MasterFILE Premier*. Web. 20 Apr. 2010.

A Plot Summary of a Play from *Masterplots II* Taken from *MagillOnLiterature*

Lutz, Reinhart. *"The Crucible."* By Arthur Miller. *Masterplots II: Drama.* N.p.: Salem, 1990. N. pag. *MagillOnLiterature*. Web. 5 July 2010.

Note that the title of Miller's play *The Crucible* is both italicized and in double quotation marks because the citation refers to an analysis of the play, not to the text of the play.

A Scholarly Journal Article from *Psychology and Behavioral Sciences Collection*

Harris, H. R. "Jane Austen's Venture into Tragedy." *Contemporary Review* 272.1589 (1998): 314-18. *Psychology and Behavioral Sciences Collection*. Web. 5 July 2010.

An Article with No Author Given from *FACTS.com*

"Facts on George W. Bush." *FACTS.com*. Web. 12 July 2010.

"Key Event: George W. Bush Signs $1.35 Trillion Tax Cut." *FACTS.com*. Web. 12 July 2010.

An Article with No Author Given from *Facts on File World News Digest* from *Facts.Com*

"Agriculture: U.S. Toughens Rules on Biotech Food." *Facts on File World News Digest* 11 May 2000: n. pag. *FACTS.com.* Web. 12 July 2010.

A Scholarly Journal Article from *JSTOR*

Carden, Mary Paniccia. "Models of Memory and Romance: The Dual Endings of Toni Morrison's *Beloved.*" *Twentieth Century Literature* 45.4 (1999): 401-27. *JSTOR.* Web. 17 June 2010.

Note that the title of Toni Morrison's novel *Beloved* is italicized in the title of the journal article.

A Newspaper Article from *LexisNexis Academic Universe: News*

Ruark, Jennifer K. "A Second Chance for Mark Twain." *Chronicle of Higher Education* 16 May 2003: 17+. *LexisNexis Academic Universe: News.* Web. 9 July 2010.

Hiaasen, Rob. "Pity the Poor Scribe When Words Fail, the Paper's Blank, the Pen Has Teeth Marks: It's Writer's Block, and There's No Sure-Fire Cure." *Los Angeles Times* 30 Dec. 2002, home ed.: 12. *LexisNexis Academic Universe: News.* Web. 5 July 2010.

1. You need not give the city of publication for national newspapers such as the *Chronicle of Higher Education*, *USA Today*, and the *Wall Street Journal*.
2. Omit the article *The* if it begins the title of a newspaper but not if it begins the title of an article in a newspaper.
3. If the database gives only the first page number of an article that is clearly longer than a single page, type a plus sign after the page number to show that the article began on one page and jumped to another page in the newspaper.

4. The database gives no section number for the article by Rob Hiaasen. You may look for the missing information in other sources and give it in square brackets or just cite the information given.

A Newspaper Article from *NewsBank NewsFile Collection*

Sawyer, Kathy. "The Shuttle's 'Smoking Gun': Test Affirms Theory That Foam Damaged Wing, Panel Says." *Washington Post* 8 July 2003, final ed.: A1. *NewsBank NewsFile Collection.* Web. 12 July 2010.

A Newspaper Article from *Business NewsBank*

Kirby, Carrie. "Microsoft to Halt Stock Options: Tech Giant to Give Shares as Expense." *San Francisco Chronicle* 9 July 2003, final ed.: B1. *Business NewsBank.* Web. 12 July 2010.

A Scholarly Journal Article from *Project Muse*

Webb, Jeff. "Literature and Lynching: Identity in Jean Toomer's *Cane.*" *English Literary History* 67.1 (2000): 204-28. *Project Muse.* Web. 30 Apr. 2010.

1. Note that the title of Jean Toomer's novel *Cane* is italicized in the title of the journal article.
2. If you are certain that your readers will recognize the acronym, you may use *ELH* instead of *English Literary History* as the journal title.

A Scholarly Journal Article from *Periodical Abstracts Research II*

Sol, Adam. "Questions of Mastery in Alice Walker's *The Temple of My Familiar.*" *Critique* 43.4 (2002): 393-404. *Periodical Abstracts Research II.* Web. 29 Apr. 2010.

Note that the title of Alice Walker's novel *The Temple of My Familiar* is italicized in the title of the journal article.

A Scholarly Journal Article with One Author from *ProQuest Nursing Journals*

Funnell, Martha M. "Preventing Type 2 Diabetes with Weight Loss

and Exercise." *Nursing* June 2003: 10. *ProQuest Nursing*

Journals. Web. 5 July 2010.

The database gives no volume or issue number for the scholarly journal cited above, so cite the month of publication in place of the volume and issue numbers, as you would cite a monthly popular magazine. The article cited above is a one-page article.

A Scholarly Journal Article with Two Authors from *ProQuest Nursing Journals*

Insel, Thomas R., and Dennis S. Charney. "Research on Major

Depression: Strategies and Priorities." *JAMA* 289.23

(2003): 3167-69. *ProQuest Nursing Journals*. Web. 8 July

2010.

In the above entry, *JAMA* refers to *Journal of the American Medical Association*. You may write out the title of the journal if you believe your reader may not recognize the acronym.

A Scholarly Journal Article with Four or More Authors from *ProQuest Nursing Journals*

Wannamethee, S. Goya, Carlos A. Camargo, Jr., JoAnn E. Manson,

Walter C. Willett, and Eric B. Rimm. "Alcohol Drinking

Patterns and Risk of Type 2 Diabetes Mellitus among

Younger Women." *Archives of Internal Medicine* 163.11

(2003): 1329-36. *ProQuest Nursing Journals*. Web. 5 July

2010.

When there are four or more authors, you may list them all in the order given on the title page or list only the first author given and type *et al.* (which means *and others*) after the author's name: Wannamethee, S. Goya, et al.

A Scholarly Journal Article
with One Author from *ScienceDirect*

Mims, Steven D. "Aquaculture of Paddlefish in the United

States." *Aquatic Living Resources* 14.6 (2001): 391-98.

ScienceDirect. Web. 11 July 2010.

A Scholarly Journal Article with Four
or More Authors from *ScienceDirect*

Gobel, Dale D., Susan M. George, Kathryn Mazaika, J. Michael

Scott, and Jason Karl. "Local and National Protection of En-

dangered Species: An Assessment." *Environmental Science and*

Policy 2.1 (1999): 43-59. *ScienceDirect.* Web. 11 July 2010.

When there are four or more authors, you may list them all in the order given on the title page or list only the first author given and type *et al.* (which means *and others*) after the author's name: Gobel, Dale D., et al.

An Article with No Author Given
from an Encyclopedia from *SIRS Discoverer*

"Greene, (Henry) Graham." *Funk and Wagnalls New Encyclopedia.*

2002 ed. *SIRS Discoverer.* Web. 9 July 2010.

If you are not certain that your reader will recognize the commonly abbreviated database name *SIRS*, you may give the name in full: *Social Issues Resources Series.*

A Weekly Magazine Article from *SIRS Knowledge Source*

Watson, Traci. "What Really Plumps You Up?" *U.S. News and World*

Report 12 Dec. 1994: 80-81. *SIRS Knowledge Source.* Web. 9

June 2010.

If you are not certain that your reader will recognize the commonly abbreviated database name *SIRS*, you may give the name in full: *Social Issues Resources Series.*

Citing Abstracts of Articles

Some reference databases give only bibliographic citations and abstracts (brief summaries) of articles published in books, scholarly journals, popular magazines, and newspapers. Use databases such as these to help you find full-text versions of the articles in other sources. **Quote from full-text articles, not from abstracts.**

An Abstract of a Scholarly Journal Article from *America: History and Life*

Benjaminson, Eric. "A Regiment of Immigrants: The 82nd Illinois
    Volunteer Infantry and the Letters of Captain Rudolph
    Mueller." *Journal of the Illinois State Historical Society*
    94.2 (2001): 137-80. Abstract. *America: History and Life.*
    Web. 10 May 2010.

America: History and Life gives bibliographic citations and abstracts (brief summaries) of articles published in scholarly journals and books on topics relating to American and Canadian history from prehistory to modern times.

An Abstract of a Scholarly Journal Article from *PsychINFO*

Oren, Dan A., Joseph F. Cubellis, and Simone Litsch. "Bright
    Light Therapy for Schizoaffective Disorder." *Journal of
    Psychiatry* 158.12 (2001): 2086-87. Abstract. *PsychINFO.*
    Web. 10 May 2010.

PsychINFO gives bibliographic citations and abstracts (brief summaries) of scholarly journal articles, technical reports, dissertations, book chapters, and books on topics relating to psychology.

The databases cited above and others like them do not provide full-text versions of the materials they index. When you have identified an article or book you want to read, type the title of the scholarly journal or book into the title search field of your library's online catalog to see whether your library subscribes to the print version of the journal in which the article appears or whether it owns the book you are interested in. You can also use the citation information from databases such as these to search for a journal article in other reference databases that offer full-text printouts of articles. A third option is to request a copy of an article or book that you need from another library through an interlibrary loan. Check your library's Web site, or ask a librarian for information about how your library handles interlibrary loans.

Citing Free Online Reference Databases

When you are citing materials taken from a free online database such as *AGRICOLA* (*Agricultural Online Access*), *ERIC* (*Educational Resources Information Center*), or *THOMAS: Legislative Information on the Internet* (named for Thomas Jefferson), follow the guidelines for citing an article from an online library subscription database, as described in the model citations discussed earlier in this chapter. MLA style no longer requires the listing of the name of the subscription service that provides access to the database, the name and location of the library providing the access, or the URL of the database.

Note that *ERIC* is available both as a subscription database and as a free database in different versions. If you can access the database without going through a library Web page, the database is free for anyone to use. Many free databases, such as *AGRICOLA, ERIC,* and *THOMAS,* are sponsored by the federal government. Check your library's Web site for a list of free online reference databases. Be aware, however, that some free databases offer only citations and abstracts (short summaries) of articles and that some may charge a fee for full-text versions of the articles.

A Historical Document from *THOMAS: Legislative Information on the Internet*

The Constitution of the United States. Text prepared by Gerald
     Murphy. Distr. Cybercasting Services Div. of the Natl.
     Public Telecomputing Network (NPTN). *THOMAS: Legislative
     Information on the Internet.* Web. 12 July 2010.

Do not italicize or type quotation marks around the titles of political documents such as the Constitution of the United States and the Declaration of Independence.

An Abstract of a Scholarly Journal Article from *AGRICOLA*

Spiegelhalter, F., F. R. Lauter, and J. M. Russell. "Detection
     of Genetically Modified Food Products in a Commercial
     Laboratory." *Journal of Food Science* 66.5 (2001): 634-40.
     Abstract. *AGRICOLA.* Web. 14 July 2010.

An Abstract of a Scholarly Journal Article from *SearchERIC.org*

Elbow, Peter. "The Cultures of Literature and Composition: What

   Could Each Learn from the Other?" *College English* 64.5

   (2002): 533–46. Abstract. *SearchERIC.org.* Web. 11 July 2010.

Citing Online Encyclopedias and Dictionaries

An Entry from an Online Encyclopedia

"Dickinson, Emily Elizabeth." *Encyclopaedia Britannica Online.*

   Encyclopaedia Britannica, 2003. Web. 30 Apr. 2010.

"Boyle, T. Coraghessan." *Grolier Multimedia Encyclopedia.*

   Vers. 3.0. Grolier, 2003. Web. 5 July 2010.

"Deconstruction." *Encyclopedia Americana.* Grolier, 2003. Web.

   23 Apr. 2010.

"American Literature." *New Book of Knowledge Online.* Grolier,

   2003. Web. 5 July 2010.

1. Give the author of the entry (if known), last name first. If no author is given, begin your citation with the title of the article.
2. Give the title of the article in double quotation marks with a period typed inside the final quotation marks.
3. Give the words in the title in the order in which they appear in the encyclopedia (names of persons inverted), following MLA guidelines for the capitalization of titles.
4. Give the title of the online encyclopedia, italicized and followed by a period and one space.
5. Give the version number if the encyclopedia has one (e.g., Vers. 3.0).
6. Give the name of the publisher of the online encyclopedia (not italicized), followed by a comma.
7. Give the date of publication, copyright, or most recent update, followed by a period.
8. Give the medium of publication, followed by a period.
9. Give the date when you accessed or printed the material (followed by a period).

A Photograph from an Online Encyclopedia

"Onassis, Jacqueline Bouvier Kennedy." Photograph. *Grolier*

   Multimedia Encyclopedia. Vers. 3.0. Grolier, 2003. Web. 17

   Apr. 2010.

1. Give the photographer's name (if known), inverted for alphabetizing and followed by a period.
2. Give the title of the photograph in double quotation marks with a period inside the end quotation marks.
3. Type the word *Photograph* (capitalized, not italicized), followed by a period.
4. Give the title of the online encyclopedia, italicized and followed by a period.
5. Give the version number if the encyclopedia has one (e.g., Vers. 3.0).
6. Give the name of the publisher of the online encyclopedia (not italicized), followed by a comma.
7. Give the date of publication, copyright, or most recent update of the encyclopedia, followed by a period.
8. Give the medium of publication, followed by a period.
9. Give the date when you accessed or printed the photograph (followed by a period).

A Definition from an Online Dictionary

"Deism." *Merriam-Webster Online*. Encyclopaedia

   Britannica, 2010. Web. 21 Apr. 2010.

1. Give the word (capitalized) in double quotation marks with a period typed inside the final quotation marks.
2. Give the title of the online dictionary, italicized and followed by a period.
3. Give the name of the publisher of the dictionary (not italicized), followed by a comma.
4. Give the date of publication, copyright, or most recent update, followed by a period.
5. Give the medium of publication, followed by a period.
6. Give the date when you accessed or printed the material (followed by a period).

See page 220 for instructions for citing listings that have several entries for a word or that have several definitions for a word.

Material Accessed with a Keyword through an Internet Service Provider (ISP) such as America Online

If you found the material that you are using by doing a keyword search on an Internet service provider such as America Online, type the word *Keyword*, a colon, and one space, and give the word that you used to search for the information that you are citing (capitalized and followed by a period).

"Frost, Robert." *Compton's Encyclopedia Online.* Vers. 3.0. 1998.

  America Online. Web. 3 May 2010. Keyword: Robert Frost.

Citing Articles from Print Reference Books

A Signed Article in a Frequently Republished General Encyclopedia or Well-Known Reference Book

Davis, Caleb W. "Miller, Arthur Ashur." *Collier's Encyclopedia.*

  1995 ed. Print.

Dowling, Herndon G. "Dinosaur." *The Encyclopedia Americana.*

  1994 ed. Print.

Foulkes, David, Wilse B. Webb, and Rosalind D. Cartwright.

  "Sleep and Dreams." *The New Encyclopaedia Britannica:*

  Macropaedia. 15th ed. 2010. Print.

Wadsworth, Frank W. "Shakespeare, William." *The World Book*

  Encyclopedia. 2000 ed. Print.

Waggoner, Hyatt H. "Dickinson, Emily." *The Encyclopedia*

  Americana. 1994 ed. Print.

1. Give the author's name, inverted for alphabetizing. (If no author's name is given, begin your citation with the title of the encyclopedia article as described below. Do not give the names of the editors of the encyclopedia.) Look for the author's name or initials at the end of the article. If initials are given, check the encyclopedia for a list of the full names of the authors.

2. Give the title of the article in double quotation marks with names of persons inverted as they appear in the encyclopedia: "Frost, Robert Lee." Follow MLA guidelines for capitalizing words in titles no matter how the title is formatted in the encyclopedia.

3. Give the title of the encyclopedia or reference book, italicized and followed by a period. Do not omit the article *The* if it begins the title.

4. For *The New Encyclopaedia Britannica,* type a colon after the title and specify whether your article came from the *Micropaedia* section or the *Macropaedia* section.

5. Give only the edition number and the date of publication for familiar reference books that frequently appear in newly updated editions. Check the copyright page to see whether the work has been frequently republished, or check the edition number. If the work is a fifteenth edition, it has obviously been updated many times. If no edition number is given on the title page and only one publication date is given on the copyright page, give full publication information, as described in the entries for reference books appearing in only one edition.

6. Give the year of the edition rather than the edition number and the year (2003 ed.) if the edition number is not specified on the title page.

7. If a frequently republished reference book is organized alphabetically, you may omit the volume and page numbers.

8. End with the medium of publication and a period.

An Unsigned Article in a Frequently Republished General Encyclopedia or Well-Known Reference Book

"Chaucer, Geoffrey." *The New Encyclopaedia Britannica:*

   Micropaedia. 15th ed. 2010. Print.

"White Shark." *The New Encyclopaedia Britannica: Micropaedia.*

   15th ed. 2010. Print.

1. If no author is given, begin your entry with the title of the article in double quotation marks with names of persons inverted as they appear in the encyclopedia: "Frost, Robert Lee."

2. Follow MLA guidelines for capitalizing words in titles no matter how the title is formatted in the encyclopedia. For example, "White Shark" was formatted in all lowercase letters in the encyclopedia. In MLA style, however, the first and last words of titles are capitalized.

3. Give the title of the encyclopedia or reference book, italicized and followed by a period. Do not omit the article *The* if it begins the title.

> **Finding an Author's Full Name in *Encyclopaedia Britannica***
>
> *The New Encyclopaedia Britannica* is divided into three sections. The *Micropaedia* contains relatively short articles. Some give the author's initials at the end of the article, and others do not list any initials. The *Macropaedia* contains long, detailed articles and always gives the initials of one or more authors at the end of the article. The third section of *Encyclopaedia Britannica* is the *Propaedia: Outline of Knowledge and Guide to the Britannica*. At the end of the *Propaedia*, you will find the full names of the authors of the articles in both the *Micropaedia* and *Macropaedia* sections.

4. For *The New Encyclopaedia Britannica*, type a colon after the title and tell whether your article came from the *Micropaedia* or *Macropaedia* section.

5. Give only the edition number and the date of publication for familiar reference books that frequently appear in newly updated editions. Check the copyright page to see whether the work has been frequently republished, or check the edition number. If the work is a fifteenth edition, it has obviously been updated many times. If no edition number is given on the title page and only one publication date is given on the copyright page, give full publication information.

6. Give the year of the edition rather than the edition number and the year (2003 ed.) if the edition number is not specified on the title page.

7. If a frequently republished reference book is organized alphabetically, you may omit the volume and page numbers.

8. End with the medium of publication and a period.

A Signed Article in a Subject-Specific Reference Book That Has Appeared in Only One Edition, such as *American Writers* or *British Writers*

O'Connor, William Van. "William Faulkner." *American Writers:*

    A Collection of Literary Biographies. Ed. Leonard Unger.

    Vol. 2. New York: Scribner's, 1974. 54-76. Print.

Sanforth, Henry T. "Ernest Hemingway." *American Writers:*

    A Collection of Literary Biographies. Ed. Leonard Unger.

    Supp. 4: Pt. 1. New York: Scribner's, 1988. 86-98. Print.

Scott-James, R. A., and C. Day-Lewis. "Thomas Hardy."

> *British Writers.* Ed. Ian Scott-Kilvert. Vol. 6. New York:

> Scribner's, 1983. 1-22. Print.

1. Give full publication information for reference books that have appeared in only one edition (no edition number is given on the title page, and only one date of publication is given on the copyright page).
2. Give the author of the article you used, followed by a period. If more than one author is given, invert only the name of the first author listed.
3. Give the title of the article in double quotation marks as it appears in the reference book (names not inverted). Type a period inside the final quotation marks.
4. Give the title of the reference book, italicized and followed by a period.
5. Type the abbreviation *Ed.* (*Edited by*), and give the name of the editor. Do not type a comma between the names if two editors are listed.
6. Type the abbreviation *Vol.,* and give the number of the volume you used, followed by a period.
7. Give the city, publisher, year of publication, and a period.
8. Give the first page number of the article, a hyphen, and the last page number (including the bibliography), followed by a period.
9. End with the medium of publication and a period.

A Signed Article from *Dictionary of Literary Biography*

Griffin, Farah Jasmine. "Gwendolyn Brooks." *American Poets since*

> *World War II.* Ed. Joseph Conte. Vol. 165 of *Dictionary of*

> *Literary Biography.* Detroit: Bruccoli-Gale, 1996. 81-91.

> Print.

Harding, Walter. "Henry David Thoreau." *The American*

> *Renaissance in New England.* Ed. Joel Myerson. Vol. 1 of

> *Dictionary of Literary Biography.* Detroit: Gale, 1978.

> 170-82. Print.

1. Each volume of the *Dictionary of Literary Biography* has a separate title and editor, so each volume should be cited separately.
2. Give the name of author of the article you used, followed by a period. If more than one author is given, invert only the name of the first author listed.

> ### Finding the Author's Name in *American Writers*
>
> In *American Writers*, the author's name is usually given after the bibliography on the last page of the article.

3. Give the title of the article in double quotation marks as it appears in the reference book (names not inverted). Type a period inside the final quotation marks.

4. Give the title of the volume in which the article appears, italicized and followed by a period.

5. Type the abbreviation *Ed.* (*Edited by*), and give the name(s) of the editor or editors of the volume. Do not type a comma between the names if there are two editors listed: Ed. James P. Smith and Mary Jones.

6. Type *Vol.*, and give the number of the volume you used, followed by *of Dictionary of Literary Biography* (title italicized) and a period.

7. Give the city, publisher, year of publication, and a period.

8. Give the first page number of the article, a hyphen, and the last page number (including the bibliography), followed by a period.

9. End with the medium of publication and a period.

An Excerpt from a Scholarly Journal Article Reprinted in *Classical and Medieval Literature Criticism*

May, Rollo. "The Therapist and the Journey into Hell." *Michigan Quarterly Review* 25.4 (1986): 629-41. Rpt. in *Classical and Medieval Literature Criticism*. Ed. Jelena O. Krstović and Zoran Minderović. Vol. 3. Detroit: Gale, 1987. 154-58. Print.

An Excerpt from a Scholarly Journal Article Reprinted in *Twentieth-Century Literary Criticism*

Heilman, Robert. "*The Turn of the Screw* as Poem." *University of Kansas City Review* 14.4 (1948): 277-89. Rpt. in *Twentieth-Century Literary Criticism*. Ed. Dennis Poupard. Vol. 24. Detroit: Gale, 1987. 336-40. Print.

Note that the title of the Henry James novel *The Turn of the Screw* is italicized in the title of the article.

An Excerpt from an Essay in an Essay Collection Reprinted in *Nineteenth-Century Literature Criticism*

Loomis, Roger Sherman. "A Defense of Naturalism." *Documents of*
    Modern Literary Realism. Ed. George J. Becker. Princeton:
    Princeton UP, 1963. 535–48. Rpt. in *Nineteenth-Century*
    Literature Criticism. Ed. Joann Cerrito. Vol. 36. Detroit:
    Gale, 1993. 311–16. Print.

An Excerpt from a Scholarly Journal Article Reprinted in *Short Story Criticism*

Fiedler, Leslie A. "William Faulkner: An American Dickens."
    Commentary 10.4 (1950): 384–87. Rpt. in *Short Story*
    Criticism: Excerpts from Criticism of the Works of Short
    Fiction Writers. Ed. Laurie Lanzen Harris and Sheila
    Fitzgerald. Vol. 1. Detroit: Gale, 1988. 151. Print.

An Excerpt from an Essay in an Essay Collection Reprinted in *Short Story Criticism*

West, Ray B., Jr. "Atmosphere and Theme in Faulkner's 'A Rose
    for Emily.'" *William Faulkner: Four Decades of Criticism.*
    Ed. Linda Welshimer Wagner. [Lansing]: Michigan State UP,
    1973. 192–98. Rpt. in *Short Story Criticism: Excerpts from*
    Criticism of the Works of Short Fiction Writers. Ed.
    Laurie Lanzen Harris and Sheila Fitzgerald. Vol. 1.
    Detroit: Gale, 1988. 148–51. Print.

The city of publication is given in square brackets because it was taken from a source other than *Short Story Criticism.*

An Article from the *CQ Researcher (Congressional Quarterly Researcher)* (Print Version)

Masci, David. "NASA's Future: Are the Space Agency's Goals Too
    Modest?" *CQ Researcher* 23 May 2003: 475–92. Print.

1. Cite an article from the *CQ Researcher* as you would an article in a popular weekly magazine. Omit the article *The* from the beginning of the title of the *CQ Researcher* but not from the beginning of the title of an article therein.
2. If the title of an article ends with a question mark, type the question mark inside the final quotation marks and do not use a period.

An Article from *Facts on File* (Print Version)

"U.S. Supreme Court Upholds 'Three-Strikes' Sentence Increases."

    Facts on File World News Digest 6 Mar. 2003: 138-39. Print.

1. Cite an article from *Facts on File World News Digest* as you would an article from a popular weekly magazine.
2. Use MLA guidelines to capitalize titles no matter how a title is formatted in a source.

Citing a Definition from a Dictionary

"Symbolism." *Merriam-Webster's Collegiate Dictionary.* 11th ed.

    2005. Print.

"Lace." Def. 2a. *The American Heritage Dictionary.* 4th ed. 2001. Print.

"Manuscript." Entry 2. *Webster's Third New International*

    Dictionary. 1981. Print.

1. Type the word being defined (capitalized and in quotation marks).
2. If the dictionary lists more than one definition and you are referring to only one of them, type the abbreviation *Def.* (*Definition*) and give the number and letter (if there is one) of the definition: Def. 2a.
3. If a dictionary lists several entries for a word, type the word *Entry* and give the number or other indicator: Entry 5.
4. Give the title of the dictionary, italicized and followed by a period and one space. Do not omit *The* from the title of a dictionary.
5. Give the edition number of the dictionary (5th ed.), followed by one space. Then give the most recent copyright date and a period. If no edition number is specified on the title page, give the year of the edition (2003 ed.), using the most recent copyright date.
6. End with the medium of publication and a period.
7. The parenthetical citation for the first entry would be ("Symbolism").
8. The parenthetical citation for the second entry would be ("Lace," def. 2a).
9. The parenthetical citation for the third entry would be ("Manuscript," entry 2).

Citing an Article from *SIRS* (*Social Issues Resources Series*) (Print Version)

Social Issues Resources Series (*SIRS*) is a loose-leaf collection of reprinted magazine and newspaper articles. Each volume of the series presents material related to a single topic of interest to researchers (e.g., *The AIDS Crisis, Alcohol, Health, Women*). Check your library Web site's list of online reference databases to see if the online version of *SIRS* is also available.

A Monthly or Bimonthly Magazine Article Reprinted in *SIRS*

Holden, Constance. "Alcoholism and the Medical Cost Crunch."

    Science Mar. 1987: 1132-33. Print. *Alcohol.* Ed. Eleanor

    Goldstein. Vol. 2. Boca Raton: SIRS, 1989. Art. 7.

1. Give the name(s) of the author(s), followed by a period and one space. Invert the name of the first author listed.
2. Give the title of the article in double quotation marks, followed by a period typed inside the final quotation marks.
3. Give the title of the magazine (italicized, not followed by a period).
4. Type the month and year of publication, a colon, and one space.
5. Give the first page number of the article, a hyphen, the last page number of the article, and a period.
6. Give the medium of publication, followed by a period.
7. Give the title of the volume you used in *SIRS* (italicized), the editor of the volume, the volume number, and the publication information on *SIRS*, followed by a period and one space.
8. Type the abbreviation *Art.*, the article number, and a period.
9. Capitalize an abbreviation that follows a period that ends a section of a bibliographical entry. Do not capitalize an abbreviation that does not follow a period that ends a section of a bibliographical entry. (See chapter 22 for more information on MLA-recommended abbreviations.)
10. The parenthetical citation for this entry would be (Holden, art. 7).

A Weekly or Biweekly Magazine Article Reprinted in *SIRS*

Gelman, David, et al. "Treating Teens in Trouble." *Newsweek*

    20 Jan. 1986: 52+. Print. *Youth.* Ed. Eleanor Goldstein. Vol.

    3. Boca Raton: Social Issues Resources Series, 1989. Art. 3.

1. If you are not certain your reader will recognize the commonly abbreviated publisher's name *SIRS* (*Social Issues Resources Series*), give the publisher's name in full or use a more recognizable abbreviation.
2. The parenthetical citation for this entry would be (Gelman, art. 3).

A Newspaper Article with an Author Given Reprinted in *SIRS*

Luber, Kristin. "The Wars between Women." *Washington Post*

26 Aug. 1984: C1+. Print. *Women.* Ed. Eleanor Goldstein.

Vol. 6. Boca Raton: SIRS, 1989. Art. 13.

The parenthetical citation for this entry would be (Luber, art. 13).

Citing Microform Databases

A Newspaper Article with an Author Given Reprinted in *NewsBank* (Microform Version)

Bryan, Robert K. "Counseling Children about AIDS." *San*

Francisco Examiner 22 Jan. 1988: n. pag. Microform.

NewsBank: Health 11 (1988): fiche 1, grids B4-7.

1. Give the name of the author(s) of the article, inverting the name of the first.
2. Give the title of the article in double quotation marks with a period typed inside the final quotation marks.
3. Give the title of the newspaper (italicized, not followed by a period). Omit the article *The* at the beginning of the title of a newspaper but not from the title of an article in a newspaper. If the city of publication is not included in the title of the newspaper, give the city in square brackets after the title. Give the postal abbreviation for the state if the city is not well known or could be confused with another city.
4. Give the day, month, and year of publication. Then type a colon, one space, and the section and page numbers of the article. If no section and page numbers are given, use the abbreviation *n. pag.*
5. Give the medium of publication (*Microform*), followed by a period.
6. Type *NewsBank,* a colon, and one space; then give the title of the section of *NewsBank,* with both title and subtitle italicized and not followed by a period.

7. Give the volume number, followed by one space. Then give the year of publication in parentheses, a colon, and one space.

8. Give the fiche number, a comma, and one space. Then give the grid numbers and a period.

9. A parenthetical citation for this entry would be (Bryan, grid B5).

A Newspaper Article with No Author Given Reprinted in *NewsBank* (Microform Version)

"Problems with Today's Health Care System." *Washington Post*

    23 June 1991: n. pag. Microform. *NewsBank: Health* 11

    (1991): fiche 3, grids C6-8.

1. If no author is given, begin your entry with the title of the article in double quotation marks with the period typed inside the end marks.

2. Give the title of the newspaper (italicized, not followed by a period). Omit the article *The* at the beginning of the title of a newspaper but not from the beginning of the title of an article in a newspaper. If the city of publication is not included in the title of the newspaper, give the city in square brackets after the title. Give the postal abbreviation for the state if the city is not well known or could be confused with another city.

3. Give the day, month, and year of publication. Then type a colon, one space, and the section and page numbers of the article. If no section and page numbers are given, use the abbreviation *n. pag.*

4. Give the medium of publication (*Microform*), followed by a period.

5. Type *NewsBank,* a colon, and one space; then give the title of the section of *NewsBank,* with both title and subtitle italicized and not followed by a period.

6. Give the volume number (not followed by a period). Then type the year of publication in parentheses, a colon, and one space.

7. Give the fiche number, a comma, and one space. Then give the grid numbers and a period.

8. A parenthetical citation for this entry would be ("Problems," grid C7).

Citing CD-ROM and DVD-ROM Databases

An Entry from an Encyclopedia on CD-ROM or DVD-ROM

"Frost, Robert Lee." *Encarta '95.* Redmond, WA: Microsoft, 1995.

    CD-ROM.

"The Early History of Blacks in America." *Compton's Encyclope-*

dia 2000. N.p.: Broderbund-Learning, 1999. CD-ROM.

"Himalaya Mountains." *Encarta Encyclopedia Standard 2003.*

Redmond, WA: Microsoft, 2003. CD-ROM.

A Map from an Encyclopedia on CD-ROM or DVD-ROM

"Swaziland." Map. *Compton's Encyclopedia 2000.* N.p.: Broder-

bund-Learning, 1999. CD-ROM.

An Abstract of a Scholarly Journal Article from *ERIC (Educational Resources Information Center)* on CD-ROM

Kim, Anna Charr. "How College Faculty Evaluate Second Language

Writing." *Research and Teaching in Developmental Education*

14.1 (1997): 35-48. Abstract. CD-ROM. *ERIC.* SilverPlatter.

1992-Mar. 1998. EJ557280.

1. Give the author or authors of the article in the order listed on the title page. Invert the name of the first author listed.
2. Type double quotation marks around the title of the journal article, and type a period inside the final quotation marks.
3. If the article has been previously published, give the publication information, following MLA guidelines for citing a print version of a scholarly journal article.
4. After the original publication information, type *Abstract* if you did not access a full-text version of the article.
5. Give the medium of publication consulted (*CD-ROM*), followed by a period.
6. Give the title of the database from which you accessed the article (italicized and followed by a period).
7. Give the name of the vendor or provider (Gale Group, SilverPlatter, UMI-ProQuest, Information Access, Congressional Information Service, Dataware Technologies, etc.). You can usually find the provider's name on the title page of the CD-ROM or DVD-ROM. If you have trouble finding this information, ask a librarian to help you.
8. Give the date of electronic publication, followed by a period.

9. Give the item number (if available) and a period.

10. If you took information from more than one disc of a multiple-disc database, give the total number of discs (e. g., 6 discs) at the end of the citation.

11. If you took information from only one of several discs, give the number of the disc you used (e. g., Disc 4) at the end of the citation.

An Abstract of a Published Dissertation from *ERIC* on CD-ROM

Unger, Thomas C. *Involving ESL Students in American Culture*

through Participation in Private School Activities. Diss.

Nova Southeastern U, 1997. Abstract. CD-ROM. *ERIC*. Silver-

Platter. 1992-Mar. 1998. ED412745.

1. Give the name of the author of the dissertation, last name first, followed by a period.

2. Give the title of the dissertation (italicized and followed by a period).

3. Type the abbreviation *Diss.* (for *Dissertation*) and give the name of the university where the dissertation was written, followed by a comma, one space, and the year of completion.

4. Type *Abstract* if you did not access a full-text version of the dissertation (unless the title of the database indicates that all the materials therein are abstracts).

5. Identify the medium of publication consulted (*CD-ROM*), followed by a period.

6. Give the title of the database (italicized): *ERIC, Dissertation Abstracts Ondisc, New York Times Ondisc*, and so on (followed by a period).

7. Give the name of the vendor or provider (Gale Group, SilverPlatter, UMI-ProQuest, Information Access, Congressional Information Service, Dataware Technologies, etc.). You can usually find the provider's name on the title page of the CD-ROM or DVD-ROM. If you have trouble finding this information, ask a librarian to help you.

8. Give the date of electronic publication, followed by a period.

9. Give the item number (if available), followed by a period.

10. If you took information from more than one disc of a multiple-disc database, give the total number of discs: 6 discs.

11. If you took information from only one of several discs, give the number of the disc you used: Disc 4.

CHAPTER 14

Parenthetical Citations

When you use an author's original interpretation or idea or an author's precise wording, you must inform your reader precisely where in your source (what page or pages) the material came from by using a parenthetical citation (also called a *parenthetical reference*). The parenthetical citation refers your reader to the complete information about that particular source given on your works-cited page.

- Most parenthetical citations contain the author's last name, followed by the page number in the source (Thompson 34) or the page number alone (34) if the author's name has been incorporated into your sentence.
- If you are referring to the entire work rather than to a specific page in the work, you may give the author's name and the title of the work in your sentence and omit the parenthetical citation. (See example on page 50.)
- Omit from the parenthetical citation any information (such as the author's name or the title of the work) already given in the introduction to your quotation, summary, or paraphrase.
- Check your works-cited list carefully to make sure that you have provided complete information on all the sources in your parenthetical citations.

Author's Name Not Given in Your Sentence

Within the parentheses type the author's name, one space, and the page number(s) from the source. Do not type a comma between the author's name and the number(s). Do not use the abbreviations *p.* and *pp.*

Pearl is "precociously intelligent" (McNamara 539).

Author's Name Given in Your Sentence

McNamara points out that Pearl is "precociously intelligent"
(539).

Author's Name Not Given in Source

Magazines and newspapers sometimes do not give the name of the author of an article, so give the title or a shortened version of the title beginning with the word by which the source was alphabetized in your works-cited list.

("Exercising" 7)

You may give the section letter as well as the page number of a newspaper article, as illustrated in the next entry.

("Problems with Children" B4)

Quotation Taken from Two Consecutive Pages

If your quotation begins at the bottom of one page and continues on the top of the next, use inclusive page numbers separated by a hyphen.

"Pearl is pure symbol, the living emblem of the sin, a human embodiment of the Scarlet Letter," writes Richard Harter Fogle (312-13).

Two or More Works by the Same Author

To make sure your reader knows which of the works you are referring to, type a comma and one space after the author's name, and give the title or a recognizable shortened form of the title beginning with the word by which the title was alphabetized in your list of works cited.

(Hawthorne, *The Scarlet Letter* 78) or (Hawthorne, *Scarlet* 78)
(Hawthorne, *The Marble Faun* 272) or (Hawthorne, *Marble* 272)

Two Authors Not Named in Your Sentence

(Hampton and Johnson 356)

Three Authors Not Named in Your Sentence

(Smith, Green, and Jones 458)

Four or More Authors Not Named in Your Sentence

Give the last name of the first author listed on the title page, followed by *et al.* (Latin for "and others"). Or you may give the last names of all the authors if you have cited all the names in your works-cited list. Be sure to give the names in the order in which they are listed on the title page of the work you are citing.

(Smithfield et al. 456)

(Smithfield, Graves, Connor, Williams, and Chaplin 56-57)

Works by Two Authors with the Same Last Name

(J. Williams 456)

(G. Williams 897)

Works by Two Authors with the Same Initial and Last Name

(James Williams 27)

(Joseph Williams 38)

Citing Several Volumes of a Multivolume Work

If you quoted or paraphrased from only one volume of a multivolume work, give the volume you used in your works-cited list. However, if you quoted or paraphrased from two or more volumes of a multivolume work, type the author's name (if not given in your sentence); then type the volume number, a colon, one space, and the page number(s).

(Wilson 2: 456-57)

(Wilson 4: 243-44)

Citing Paragraphs, Articles, Screens, Grids, or Items

If you need to specify anything other than a page number, type a comma and one space after the author's name and either type the appropriate word or use the MLA-recommended abbreviation (*par.* for *paragraph*, *pars.* for *para-*

graphs, art. for *article*) followed by the number(s). (See chapter 22 for a list of MLA-recommended abbreviations.)

```
(Franklin, par. 7)

(Franklin, pars. 8-9)

(Luber, art. 25)

(Millworth, screens 4-5)

(Brown, grids 7-9)
```

Citing Several Works

Use semicolons followed by one space to separate the citations. This information could also be given in a footnote or an endnote (also called a *note*), which is a much better choice if your parenthetical citation will be long. (See chapter 15 for more information on formatting footnotes and endnotes.)

```
(Smith 345; Green 248; Thompson 786)
```

A Work with an Organization as Author

Either give the name of the organization in your sentence with a page reference in the parenthetical citation or give the name (shortened or in full) in the parenthetical citation along with the page reference.

```
(United States Environmental Protection Agency 15)

(EPA 15)

(American Psychological Association 56)
```

An Entire Work

If you are referring to the entire work rather than to a specific page in the work, give the author's name and the title of the work in your sentence. No parenthetical citation is necessary.

Nonprint Sources

If you are citing a film, a television program, a radio program, a concert, a performance, a speech, or some other source with no page numbers, give the title of the source and information about the performers, directors, narrators, radio hosts, conductors, speakers, or other persons in your text. If that method does not seem appropriate, give the title of the source alone in your parenthetical citation since there are no page numbers to give.

(*Braveheart*)

A Quotation from a Literary Work Available in Many Editions

Give the reader enough information to locate the quotation in any edition of the work. After the page number from the edition you used, type a semicolon and use MLA-recommended abbreviations to specify the chapter (*ch.*), book (*bk.*), paragraph (*par.*), part (*pt.*), section (*sec.*), scene (*sc.*), and so on. (See chapter 22 for a list of MLA-recommended abbreviations.)

Hawthorne describes Pearl as "the scarlet letter endowed with life" (70; ch. 7).

A Quotation from a Short Poem

In your first parenthetical citation, type *line* or *lines* (lines 4-8). Once you have informed your reader that you are giving line numbers rather than page numbers, you may give the line numbers alone (4-8). Do not use the abbreviations *l.* or *ll.* because they can be confused with numbers.

Robert Herrick urges his readers to savor each moment when he writes, "Gather ye rosebuds while ye may, / Old Time is still a-flying / And this same flower that smiles today, / Tomorrow will be dying" (lines 1-4).

A Quotation from a Long Poem

If a poem is long enough to be divided into books or cantos, type the title of the poem (italicized), the book or canto number, a period followed by no space, and the line or line numbers. The citation that follows refers to book 7, lines 24 through 28 of Homer's *Odyssey*.

(*Odyssey* 7.24-28)

A Quotation from a Shakespearean or Other Classic Verse Play

Italicize the title of the play. If you abbreviate the title of the play, italicize the abbreviation. (See chapter 22 for a list of MLA-recommended abbreviations of the titles of Shakespeare's works.) Give the act, scene, and line numbers in Arabic numerals separated by periods. The citations below refer to Shakespeare's *Hamlet,* act 3, scene 1, lines 6 through 8.

(*Hamlet* 3.1.6-8)

(*Ham.* 3.1.6-8)

A Quotation from the Bible

Give the name of the book and then the chapter and verse in Arabic numerals separated by periods. Do not italicize the titles of books of the Bible. You may abbreviate the names of books of the Bible: *Gen.* for Genesis, for example. (See chapter 22 for a list of MLA-recommended abbreviations for books of the Bible.) The citations below refer to the book of Genesis, chapter 2, verses 10 through 12.

(Genesis 2.10-12)

(Gen. 2.10-12)

An Online Source

If a Web site has page numbers or paragraph numbers, use them in your parenthetical citations. Many Web documents, however, are not paginated, nor do they have numbered paragraphs. For those documents, you do not have to give a page or paragraph number in your parenthetical citation; just name the author(s) either in your sentence or in the parenthetical citation at the end of your sentence (e.g., Brower). You may also use the MLA abbreviation *n. pag.* to assure your reader that no pages were given for you to cite (e.g., Brower n. pag.).

Some instructors will ask you to turn in photocopies of all print materials and printouts of Web materials cited in your paper. An instructor who is checking your citations for accuracy may ask you to identify the pages in the Web site printouts from which you quoted, paraphrased, or summarized information. In this case, follow your instructor's guidelines for giving printout page numbers in your parenthetical citations. MLA allows you to give additional information beyond the minimum requirements if you think such information will be useful to your reader or if your professor requests it.

Web document with page numbers: (Carrington 7) (Carrington 2-3)

Web document with paragraph numbers: (Roberts, par. 8) (Roberts, pars. 8-10)

Web document with no page or paragraph numbers: (Carter) or (Carter n. pag.)

Printout page references requested by your professor: (Carter 3)

Quoting/Paraphrasing/Summarizing from an Indirect Source

If you are reading Robert T. Brown's book analyzing the novels of Thomas Hardy, Brown's words and ideas are your **original** source of information. If Brown quotes from Charles K. Smith to support a point he is making and you wish to quote Smith's words in your paper, you are using an **indirect** source. If your instructor has asked you not to use indirect sources in your paper, then you must find Charles K. Smith's article or book so that you can quote from the original source. If your instructor has no objections to your quoting from an indirect source, follow the guidelines discussed here.

Short Quotation (One to Four Lines) Taken from an Indirect Source

1. The material you are quoting will be in double quotation marks in your source. Use double quotation marks around the quoted material to show that you are quoting, and change the double quotation marks in your source to single quotation marks to show that the material was quoted in your source.
2. If you are quoting a brief passage from a long, block quotation in your source, you must enclose that material in both single quotation marks (to show that the material was quoted in the source rather than written by the author of the source) and double quotation marks (to show that you are quoting the material).

Long Quotation (More Than Four Lines) Taken from an Indirect Source

If the material you are quoting takes up more than four lines of space when typed into your paper, indent the quotation one inch (or ten spaces on a typewriter) from the left margin, and enclose the block material in double quotation marks in your paper to show that it was quoted in your source.

Parenthetical Citations for Quotations
Taken from an Indirect Source

You will also need to identify both the writer of the words you are quoting and the author of the essay, article, or book from which you are quoting. If Robert T. Brown quoted Charles K. Smith in your source and you wish to use Smith's words, use one of the parenthetical citations that follow.

Smith named in your sentence:

(qtd. in Brown 346)

Smith not named in your sentence:

(Smith qtd. in Brown 346)

Smith paraphrased by Brown and named in your sentence:

(para. in Brown 346)

Smith paraphrased by Brown and not named in your sentence:

(Smith para. in Brown 346)

General Knowledge of a Subject: No Parenthetical Citation Needed

1. You need not give a parenthetical citation when you present general knowledge material in your own words.

2. For example, if you are writing a literary analysis, you may describe events that occur in the story, novel, play, or poem without a parenthetical citation as long as you do not use the author's precise wording.

3. Biographical information about a famous person can be found without a parenthetical citation, footnote, or endnote in many sources. Therefore, you may give general information about someone's life (where the person was born; where he or she was educated; whom he or she married; when he or she died; when a particular novel, story, poem, or play was published) without a parenthetical citation as long as you do not use the precise wording of your source.

4. If you see information discussed in several of your sources without being credited to other sources, you may safely assume that the

information is general knowledge and need not be cited to a source in your paper.

5. Remember, however, that the precise wording of a source must always be cited to the person who wrote the words because not to do so is plagiarism. (See chapter 21 for more information about plagiarism.)

6. If you are not sure whether the information you are using is general knowledge, the best plan is to give a parenthetical citation rather than to risk being accused of plagiarizing from your sources.

Punctuating Parenthetical Citations: Short Quotations

Citation at the End of a Short Quotation

Place the parenthetical citation before the period that ends the sentence.

That Linda Loman truly loves her husband seems obvious when she tells Biff and Happy, "He's just a big stupid man to you, but I tell you there's more good in him than in many other people" (Miller 1797).

Citation in the Middle of a Quoted Sentence

If the quotation appears in the first half of the sentence, place the parenthetical citation as close as possible to the quotation and **before any punctuation** that appears in the middle of the sentence.

Although, as Hawthorne tells us, "Pearl . . . could have borne a fair examination in the New England Primer" (77; ch. 8), she refuses to give the expected answer to Mr. Wilson's question as to who created her.

Citation after a Question Mark or Exclamation Point

A question mark or exclamation point that ends a quotation should be typed inside the final quotation marks. Then type one space, the parenthetical citation, and a period to end the sentence.

As they make plans to run away together, Hester promises Arthur that they can escape their shame: "'Let us not look back. . . .

The past is gone! Wherefore should we linger upon it now?'"
(Hawthorne 137; ch. 18).
Biff is so upset that he literally screams at his father,
"We never told the truth for ten minutes in this house!"
(Miller 1832).

Punctuating Parenthetical Citations: Long, Block Quotations

1. Place the parenthetical citation **after the period or other punctuation** that ends a block quotation.
2. Note that the double quotation marks used to punctuate the dialogue in the novel are used precisely as printed in the source in the block quotation that follows.
3. Note that the second paragraph in this quotation is indented an additional one-quarter inch (on a computer) or an additional three spaces (on a typewriter) from the left margin to mark the change of paragraphs in the source.
4. The first line of the quotation is not indented an additional one-quarter inch (or three spaces) because it was not the first sentence in the paragraph in which it was printed in the novel. If the first line of the quotation had also been the first sentence in the paragraph in the novel, it would have been indented an additional one-quarter inch (or three spaces) from the left margin.

Hawthorne makes it clear that Chillingworth's revenge is the worst sin in *The Scarlet Letter*:

> "We are not, Hester, the worst sinners in the world. There is one worse than even the polluted priest! That old man's revenge has been blacker than my sin. He has violated, in cold blood, the sanctity of a human heart. Thou and I, Hester, never did so!"
>
> "Never, never!" whispered she. "What we did had a consecration of its own. We felt it so! We said so to each other! Hast thou forgotten it?"
> (133; ch. 17)

CHAPTER 15

Endnotes and Footnotes

Endnotes and footnotes are used to give information that does not fit well into the text of your paper but may be of interest to your reader. Notes that give additional information are called **content notes.** Notes that list additional or indirect sources are called **bibliographic notes.** Endnotes are typed in a list at the end of the paper, and footnotes are typed at the bottoms of the pages. You need not use endnotes or footnotes, but if you wish to give additional information, endnotes are easier to organize and are preferred by most instructors.

Notes can be used for the following purposes:

- To give additional information or further explanation
- To define a term your reader might not understand
- To comment on or evaluate a source
- To give the source of additional information
- To give the source of a contrasting interpretation
- To list multiple sources
- To give full publication information for an indirect source

    1. For a contrasting interpretation of Hamlet's state of mind in this scene, see Harrison 56-58.

    2. For a more complete discussion of Plath's relationship to Hughes, see Smith 89-94; Johnson 234-39; and Brewer 95-105.

    3. Charles K. Smith, *Thomas Hardy: The Early Novels* (New York: Oxford UP, 1998) 276.

Formatting a Superscript Number in Microsoft Word

In Microsoft Word, highlight or select the footnote or endnote number you wish to appear in superscript (on the top half of the line). Click on **Format,** and then click on **Font.** Check **Superscript,** and then click **OK.**

Formatting Footnotes and Endnotes in Microsoft Word

Most word-processing programs will format footnotes and endnotes for you. In Microsoft Word, you will find the footnote/endnote function under the **Insert** menu. Click on **Reference,** and follow the instructions. Click on **Help** at the top of your screen for additional instructions.

Endnotes

1. Center the word *Notes* one inch from the top of a new page, double-space, and begin your list of notes.
2. Double-space everything on your endnote page.
3. The first line of an endnote is indented one-half inch (on a computer) or five spaces (on a typewriter) from the left margin; subsequent lines begin flush with the left margin.
4. Type the endnote (or footnote) number on the top half of the line at the end of the sentence (after the period) or phrase in your paper to which the note refers. This is called a *superscript number*.
5. Type the matching endnote number, a period, and a space at the beginning of the note on the endnote page. Then continue with the material in the endnote.
6. Number the endnote page as a part of your text, and place this page after the last page of your paper and before the list of works cited.

Footnotes

1. Footnotes are typed at the bottoms of the pages.
2. Indent the first line as noted above and type the footnote number, a period, and one space. Then continue with the material in the footnote.
3. Leave four lines (two double spaces) between your text and the first footnote.
4. Single-space the material in each footnote, but double-space between the footnotes.
5. If you need to continue a footnote from one page to the next, double-space after the text for the next page ends, type a line across the page, and double-space again. Then begin the footnote continued from the previous page, followed by the rest of the footnotes for that page.
6. Number footnotes consecutively throughout the paper.

CHAPTER 16

Quotations

Avoiding the Use of Too Many Quotations

Avoid using an excessive number of quotations in your paper. Most of the paper should be your own explanation or analysis of the subject presented in your own words.

Use quotations for the following reasons:

- To vividly illustrate a point you want the reader to see
- To back up what you have said with an expert's opinion
- To prove to your reader that you have adequately researched your topic by incorporating expert opinions into your text
- Because the writer in your source has explained a point so precisely and beautifully that a paraphrase or summary would not do justice to the original

Sometimes, using a quotation is much more vivid than explaining an idea in your own words.

Explanation of an idea in your own words:

Biff tells his father that they are both ordinary men--not winners.

Quotation:

Biff tells his father, "Pop! I'm a dime a dozen, and so are you!" (Miller 1833).

Your explanation combined with the author's vivid wording:

Biff tells his father that they are both ordinary men--not winners: "Pop! I'm a dime a dozen, and so are you!" (Miller 1833).

Punctuating a Short Quotation Ending in a Question Mark or an Exclamation Point

If a short quotation ends with a question mark or an exclamation point, type the end quotation mark after the question mark or exclamation point, type one space after the end quotation mark, and type the parenthetical citation, followed by a period: "last word?" (34). OR "last word!" (34).

As the novel ends, Hawthorne tells us that "Hester Prynne had returned [to Boston], and taken up her long-forsaken shame. But where was little Pearl?" (176; ch. 24).

By the last pages of the novel, Hester's scarlet symbol is looked upon with "awe" and "reverence" and brings troubled people to her door in search of comfort and advice: "[P]eople brought all their sorrows and perplexities . . . to Hester's cottage demanding why they were so wretched, and what the remedy!" (Hawthorne 177; ch. 24).

If the material ending with a question mark or exclamation point is dialogue and therefore already in quotation marks in the text of the work from which you are quoting, type the question mark or exclamation point inside both the single and the double quotation marks; then type one space, the parenthetical citation, and a period: "'last word?'" (105). OR "'last word!'" (105).

When the Rev. Dimmesdale invites Hester and Pearl to stand beside him on the scaffold at night, Pearl asks the minister, "'Wilt thou stand here with mother and me, tomorrow noontide?'" (Hawthorne 105; ch. 12).

Foreshadowing the end of the novel, Dimmesdale replies, "'I shall, indeed, stand with thy mother and thee one other day, but not tomorrow!'" (Hawthorne 105; ch. 12).

Short Quotations

- One to four lines in length when the quoted material is typed into your paper.
- In double quotation marks within the regular text of the paper.
- Double-spaced.
- Not indented.
- Words or phrases that appear in double quotation marks in your source should be typed in single quotation marks in your text.
- Words italicized or printed in bold in your source should be italicized or formatted in bold in your paper.
- An ellipsis (three spaced periods) should be used to indicate that material that is not already obvious has been omitted from the quotation.
- The parenthetical citation should be placed at the end of the quotation and before the nearest internal or the final punctuation mark.
- Always connected to your text by an introduction or lead-in of some sort—naming the writer or speaker, if possible.

```
In the beginning moments of his short story "The Open Boat,"
Stephen Crane emphasizes the violence of the sea: "These waves
were most wrongfully and barbarously abrupt and tall, and each
froth-top was a problem in small boat navigation" (1492).
```

Long, Block Quotations

- More than four lines in length when the quoted material is typed into your paper.
- Indented one inch (or ten spaces on a typewriter) from the left margin.
- Not indented from the right margin.
- Double-spaced.
- No quotation marks are necessary (unless they appear in the text you are quoting) because indenting the material identifies it as a quotation.
- Any single or double quotation marks should be copied exactly as they appear in your source.
- Any words italicized or printed in bold should be reproduced exactly as they appear in your source.
- An ellipsis (three spaced periods) should be used to indicate that material that is not already obvious has been omitted from the quotation.

- The parenthetical citation should be placed at the end of the quotation and after the final punctuation mark.
- Always connected to your text with an introduction or lead-in of some sort—naming the writer or speaker, if possible.

Michael J. Colacurcio writes:

> So teasing do Hawthorne's connections and analogies come to seem, that we are eventually led to wonder whether *The Scarlet Letter* shows only this one set of historical footprints. If Hester Prynne bears relation to Ann Hutchinson, would it be too outrageous to look for similarities between Arthur Dimmesdale and John Cotton, that high Calvinist who was variously asserted and denied to be the [Hutchinson's] partner in heresy? And . . . might there not be some fundamental relation between the deepest philosophicel [sic] and theological "issues" raised by the Antinomian Controversy and the "themes" of Hawthorne's romance? (216)

1. In the preceding quotation, the student writer has given the literary critic's full name in the lead-in to the quotation rather than giving only the critic's last name at the end in the parenthetical citation. If the student had cited material from this writer earlier in the paper, he or she would give only the last name in the introduction to the quotation (e.g., *Colacurcio writes:*).
2. The title of the novel (*The Scarlet Letter*) is in italics.
3. The word *Hutchinson's* has been placed in square brackets to clarify who "the partner in heresy" (of John Cotton) was thought to have been.
4. An ellipsis (three spaced periods) is used to indicate that a phrase was omitted between the word *And* and the word *might*.
5. The Latin word *sic* (not italicized) in square brackets is used to show that the word *philosophical* was misspelled in the source and is not the student's error.
6. The double quotation marks around the words *issues* and *themes* are copied exactly as they appear in the original text that is being quoted.

7. The parenthetical citation is placed **after** the punctuation mark ending the quoted material.

Indenting Paragraphs in a Block Quotation

1. If you quote two or more entire paragraphs from your source, indent the first sentence of each new paragraph an additional one-quarter inch (one and one-quarter inches total) from the left margin if you are working on a computer. On a typewriter, indent each new paragraph an additional three spaces (thirteen spaces total) from the left margin.

2. If the first sentence of your quotation is not the first sentence in a new paragraph in your source, however, do not indent it more than the usual one inch (or ten spaces on a typewriter) from the left margin. Indent only the first sentence of the second or third paragraphs the additional one-quarter inch (or three spaces).

In this scene the correspondent realizes for perhaps the first time that if he drowns in the sea, nature will continue without interruption, not even taking notice of his absence:

> When it occurs to a man that nature does not regard him as important, and that she feels she would not maim the universe by disposing of him, he at first wishes to throw bricks at the temple, and he hates deeply the fact that there are no bricks and no temples. Any visible expression of nature would surely be pelleted with his jeers.
>
> Then, if there be no tangible thing to hoot, he feels, perhaps, the desire to confront a personification and indulge in pleas, bowed to one knee, and with hands supplicant, saying, "Yes, but I love myself."
>
> A high cold star on a winter's night is the word he feels that she says to him. Thereafter he knows the pathos of his situation. (Crane 1503)

1. Note that three full paragraphs are quoted from Stephen Crane's short story "The Open Boat."

2. Each paragraph is indented one and one-quarter inches from the left margin.

3. No quotation marks are used at the beginning or at the end of the quotation because the block format identifies the material as a quotation.

4. Note that the double quotation marks from the source are duplicated exactly as they appear in Crane's text. (If this had been a short quotation, the writer would have changed Crane's double quotation marks to single quotation marks.)

5. Note that the parenthetical citation is typed **after the period** that ends the quotation. (If this had been a short quotation, the citation would have been typed before, not after, the period that ends the sentence.)

Quoting Dialogue from a Novel or Short Story: Short Quotations

Dialogue quoted from a novel or short story should be placed in both single and double quotation marks. The double quotation marks tell your reader that you are quoting material from your source, and the single quotation marks replace the double quotation marks that appeared in your source.

In the forest scene Hawthorne describes Pearl's intuitive sense of what Dimmesdale must do to save his soul: "'Doth he love us?' said Pearl, looking up with acute intelligence into her mother's face. 'Will he go back with us, hand in hand, we three together into the town?'" (144; ch. 18).

Quoting Dialogue from a Play: Short Quotations

Dialogue quoted from a play will usually be printed without quotation marks in your source. In a short quotation, use double quotation marks around dialogue in a play.

In a desperate attempt to escape from what he perceives as a futile pursuit of the American Dream, Biff pleads with

> ## Naming the Writer or Speaker in the Introduction to a Quotation
>
> 1. As a general rule, give the name of the writer of the words that you are quoting in your introduction to the quotation rather than in the parenthetical citation.
> 2. If it seems appropriate, you can also include the writer's credentials in your lead-in to the quotation to explain why your reader should believe the opinions expressed by this writer.
> 3. Avoid, however, pointing out what will already be obvious to your reader. For example, you need not tell the reader of a literary analysis essay that you are quoting literary critics. Just give the critic's name in your lead-in.
> 4. The first time you quote (or paraphrase or summarize) from a literary critic or other expert writer, give his or her full name in the introduction to the material you are quoting. Thereafter, you may give only the writer's last name in your introductory material.
> 5. When you quote dialogue in papers analyzing literary works, identify in your introduction to the quotation the character who is speaking.

```
his father: "Will you let me go, for Christ sake? Will you
take that phony dream and burn it before something happens?"
(Miller 1833).
```

Quoting Dialogue from a Play: Long Quotations

1. If you wish to quote dialogue spoken by two or more characters in a play, indent the material you are quoting one inch (or ten spaces on a typewriter) from the left margin.
2. Type each character's name in all capital letters and follow with a period and a space. Then type the character's speech, indenting all lines after the first in the speech an additional one-quarter inch (one and one-quarter inches total) from the left margin on a computer and three additional spaces (thirteen spaces total) from the left margin on a typewriter.
3. Then indent one inch (or ten spaces on a typewriter) from the left margin, and type the second character's name in all capital letters followed by a period, one space, and that character's speech.
4. Except for the character identifications, reproduce any words italicized or printed in bold exactly as they appear in your source. In the following quotation, note that the stage directions, which appear in italics in the text of the play, have been reproduced in italics in the student's quotation.

Willy believes his brother Ben has achieved the American Dream
and is therefore "a great man":

> WILLY. No! Boys! Boys! *(Young Biff and Happy appear.)*
> Listen to this. This is your Uncle Ben, a great
> man! Tell my boys, Ben!
>
> BEN. Why, boys, when I was seventeen I walked into
> the jungle, and when I was twenty-one I walked
> out. *(He laughs.)* And by God I was rich.
>
> WILLY. *(to the boys)* You see what I been talking about?
> The greatest things can happen! (Miller 1791)

Quoting Poetry: Short Quotations

1. One to three lines of poetry may be incorporated into the text of your
   paper in quotation marks. Type a space, a slash, and another space between each line to identify the line breaks.
2. Type single quotation marks around any words, phrases, or sentences
   that appear in double quotation marks in your source. Reproduce any
   italics or bold appearing in your source.

In his sonnet "My mistress' eyes are nothing like the sun,"
Shakespeare suggests that a man who is truly in love accepts
his beloved just as she is: "And yet, by heaven, I think
my love as rare / As any she belied with false compare"
(lines 13-14).

3. However, if you wish to place special emphasis on one to three lines of
   poetry, indent the lines one inch (or ten spaces on a typewriter) from the
   left margin and reproduce the lines exactly as they appear in your source.

Shakespeare suggests in his sonnet "My mistress' eyes are nothing like the sun" that one who is truly in love accepts his
beloved just as she is:

> And yet, by heaven, I think my love as rare
> As any she belied with false compare. (lines 13-14)

Quoting Poetry: Long Quotations

1. If you are quoting more than three lines of poetry, indent the lines one inch (or ten spaces on a typewriter) from the left margin, and type the lines exactly as they appear in your source except that the lines should be double-spaced.

2. Do not use quotation marks around the lines because indenting the poetry identifies the lines as quoted material.

3. If any quotation marks appear in the poetry, reproduce them as they appear in your source. Reproduce exactly any italics or bold.

In Keats's "Ode on a Grecian Urn," the young lovers will be
forever young and in love:

> Fair youth, beneath the trees, thou canst not leave
> Thy song, nor ever can those trees be bare;
> Bold lover, never, never canst thou kiss,
> Though winning near the goal—yet, do not grieve;
> She cannot fade, though thou hast not thy bliss,
> For ever wilt thou love, and she be fair!
>
> (lines 15-20)

4. If the lines you are quoting are too long to fit on a single line in your text, you may reduce the indentation from the left margin to less than one inch (or to fewer than ten spaces on a typewriter) if this reduction will allow the lines to fit. If this plan does not work, continue the line of poetry onto the next line, and indent an additional one-quarter inch (or three additional spaces on a typewriter) to show your reader that this material is still part of the same line.

Walt Whitman describes the horrors of the Civil War in these
lines from his poem "The Wound-Dresser":

> I dress the perforated shoulder, the foot with the
> bullet-wound,
> Cleanse the one with a gnawing and putrid gangrene, so
> sickening, so offensive,

```
While the attendant stands behind aside me holding the
    tray and pail.
I am faithful. I do not give out.
The fractured thigh, the knee, the wound in the
    abdomen,
These and more I dress with impassive hand, (yet deep
    in my breast a fire, a burning flame). (lines 50-56)
```

5. If the lines of the poem are arranged in an unusual way in your source, reproduce the spatial arrangement of the lines as closely as you can, reducing the indentation to less than one inch (or fewer than ten spaces) if necessary.

```
In these lines, George Herbert describes God's power to help
the sinner overcome adversity:
                    With thee
               Let me combine,
            And feel this day thy victory
            For if I imp my wing on thine,
        Affliction shall advance the flight in me. (lines 16-20)
```

Parenthetical Citation for a Short Poetry Quotation

1. In your first parenthetical citation, type *line* or *lines* (lines 4-8). Once you have informed your reader that you are giving line numbers rather than page numbers, you may give the line numbers alone (4-8). Do not use the abbreviations *l.* and *ll.* because they could be confused with numbers.

2. Type the parenthetical citation before the period that ends the sentence.

```
William Blake asks whether God created both good and evil in
this line from "The Tyger": "Did he who made the Lamb make
thee?" (line 20).
```

Parenthetical Citation for a Long, Block Poetry Quotation

1. At the end of the quotation, type a period or other end punctuation, one space, and the parenthetical citation (not followed by a period).

2. If you use an ellipsis to show that you omitted the final words in a poetic sentence, leave no space before the first period of the ellipsis. Type one space after the ellipsis, and type a fourth period to end the poetic sentence. Type one space after the fourth period, and give the parenthetical citation (not followed by a period).

3. If the parenthetical citation will not fit on the last line, type it on the next line so that it ends at the right margin.

These lines from Ken McLaurin's poem "Cancer" suggest that the traumatic experiences of one's life can never truly be escaped:

> You tell yourself what's done is done—
>
> we bury the dead in many ways.
>
> But the snug fit of bone doesn't leave
>
> your hand, deforming every fist you try,
>
> every touch you offer. And when
>
> you meet strangers or the long absent,
>
> you give them that hand to squeeze
>
> its bones close to theirs, and always
>
> in between, you feel that other. (lines 14-22)

Using an Ellipsis to Omit Lines of Poetry

If you wish to omit one or more lines from a block poetic quotation, type a line of spaced periods to identify the location of the omitted material. Note that because the parenthetical citation in the following example would not fit on the last line quoted, it is typed so that it ends flush with the right margin. Also note that it is not followed by a period.

Because poet John Donne believes in the immortality of his soul, he has no fear of death:

> Death be not proud, though some have called thee
>
> Mighty and dreadful, for thou art not so;

For those whom thou think'st thou dost overthrow

Die not, poor death, nor yet canst thou kill me.

. . . .

One short sleep past, we wake eternally,

And death shall be no more; death, thou shalt die.

(lines 1-4, 13-14)

CHAPTER 17

Using Square Brackets in Quotations

Because you must quote precisely, any changes that you make to a quotation must be placed in square brackets. If square brackets are not available on your keyboard, leave spaces and add them with a pen.

Use Brackets to Explain Something That Might Be Unclear to Your Reader or to Give Additional Information

Although, as Hawthorne tells us, "Pearl . . . could have borne a fair examination in the New England Primer [a popular textbook that taught religious precepts to the Puritan children]" (77; ch. 8), she refuses to give the expected answer to Mr. Wilson's question as to who created her.

The bracketed explanation identifying the *New England Primer* could also be placed in a footnote or endnote, which is a better choice if the explanatory material is lengthy.

Use Brackets to Clarify a Pronoun

If the noun to which a pronoun in your quotation refers (the antecedent of the pronoun) might be unclear to your reader, identify the noun in square brackets after the pronoun or replace the unclear pronoun with the noun in square brackets.

Hawthorne writes, "Tempted by a dream of happiness, he [Dimmesdale] had yielded himself with deliberate choice, as he had never done before, to what he knew was deadly sin" (150; ch. 18).

Use Brackets to Change Verb Tenses

It is common practice to analyze literary works in present tense. Thus, you would write, "Pearl **is** a difficult child" rather than "Pearl **was** a difficult child" in an analysis of Hawthorne's *The Scarlet Letter.* If you are quoting a critic who has used a past tense verb in a particular sentence, you may change the tense of the critic's verb by typing the tense you wish to use in square brackets. This bracketed change of tense avoids an awkward verb tense shift in your text.

As a general rule of thumb, however, avoid changing the tense of verbs in the text of a literary work you are analyzing. One way to avoid the need to change tenses in brackets is to quote short phrases from the source rather than entire sentences.

Original sentence containing an awkward verb tense shift:

As Frederick C. Crews points out, "Hawthorne carried symbolism to the border of allegory but did not cross over" (369).

Verb tense changed in brackets to avoid a verb tense shift:

As Frederick C. Crews points out, "Hawthorne [carries] symbolism to the border of allegory but [does] not cross over" (369).

Short phrases quoted to avoid the need for a bracketed tense change:

Frederick C. Crews points out that although Hawthorne often takes his symbolism "to the border of allegory," he does not "cross over" (369).

Use Brackets to Change a Capital Letter to a Lowercase Letter

Sometimes when you are quoting, your sentence structure requires a lowercase letter rather than a capital letter or vice versa. You may change the capital letter in your source to a lowercase letter in square brackets. For example, when the lead-in to your quotation ends in *that,* the quoted material should begin with a lowercase letter to be grammatically correct.

When Hawthorne tells us that "[t]he scarlet letter had not done its office" (114; ch. 13), he means that Hester has not yet learned the lesson the scarlet letter was intended to teach her.

Use Brackets to Change a Lowercase Letter to a Capital Letter

In the quotation below, note that no ellipsis is needed before the word *[L]ittle* because the bracketed letter informs the reader that the words preceding the bracketed letter were omitted from the quoted sentence.

Hawthorne describes Hester's acceptance of the pain inflicted upon her by the scarlet letter in this scene:

> [L]ittle Pearl paused to gather the prickly burrs from a tall burdock, which grew beside the tomb. Taking a handful of these, she arranged them along the lines of the scarlet letter that decorated the maternal bosom, to which the burrs, as their nature was, tenaciously adhered. Hester did not pluck them off.
>
> (92; ch. 10)

Use [sic] to Indicate an Error in Your Source

You must quote precisely from your sources. Therefore, if you find a logical, typographical, spelling, grammatical, punctuation, or other type of error in the material you wish to quote, do not correct it. Instead, type the word *sic* (Latin for "thus") in square brackets after the error to show your reader that the error was in your source and is not your copying or typing error.

Note that in the quotation that follows, the word *religious* was misspelled in the source. The error is identified as a typographical error in the source by the placement of [sic] after the misspelled word.

Hawthorne tells us that had it not been for her sin, Hester "might have come down to us in history, hand in hand with Ann Hutchinson, as the foundress of a religous [sic] sect" (113; ch. 13).

Do Not Use [sic] after Intentional Errors
Such as Dialect Spellings

In the last lines of the novel Huck tells us, "[T]here ain't
nothing more to write about, and I am rotten glad of it, because if I'd a knowed what a trouble it was to make a book I
wouldn't a tackled it and ain't agoing to no more" (Twain 1380;
ch. 43).

CHAPTER 18

Using an Ellipsis to Omit Words

If you wish to omit words, phrases, or sentences from a quotation that appears to be a complete sentence or paragraph, you must inform your reader that you have omitted material by using an ellipsis (three spaced periods). Unless you are quoting single words or brief phrases or unless the omission is already obvious to your reader, as described in some of the examples in this chapter, you need to use an ellipsis.

You may not change the meaning the author intended by using an ellipsis.

If you have omitted material from a sentence and what remains appears to be a complete sentence, you must use an ellipsis to inform your reader that a portion of the material in the original sentence has been omitted. In addition, even though some of the sentence has been omitted, the portion of the sentence that remains must be grammatically correct, faithful to what the writer of the quoted material intended to say, and clear in meaning to your reader.

If you have omitted material from a series of sentences or from a paragraph or more used in a block quotation and what remains appears to contain no obvious omissions, you must use an ellipsis to inform your reader that a portion of the material has been omitted. Despite your omission(s), the material that remains must be grammatically correct, faithful to what the writer of the quoted material intended to say, and clear in meaning to your reader.

If you are quoting single words or brief phrases, the combination of your words and the quoted words and phrases must be grammatically correct and clear to your reader.

1. To create an ellipsis, type a period, a space, a period, a space, and a period: . . .
2. If the ellipsis falls in the middle of a sentence, leave one space before the ellipsis and another space after the ellipsis.
3. If material has been omitted at the end of a short quotation, leave one space before the first ellipsis period and type the quotation mark immediately

after the third period of the ellipsis. Then type the parenthetical citation in parentheses followed by a period to end the sentence:
. . ." (324).

4. If material has been omitted from the end of the final sentence of a block quotation, leave no space before the first ellipsis period, and type the three spaced ellipsis periods, one space, and a fourth period to end the sentence. After the fourth period, type one space followed by the parenthetical citation. Do not type a period after the parenthetical citation that ends a block quotation: last word. . . . (304-05)

5. If you wish to omit material from a quotation that already contains an ellipsis, format your ellipsis in square brackets to distinguish it from the ellipsis used by the author whom you are quoting.

6. It is also acceptable, according to the 2008 MLA guidelines, to format all ellipses in square brackets if your professor prefers that all alterations in source materials are consistently formatted in brackets, as described in chapter 17: [. . .]

7. Follow the guidelines described above to omit material from quoted poetry.

8. If you wish, however, to omit one or more lines from a block poetry quotation, type a line of spaced periods equal in length to the line of poetry that precedes the ellipsis.

Read the following analysis of Pearl, the daughter of Hester Prynne, Nathaniel Hawthorne's most famous heroine, carefully so that you will understand the examples that follow.

Original material from Richard Harter Fogle's book:

> Pearl is pure symbol, the living emblem of the sin, a human embodiment of the Scarlet Letter. Her mission is to keep Hester's adultery always before her eyes, to prevent her from attempting to escape its moral consequences. Pearl's childish questions are fiendishly apt; in speech and in action she never strays from the control of her symbolic function; her dress and her looks are related to the letter. When Hester casts the letter away in the forest, Pearl forces her to reassume it by flying into an uncontrollable rage. Yet despite the undeviating arrangement of every

> circumstance which surrounds her, no single action
> of hers is ever incredible or inconsistent with the
> conceivable actions of any child under the same con-
> ditions. (312-13)

No Ellipsis Needed with Quoted Phrases

You do not need to use an ellipsis or ellipses when you are quoting brief phrases from your source. The lowercase letters and incomplete sentence structures will make it clear to your reader that you have not quoted the entire sentence from your source.

> As Richard Harter Fogle points out, Hawthorne uses Pearl as
> "a human embodiment of the Scarlet Letter" (313).

Omitting Words from the Beginning of a Quoted Sentence

When you omit material from your source, be careful not to create an unclear sentence, a grammatically incorrect sentence, or a sentence fragment. Note that in the quotation that follows, the quoted material is a grammatically correct sentence even though some material has been omitted.

When you introduce a quotation using wording ending in *that,* use a lowercase letter at the beginning of the quotation. The lowercase letter informs your reader that material has been omitted from the beginning of the quoted sentence. Because the omission is obvious, no ellipsis is needed.

> Richard Harter Fogle explains that "in speech and in action
> [Pearl] never strays from the control of her symbolic function;
> her dress and her looks are related to the [scarlet] letter"
> (313).

In the next example, the lowercase letter that appears in Fogle's sentence is changed to a capital letter inside square brackets because the quoted material is a grammatically complete sentence, which must begin with a capital letter. The bracketed letter informs the reader that material has been omitted from the beginning of the quoted sentence. Therefore, no ellipsis is needed.

> According to Richard Harter Fogle, "[I]n speech and in action
> [Pearl] never strays from the control of her symbolic function;

her dress and her looks are related to the [scarlet] letter"
(313).

Use an ellipsis to show that material has been omitted from the beginning of a quotation when the quotation appears to be a complete sentence and when without the ellipsis your reader would not be able to tell that material has been omitted. In the example below, *Pearl* was not the first word of Fogle's sentence.

Fogle notes that when Hester removes the symbol of her adultery in the forest scene, ". . . Pearl forces her to reassume it by flying into an uncontrollable rage" (313).

Ellipsis Used to Omit Words in the Middle of a Sentence in a Short Quotation

If the ellipsis falls in the middle of a quoted sentence, leave one space before the ellipsis and another space after the ellipsis. Note that even with the omission, the following quotation is a clear, grammatically correct sentence.

As Richard Harter Fogle points out, "Pearl is . . . the living emblem of the sin, a human embodiment of the Scarlet Letter" (312-13).

Make sure that what remains of the sentence is punctuated correctly, either by using the punctuation as it appears in the source or by altering the punctuation so that what remains is correctly punctuated.

"Pearl is pure symbol, . . . a human embodiment of the Scarlet Letter," writes Fogle (312-13).

Ellipsis Used to Omit Words at the End of a Sentence in a Short Quotation

If material has been omitted at the end of a sentence in a short quotation, leave one space before the first ellipsis period and type the quotation mark immediately after the third period of the ellipsis. After the quotation mark, type one space and the parenthetical citation in parentheses and follow with a period to end the sentence: . . ." (324).

Richard Harter Fogle believes that "Pearl's childish questions are fiendishly apt; in speech and in action she never strays from the control of her symbolic function . . ." (313).

If the author identification is placed at the end of the quoted material, type a comma immediately after the third period of the ellipsis and then type the end quotation mark followed by one space, the author identification followed by one space, and the parenthetical citation followed by a period to end the sentence.

"Pearl is pure symbol, the living emblem of the sin, a human embodiment of the Scarlet Letter. Her mission is to keep Hester's adultery always before her eyes . . .," writes Richard Harter Fogle (312-13).

Ellipsis Used to Omit One or Several Sentences from the Middle of a Block Quotation

After the end period for the sentence preceding the omission, type one space, the ellipsis (three spaced periods), and another space. Then begin the next sentence you wish to quote.

Richard Harter Fogle writes:

> Pearl is pure symbol, the living emblem of the sin, a human embodiment of the Scarlet Letter. Her mission is to keep Hester's adultery always before her eyes, to prevent her from attempting to escape its moral consequences. . . . When Hester casts the letter away in the forest, Pearl forces her to reassume it by flying into an uncontrollable rage. (312-13)

Ellipsis Used to Omit Material from the Middle of One Sentence to the End of Another in a Block Quotation

Leave no space before the first period of the ellipsis. After the ellipsis, type one space, a fourth period to end the sentence, and another space. Then begin the next sentence.

Richard Harter Fogle explains that

> Pearl is pure symbol, the living emblem of the sin, a human embodiment of the Scarlet Letter. Her mission is to keep Hester's adultery always before her eyes. . . . When Hester casts the letter away in the forest, Pearl forces her to reassume it by flying into an uncontrollable rage. Yet despite the undeviating arrangement of every circumstance which surrounds her, no single action of hers is ever incredible or inconsistent with the conceivable actions of any child under the same conditions. (312-13)

Ellipsis Used to Omit Material from the Middle of One Sentence to the Middle of Another Sentence in a Block Quotation

Leave one space before and another space after the ellipsis.

Since you are creating a new sentence out of two partial sentences in your source, make sure the sentence that remains is correctly punctuated by retaining the punctuation in the source or by altering the punctuation as necessary. If the semicolon had been omitted before the ellipsis in the example below, the remaining sentence would be a run-on or fused sentence.

According to Richard Harter Fogle,

> Pearl is pure symbol, the living emblem of the sin, a human embodiment of the Scarlet Letter. Her mission is to keep Hester's adultery always before her eyes,

> to prevent her from attempting to escape its moral
> consequences. Pearl's childish questions are fiend-
> ishly apt; . . . no single action of hers is ever
> incredible or inconsistent with the conceivable
> actions of any child under the same conditions.
> (312-13)

Ellipsis Used to Omit Material from the End of a Block Quotation

If material has been omitted from the end of the final sentence of a block quotation, leave no space before the first ellipsis period; type the three spaced ellipsis periods, one space, and a fourth period to end the sentence. After the fourth period, type one space and then type the parenthetical citation. Do not type a period after the parenthetical citation that ends a block quotation: last word. . . . (304-05)

According to Richard Harter Fogle,

> Pearl is pure symbol, the living emblem of the sin,
> a human embodiment of the Scarlet Letter. Her mission
> is to keep Hester's adultery always before her eyes,
> to prevent her from attempting to escape its moral
> consequences. Pearl's childish questions are fiend-
> ishly apt; in speech and in action she never strays
> from the control of her symbolic function. . . .
> (312-13)

Using a Bracketed Ellipsis

1. To format an ellipsis in square brackets, leave one space before the opening bracket; type the bracket, a period, a space, a period, a space, a period, the closing bracket, and another space: [. . .]
2. If a parenthetical citation is needed after a bracketed ellipsis at the end of a short quotation, type the end quotation mark immediately after the closing bracket, type one space, and give the parenthetical citation in parentheses followed by a period: [. . .]" (344).

3. If a parenthetical citation is needed after a bracketed ellipsis at the end of a block quotation, type the bracketed ellipsis, a period, and one space. Then type the parenthetical citation in parentheses (not followed by a period): [. . .]. (304-05)

Bracketed Ellipsis Used to Omit Material from a Quotation Already Containing an Ellipsis

Literary critics regularly quote from the text of whatever work they are analyzing. If a portion of what you are quoting was written by the critic and other portions of your quotation were taken by the critic from the text of the work being analyzed and if the quoted material from the text of the work contains an ellipsis used by the critic, format any ellipses you wish to use in square brackets to distinguish your ellipses from the ellipses of the critic.

You may quote a mixture of a critic's words and words quoted from the literary work being analyzed, but if your entire quotation comes from the text of the literary work, quote from your textbook or from whatever text of the work you are citing as the basis for your analysis.

In the following example, Frederic I. Carpenter quotes from *The Scarlet Letter* as he analyzes the scene in which Hester Prynne tries to convince Arthur Dimmesdale to leave Boston in search of a better life. Carpenter's ellipsis is not formatted in square brackets. The bracketed ellipses identify the omissions of the student writer quoting from Carpenter.

According to Frederic I. Carpenter,

> Hester [. . .] envisions the transcendental ideal of positive freedom, instead of the romantic ideal of mere escape. She urges her lover to create a new life with her in the wilderness: "Doth the universe lie within the compass of yonder town? [. . .]" And she seeks to arouse him to a pragmatic idealism equal to the task: "Exchange this false life of thine for a true one! . . . Preach! Write! Act! Do anything save to lie down and die!" Thus Hester Prynne embodies the authentic American dream of a new life in the wilderness of the new world, and of self-reliant action to realize that ideal. (299-300)

Bracketed Ellipsis Used to Omit Material from a Critical Analysis Containing an Indirect Quotation Already Containing an Ellipsis

Literary critics often quote from the analyses of other critics. If a portion of what you are quoting was written by the critic whose analysis you are reading and other portions of your quotation were taken from a second critic whose analysis the first critic is discussing and if the material quoted from the second critic contains an ellipsis, format any ellipses you wish to use in square brackets to distinguish your ellipses from the ellipses of the critic who wrote the article or book you are citing.

In the following example, Nina Baym uses an ellipsis while quoting from Darrel Abel's analysis of *The Scarlet Letter*. The ellipsis not formatted in brackets identifies Baym's omission. The bracketed ellipses identify materials omitted by the student writer quoting Baym's analysis.

An ellipsis used in the middle of a block quotation can be used to denote the omission of any amount of text—from a single word to a brief phrase, a single sentence, or a number of sentences.

In the quotation below, the first bracketed ellipsis denotes the omission of a brief phrase from material quoted from Abel (an indirect quotation), the second bracketed ellipsis denotes the student writer's omission of a single sentence written by Baym, and the third bracketed ellipsis denotes the student writer's omission of several sentences written by Baym.

Nina Baym disputes Darrel Abel's claim that Arthur Dimmesdale, not Hester Prynne, is the protagonist of *The Scarlet Letter:*

> Abel makes the best case he can for Dimmesdale as protagonist in "Hawthorne's Dimmesdale," necessarily at the expense of order, proportions, and emphasis in the plot. In fact, Abel goes so far as to assert that, for all practical purposes, *The Scarlet Letter* has no plot at all. "The situation is presented . . . in exposition and spaced scenes which picture the positions that the exposition prepares. Hawthorne's narrative does not have the dramatic continuity of a

moving picture; it has the static consecutiveness
of a series of lantern slides [. . .]." Because
there is no plot per se, it is permissible for the
critic to infer a plot from the sequence of lantern
slides, and Abel infers that the "plot" of *The Scarlet Letter* consists of the "struggle between God and
the Devil for the soul of Arthur Dimmesdale." [. . .]
As I have suggested above, more than half of the
story has nothing to do with Dimmesdale [. . .].
Whether we look at it as a plot of forbidden love
or a plot of false appearances, we must see that
Dimmesdale is the less weighty of the two characters.
(406-07)

Ellipsis Used to Omit One or More Lines from a Block Poetry Quotation

If you wish to omit one or more lines from a block poetry quotation, type a line of spaced periods equal in length to the line of poetry that precedes the ellipsis.

Ken McLaurin describes a child's fear of death in these lines
from "Storm Pit":
        As a child I went down into earth
        when the west turned black with clouds.
        I was jealous when Mama held Daddy's head
        in her lap, and scared like him, praying.

        . . . .
        I worried about floods, whether ferry existed
        to carry my soul unburied in that gloomy hole.
        The sky raging, I worried if I had a soul.
        As a child I went down into earth. (lines 1-4, 15-19)

Ellipsis Used to Omit Material from the End of a Block Poetry Quotation

If material has been omitted from the end of the final sentence of a block poetry quotation, leave no space before the first ellipsis period; type the three spaced ellipsis periods, one space, and a fourth period to end the sentence. After the fourth period, type one space followed by the parenthetical citation. Do not type a period after the parenthetical citation that ends a block quotation: last word. . . . (lines 106-11)

In the example below, one line has been omitted after the word *pain* (indicated by a full line of ellipsis points), four lines have been omitted after the word *ptomaine* (indicated by a full line of ellipsis points), and the words after *names* in the poetic sentence have been omitted. Therefore, the dash that appears after the word *names* in the poem has been changed to a period with no spaces before it, followed by three additional spaced periods, one space, and the parenthetical citation in parentheses (not followed by a period).

In his poem "The Bee Constellation," Ken McLaurin describes the speaker's childhood memory of his mother and her quilting bee companions as they discuss the exotically named ailments of the inhabitants of their community:

> Centered under the great belly of cloth
>
> I watched needles flash
>
> stitching a zodiac I connected
>
> to the language of pain.
>
> . . . .
>
> [F]our quilters (my mother one of them)
>
> exhausted the list of the sick:
>
> milk leg, phlebitis, pleurisy, ptomaine.
>
> . . . .
>
>   All summer
>
> their bodies the four directions walling me,
>
> I played, the voices no more than the wind outside
>
> except for the gusts of exotic names. . . .
>
>   (lines 1-4, 6-8, 13-16)

CHAPTER 19

Punctuating Quotations

When you quote, reproduce the internal punctuation of the original material exactly, except that in a short quotation you may change double quotation marks in your source to single quotation marks to show that the material appeared in double quotation marks in your source. You may also alter the internal and end punctuation of a quotation so that the combination of the quoted material and your words is punctuated correctly.

Your lead-in or explanatory material combined with the quoted material must read as a correctly punctuated, grammatically correct sentence.

Using Single Quotation Marks inside Double Quotation Marks

In a short quotation, use single quotation marks inside double quotation marks to indicate that the material was already in quotation marks in the text from which you are quoting.

```
" 'If we don't all get ashore--' said the captain. 'If we don't
all get ashore, I suppose you fellows know where to send news
of my finish?' " (Crane 1497).
```

Altering End Punctuation

You may alter the end punctuation of a quotation so that the combination of the quoted material and your words is punctuated correctly.

Sentence as printed in Hawthorne's "Young Goodman Brown":

```
A stern, a sad, a darkly meditative, a distrustful, if not
a desperate man did he become from the night of that fearful
dream. (428)
```

Quotation incorporated into your paper (internal punctuation remains the same; end period has been changed to a comma):

"A stern, a sad, a darkly meditative, a distrustful, if not
a desperate man did he become from the night of that fearful
dream," writes Hawthorne (428).

Placing Commas and Periods inside Ending Quotation Marks

Commas and periods are always typed inside ending quotation marks.

"I enjoyed the book I read last night," she said.
She said, "I enjoyed the book I read last night."

The end period is placed after the parenthetical citation at the end of a short quotation, however.

"It would be difficult to describe the subtle brotherhood of
men that was here established on the seas. [I]t dwelt in the
boat, and each man felt it warm him," explains the correspondent in Crane's "The Open Boat" (1495).

Placing Commas and Periods inside Single and Double Ending Quotation Marks

A comma or period should be typed inside the single quotation mark when single and double quotation marks are used together.

"I enjoyed reading Poe's 'Annabel Lee,'" she said.
She said, "I enjoyed reading Poe's 'Annabel Lee.'"

Placing Semicolons and Colons outside Ending Quotation Marks

Semicolons and colons are always typed outside ending quotation marks.

He asked if I had read Poe's "Annabel Lee"; I told him that I
had memorized it when I was a child.

Placing Question Marks and Exclamation Points
When Used with Ending Quotation Marks

Question marks and exclamation points are typed inside the ending quotation marks when the quoted material is a question or exclamation.

"Did you read the story I told you about?" he asked.

A question mark or an exclamation point is typed inside both the single and the double quotation marks when both marks are used.

The captain called to the correspondent, "'Come to the boat!

Come to the boat!'" (Crane 1507).

Question marks and exclamation points are typed outside the final quotation marks when your sentence is a question or exclamation but the quoted material is not.

Are you sure he said, "I'm going to the movies"?

If both your sentence and the quoted material are questions or exclamations, place the question mark or exclamation point inside the final quotation marks if they fall at the end of the sentence. Do not use two question marks or exclamation points.

Are you sure he asked, "Do you think she would go out with me?"

Punctuating a Short Quotation Ending
in a Question Mark or an Exclamation Point

If a short quotation ends with a question mark or an exclamation point, type the end quotation mark after the question mark or exclamation point, type one space after the end quotation mark, and type the parenthetical citation, followed by a period: "last word?" (34). OR "last word!" (34).

As the novel ends, Hawthorne tells us that "Hester Prynne had

returned [to Boston], and taken up her long-forsaken shame. But

where was little Pearl?" (176; ch. 24).

```
By the last pages of the novel, Hester's scarlet symbol is

looked upon with "awe" and "reverence" and brings troubled

people to her door in search of comfort and advice: "[P]eople

brought all their sorrows and perplexities . . . to Hester's

cottage demanding why they were so wretched, and what the

remedy!" (Hawthorne 177; ch. 24).
```

If the material ending with a question mark or exclamation point is dialogue and therefore already in quotation marks in the text of the work from which you are quoting, type the question mark or exclamation point inside both the single and the double quotation marks, and then type one space, the parenthetical citation, and a period: "'last word?'" (105). OR "'last word!'" (105).

```
When the Rev. Dimmesdale invites Hester and Pearl to stand

beside him on the scaffold at night, Pearl asks the minister,

"'Wilt thou stand here with mother and me, tomorrow noon-

tide?'" (Hawthorne 105; ch. 12).
```

```
Foreshadowing the end of the novel, Dimmesdale replies,

"'I shall, indeed, stand with thy mother and thee one other

day, but not tomorrow!'" (Hawthorne 105; ch. 12).
```

Punctuating Quotation Lead-Ins

When you place your author/speaker identification or other type of explanatory lead-in at the beginning of a quotation, you might think of your quotation as the meat in a sandwich. The quotation (the meat) is sandwiched between two slices of bread—the lead-in to the quotation and the parenthetical citation, which refers your reader to the complete information about your source presented in your works-cited list.

Although the lead-in is most often placed at the beginning of a quotation, the author/speaker identification or explanatory information about a quotation may, for variation, be placed in the middle or at the end of your quotation. This explanatory information connects your quotation to your text by identifying the writer or speaker of the words you are quoting or by explaining how the quotation relates to the point you are trying to explain by using the quotation.

An Author/Speaker Identification Lead-In with a Comma

Hawthorne explains, "Now Pearl knew well enough who made
her . . ." (77; ch. 8).

A Lead-In Ending in the Word *That*

When your lead-in ends in the word *that,* you do not need a comma before
the quotation.

Hawthorne tells us that ". . . Pearl knew well enough who made
her . . ." (77; ch. 8) because her mother had taught her about
the Puritan beliefs.

Author Identification in the Middle of the Quotation

When you position your author/speaker identification or explanatory material in the middle of the quotation, set it off with commas on both sides.

"With sudden and desperate tenderness," writes Hawthorne,
"she threw her arms around him, and pressed his head against
her bosom; little caring though his cheek rested on the scarlet
letter" (132; ch. 17).

Author Identification between Two
Complete Sentences from Your Source

Use a semicolon between two independent clauses (two grammatically complete
sentences) to avoid creating a comma splice when your author/speaker identification or explanatory material falls between the two independent clauses.

"The tendency of her fate and fortunes had been to set her
free," writes Hawthorne; "[t]he scarlet letter was her
passport into regions where other women dared not tread"
(136; ch 18).

Speaker Identification between Two Dialogue Sentences

To avoid a comma splice, use a semicolon after the speaker identification.

"'Preach! Write! Act!'" Hester tells her beloved Arthur;
"'[d]o anything, save to lie down and die!'" (135; ch. 17).

A Full-Sentence Lead-In Ending with a Colon

Use a colon after a full sentence lead-in to a quotation.

Hawthorne describes Hester's all-too-brief moment of freedom
from the scarlet letter in the forest scene: "So speaking, she
undid the clasp that fastened the scarlet letter, and, taking
it from her bosom, threw it to a distance among the withered
leaves" (137; ch. 18).

CHAPTER 20

Paraphrasing and Summarizing

Paraphrasing

To paraphrase means to express in your own words the idea of another person. When you paraphrase, you replicate the idea of the writer in your source without using any characteristic wording from your source. If you need to use some of the unique words or original phrases from your source, simply place them in quotation marks. A good rule of thumb when paraphrasing is not to use any three words in the same order in which they are found in your source.

Even though you are expressing the idea in your own words, you must inform your reader that you took the idea from a source

1. by identifying the writer at the beginning of your sentence so that your reader will know that the idea being expressed is not your own
2. by placing a parenthetical citation after the paraphrased material and inside the final punctuation mark of the sentence

Original sentence written by John Caldwell Stubbs:

Seeing himself as an aging husband who wronged Hester by bringing her to a loveless marriage, he can forgive her adultery as no more than a counter-balancing wrong. (385)

Direct Quotation (Precise Wording of Critic)

John Caldwell Stubbs writes, "Seeing himself as an aging husband who wronged Hester by bringing her to a loveless marriage, he [Chillingworth] can forgive her adultery as no more than a counter-balancing wrong" (385).

Paraphrase of Critic's Interpretation

John Caldwell Stubbs points out that Chillingworth is able to forgive Hester's adultery because he realizes that he has also wronged her by enticing her into marrying him--a much older man she has never loved (385).

Summarizing

To summarize is to present in your own words a shortened version (one or several sentences) of one or more paragraphs from your source

1. by identifying the writer at the beginning of your summary so that your reader will know that the ideas being expressed are not your own
2. by placing a parenthetical reference after the summarized material and inside the final punctuation mark of the final sentence of the summary

Original paragraph written by John Caldwell Stubbs:

> In precisely this context are Hester and Chillingworth presented to us. They are part of the series of opposed images. Hester is almost literally an intensification of the young wife. She carries her child in her arms. The striking richness of her attire and her dark hair make her woman on the large scale. Hawthorne likens her to the madonna of Renaissance art. Her role as representative of unrestricted, natural emotions is made all the more clear by contrast with the beadle marching before her as an embodiment of "the whole dismal severity of the Puritan code of law." The role of the beadle is quickly subsumed by Chillingworth. Seeing himself as an aging husband who wronged Hester by bringing her to a loveless marriage, he can forgive her adultery as no more than a

counter-balancing wrong. But he burns to make the escaped lover suffer. Here he becomes Hester's ultimate
adversary. In his demoniacal drive, he embodies the
severest aspects of the hard justice of the Puritans
to which Hester stands irrevocably opposed. (385)

Summary of Critical Interpretation

John Caldwell Stubbs points out that Hawthorne sets up a symbolic opposition between Hester and her wronged husband, Roger
Chillingworth. Whereas Hester represents the sort of person who
always follows the intuitive dictates of her heart, Roger represents the harsh Puritan justice that attempts to dictate the
path one must follow (385).

Summary Using Some of the Critic's Memorable Phrases

John Caldwell Stubbs points out that Hawthorne sets up a
symbolic opposition between Hester and her wronged husband,
Roger Chillingworth. Whereas Hester is "representative of
unrestricted, natural emotions," Roger "embodies the severest
aspects of the hard justice of the Puritans" (385).

Choosing What to Paraphrase or Summarize

If you are writing a literary analysis, you will find that the critics you are
reading will summarize events that occurred in the plot prior to analyzing
the meaning of those events. You should avoid paraphrasing or summariz-
ing these ideas because you can describe events from the plot in your own
words without parenthetical citations. What happens in the story, novel, or
play is considered general knowledge about your subject because anyone
who reads the work will know what happened in the plot.

Paraphrase or summarize the critic's interpretation of the meaning of
the work he or she is analyzing, not the supportive illustrations and plot
summaries.

Poor Choice of Material to Paraphrase

Robert Thomas points out that Willy Loman commits suicide at
the end of *Death of a Salesman* (85).

Anyone who has read *Death of a Salesman* knows that Willy Loman commits suicide at the end of the play. You can explain this plot element without referring to a critic or using a parenthetical citation.

Better Choice of Material to Paraphrase

Robert Thomas believes that Willy's suicide at the end of the
play is a misguided act of love for his family (85).

Here the critic is expressing an interpretation of Willy's motivation in committing suicide, so this is a better choice of material to paraphrase.

CHAPTER 21

Avoiding Plagiarism

When you take **original ideas, opinions,** or **interpretations** or **an author's precise wording** from a source, you must let your reader know whose idea or wording you are using by giving a parenthetical citation and by citing the complete information about your source in the list of works cited located at the end of your paper.

Not to distinguish your ideas and wording from those of your sources is plagiarism.

If even one sentence in your paper is plagiarized, your instructor must conclude that every other sentence in your paper may be plagiarized. Therefore, your paper is unacceptable and may earn a failing grade. Because plagiarism is considered cheating, you may also earn a failing grade in the course and be in violation of your school's honor code. The only way to avoid plagiarizing is to be absolutely certain you credit your sources properly when you use the precise wording of your sources and use ideas or interpretations that are not your own and not general knowledge.

Original sentence written by John Caldwell Stubbs:

Seeing himself as an aging husband who wronged Hester by bringing her to a loveless marriage, he can forgive her adultery as no more than a counter-balancing wrong. (385)

Plagiarized sentence (plagiarized [stolen] phrases appear in blue):

Chillingworth sees himself as an aging husband who sinned against Hester by bringing her to a loveless marriage.

This sentence is plagiarized because

1. no quotation marks identify the phrases taken from the source. Therefore, the writer is leading the reader to believe that the idea expressed and the wording of this sentence are original rather than borrowed from a source.

2. the critic's name is not given in the introduction to the sentence
3. no parenthetical citation identifies the critic or the page on which those phrases appeared in the source

Plagiarized sentence (plagiarized phrases appear in blue):

John Caldwell Stubbs points out that Chillingworth sees himself as an aging husband who sinned against Hester by bringing her to a loveless marriage (385).

Although the critic's name and the page number of the source are given, this sentence is also plagiarized because the precise words of the critic have been used without quotation marks to distinguish those words from the student's own words. The student is leading the reader to believe that the sentence is paraphrased when in reality the student is stealing the critic's copyrighted phrases.

Plagiarizing Papers from the Internet

You might be tempted to download and turn in as your own one of the student papers you find on the Internet. To do so would be a violation not only of your personal sense of honor but also of your school's honor code. Turning in someone else's work as your own is cheating. Even turning in a paper that you wrote for another class without asking the professor for permission to do so is considered cheating at most universities. If you are caught plagiarizing in any of these ways, you will almost certainly earn a failing grade on the paper and, most likely, a failing grade in the course as well. If you are found guilty of violating your school's honor code, you could be expelled.

You should be aware that your professor has access to a number of Web sites that specialize in detecting plagiarism in student papers. Don't risk your reputation as an honest person. Do your own work, and be conscientious about crediting any sources from which you borrowed materials. When in doubt, give a citation. It's better to be safe than sorry.

CHAPTER 22

MLA-Recommended Abbreviations

Use MLA-recommended abbreviations in your works-cited or works-consulted list. Avoid using abbreviations in the text of an MLA-style paper except in tables, parentheses, or parenthetical citations or when an abbreviation is typically used to describe information (*a.m., p.m., mph, rpm*). Clarity is more important than brevity, however. Spell out in full any term you believe your reader may not understand.

The following are typically abbreviated in MLA-style works-cited and works-consulted lists:

- The names of all months with the exception of May, June, and July
- The names of states (using postal abbreviations without periods)
- The names of Canadian provinces
- The names of countries
- The names of well-known publishers (shortened following MLA guidelines)
- Additional terms as noted in the following lists

You may abbreviate the following within the text of an MLA-style paper:

- Titles of well-known literary works mentioned repeatedly (e.g., works of Shakespeare and Chaucer)
- Titles of books of the Bible and other well-known religious works mentioned repeatedly
- Time and other designations typically abbreviated (*a.m., p.m., AD, BC, BCE, mph, rpm*)

General Guidelines

- Omit periods and spaces in abbreviations consisting of all capital letters (*CD, LP, DVD, VCR, SC, NC, USA, USSR, AD, BC*).

■ When you abbreviate one or two words by using all lowercase letters or a combination of capital and lowercase letters, end the abbreviations with periods (*abbr., bk., Scot., Swed., So. Amer., No. Amer., Gt. Brit.*).

■ If each lowercase letter stands for a different word in a series of words, type a period after each letter, but not a space (*a.m., p.m., n.p., n.d., i.e.*). Note, however, that MLA leaves one space after the *n.* in the abbreviation meaning "no pagination" (*n. pag.*).

■ Notable exceptions to this rule are abbreviations found in your dictionary, such as *rpm* for "revolutions per minute" and *mph* for "miles per hour."

■ Leave one space after any period that follows an initial in a person's name (T. S. Eliot, not T.S. Eliot; J. R. R. Tolkien).

■ In a bibliographical citation, an abbreviation that follows the period that ends a section of the entry is always capitalized (*The Poetry of Robert Frost. Ed.* Robert T. Watkins.).

■ In a bibliographical citation, an abbreviation that does not follow the period that ends a section of the entry always begins with a lowercase letter (White, Richard P., and Francis W. Taylor, *eds.*).

The following terms are often abbreviated in MLA-style documentation:

Abr. ed.	Abridged edition	BCE	before the common era (eighth century BCE)
AD	after the birth of Christ (Latin: *anno Domini,* "in the year of the Lord"); used before Arabic numerals (AD 1015) and after centuries (tenth century AD)		
		bk.	book
		bks.	books
		c.	circa, around (approximate date: c. 1645)
adapt.	adapter, adaptation		
Adapt.	Adapted by	CD	compact disc
a.m.	before noon (Latin: *ante meridiem*)	CD-ROM	compact disc read-only memory
		CE	common era (ninth century CE)
anon.	anonymous		
app.	appendix	cf.	compare
art.	article	ch.	chapter
arts.	articles	chs.	chapters
Assn.	Association	chor.	choreographer
b.	born	Chor.	Choreographed by
BC	before the birth of Christ (as in "350 BC" or "tenth century BC")	col.	column
		comp.	compiler

Comp.	Compiled by	i.e.	that is (Latin: *id est*)
cond.	conductor	illus.	illustration; illustrator
Cond.	Conducted by	Illus.	Illustrated by
Conf.	Conference	introd.	introduction
cont.	continued; contents	Introd.	Introduced by
d.	died	jour.	journal
def.	definition	l.	line of poetry (use *line* instead)
Dev.	Developed by		
dir.	director	ll.	lines of poetry (use *lines* instead)
Dir.	Directed by		
Diss.	Dissertation	Lib.	Library
distr.	distributor	LP	long-playing phonograph record
Distr.	Distributed by		
doc.	document	misc.	miscellaneous
DVD	digital videodisc	MS	manuscript
ed.	editor, edition	MSS	manuscripts
eds.	editors	n	note (footnote or end-note) ("37n2" means "note 2 on page 37")
Ed.	Edited by		
2nd ed.	second edition		
3rd ed.	third edition	nn	notes (footnotes or endnotes) ("37nn2-4" means "notes 2, 3, and 4 on page 37")
4th ed.	fourth edition		
e.g.	for example (Latin: *exempli gratia*)		
		narr.	narrator
e-mail	electronic mail	Narr.	Narrated by
enl.	enlarged	NB	take note of; notice (Latin: *nota bene*)
Enl. ed.	Enlarged ed.		
esp.	especially	n.d.	no date of publication given
et al.	and others (Latin: *et alii* or *et aliae*)		
		N.p.	no city (place) of publication given
etc.	and so forth (Latin: *et cetera*); avoid using in text		
		n.p.	no publisher given
		n. pag.	no pages (pagination) given; one space after *n.*
ex.	example		
fig.	figure	ns	new series of a journal
fwd.	foreword; forwarded	os	old or original series of a journal
Fwd. by	Foreword by; Forwarded by		
		P	Press
gen. ed.	general editor	p.	page

pp.	pages		sess.	session
par.	paragraph		sic	thus; error in source
para. by	paraphrased by		soc.	society
pars.	paragraphs		st.	stanza
perf.	performer		trans.	translator
Perf.	Performed by		Trans.	Translated by
PhD	doctor of philosophy		TS	typescript
p.m.	after noon		TSS	typescripts
	(Latin: *post meridiem*)		U	University
pref.	preface		UP	University Press
Pref.	Preface by		URL	uniform resource locator; Web site address
proc.	proceedings			
prod.	producer		VHS	videocassette recorder (video home system)
Prod.	Produced by			
pt.	part		vers.	version
qtd.	quoted		Vol.	volume
Rev. ed.	Revised edition		vols.	volumes
Rev. of	Review of		vs.	versus; against
Rpt. in	Reprinted in		v.	versus; against; preferred form for citing legal cases
sec. (sect.)	section			
ser.	series		Writ.	Written by

Abbreviating Months

Write out the names of months within the text of your paper, but abbreviate the names of all months with the exception of May, June, and July in your works-cited or works-consulted list.

Jan.	January	May	May	Sept.	September
Feb.	February	June	June	Oct.	October
Mar.	March	July	July	Nov.	November
Apr.	April	Aug.	August	Dec.	December

Abbreviating Days of the Week and Other Time Descriptors

Write out the names of days of the week within the text of your paper. Write out time descriptors such as *minute*, *week*, *month*, and *year* unless those time descriptors are typically abbreviated (*a.m.*, *p.m.*, *AD*, *BC*). Abbreviate the names of all days or time designations in your works-cited or works-consulted list.

Sun.	Sunday	a.m.	before noon
Mon.	Monday	p.m.	after noon
Tues.	Tuesday	AD	after the birth of Christ (Latin: *anno Domini,* "in the year of the Lord"); used before an Arabic numeral (AD 17) and after a century (tenth century AD)
Wed.	Wednesday		
Thurs.	Thursday		
Fri.	Friday		
Sat.	Saturday		
sec.	second	BC	before the birth of Christ; used after an Arabic numeral (14 BC) and after a century (ninth century BC)
min.	minute		
hr.	hour	BCE	before the common era; used after an Arabic numeral (17 BCE) and after a century (tenth century BCE)
wk.	week		
mo.	month		
yr.	year	CE	common era; used after Arabic numerals and centuries
cent.	century		

Abbreviating States

Do not abbreviate the names of states in the text of your paper, but use the postal abbreviation for the name of a state used in a bibliographical citation, in a postal address, and in parentheses.

AK	Alaska	ID	Idaho
AL	Alabama	IL	Illinois
AR	Arkansas	IN	Indiana
AZ	Arizona	KS	Kansas
CA	California	KY	Kentucky
CO	Colorado	LA	Louisiana
CT	Connecticut	MA	Massachusetts
DC	District of Columbia	MD	Maryland
DE	Delaware	ME	Maine
FL	Florida	MI	Michigan
GA	Georgia	MN	Minnesota
HI	Hawaii	MO	Missouri
IA	Iowa	MS	Mississippi

MT	Montana	RI	Rhode Island
NC	North Carolina	SC	South Carolina
ND	North Dakota	SD	South Dakota
NE	Nebraska	TN	Tennessee
NH	New Hampshire	TX	Texas
NJ	New Jersey	UT	Utah
NM	New Mexico	VA	Virginia
NV	Nevada	VT	Vermont
NY	New York	WA	Washington
OH	Ohio	WI	Wisconsin
OK	Oklahoma	WV	West Virginia
OR	Oregon	WY	Wyoming
PA	Pennsylvania		

Abbreviating Provinces of Canada

Abbreviate the names of provinces of Canada in bibliographic citations. Do not abbreviate the names of Canadian provinces in the text of your paper except in a postal address or in parentheses.

AB	Alberta	NT	Northwest Territories
BC	British Columbia	ON	Ontario
MB	Manitoba	PE	Prince Edward Island
NB	New Brunswick	QC	Québec, Quebec
NL	Newfoundland and Labrador	SK	Saskatchewan
		YT	Yukon Territory
NS	Nova Scotia		

Abbreviating the Names of Countries and Continents

Give the full name of a country or continent when you mention it in a sentence in your paper. You may abbreviate the name of a country in documentation, in a postal address, or in parentheses. You may abbreviate USSR in all situations.

Afr.	Africa	Arg.	Argentina
Alb.	Albania	Arm.	Armenia
Ant.	Antarctica	Aus.	Austria

Austral.	Australia	No. Amer.	North America
Belg.	Belgium	Norw.	Norway
Braz.	Brazil	NZ	New Zealand
Bulg.	Bulgaria	Pan.	Panama
Can.	Canada	Pol.	Poland
Den.	Denmark	Port.	Portugal
Ecua.	Ecuador	PR	Puerto Rico
Eng.	England	PRC	People's Republic of China
Eur.	Europe	Russ.	Russia
Fr.	France	Scot.	Scotland
Ger.	Germany	So. Amer.	South America
Gr.	Greece	Sp.	Spain
Gt. Brit.	Great Britain	Swed.	Sweden
Hung.	Hungary	Switz.	Switzerland
Ire.	Ireland	Turk.	Turkey
Isr.	Israel	UK	United Kingdom
It.	Italy	US	United States
Jpn.	Japan	USA	United States of America
Leb.	Lebanon	USSR	Union of Soviet Socialist Republics
Mex.	Mexico		
Neth.	Netherlands		

Abbreviating the Names of Books of the Bible and Other Religious Works

You may abbreviate books of the Bible (Bib.) in parenthetical citations and in your works-cited or works-consulted list. If you refer to a particular book repeatedly or to many books of the Bible within the text of your paper, give the title of the book in full the first time you refer to it, and inform your reader in parentheses that hereafter you will refer to the work using an abbreviated form of the title: Genesis (Gen.).

When creating a parenthetical citation for a quotation from the Bible, give the full or abbreviated name of the book followed by one space, the chapter in Arabic numerals followed by a period and no space, and the verse or verses in Arabic numerals: (Exodus 3.4-6) or (Exod. 3.4-6).

Do not italicize or put quotation marks around the names of religious works (e.g., the Bible, the Koran, the Talmud), versions of religious works (the King James Version of the Bible), or divisions of religious works (the New Testament, the Gospels).

Do not italicize or use quotation marks around the titles of books of the Bible (Genesis, Exodus) and other religious writings.

Italicize the title of a specific published edition of a religious work, and cite it in your works-cited list as you would any other published book.

Books of the Old Testament (OT)

Gen.	Genesis	Eccles.	Ecclesiastes
Exod.	Exodus	Song of Sol.	Song of Solomon
Lev.	Leviticus	Cant. of Cant.	Canticle of Canticles
Num.	Numbers	Isa.	Isaiah
Deut.	Deuteronomy	Jer.	Jeremiah
Josh.	Joshua	Lam.	Lamentations
Judg.	Judges	Ezek.	Ezekiel
Ruth	Ruth	Dan.	Daniel
1 Sam.	1 Samuel	Hos.	Hosea
2 Sam.	2 Samuel	Joel	Joel
1 Kings	1 Kings	Amos	Amos
2 Kings	2 Kings	Obad.	Obadiah
1 Chron.	1 Chronicles	Jon.	Jonah
2 Chron.	2 Chronicles	Mic.	Micah
Ezra	Ezra	Nah.	Nahum
Neh.	Nehemiah	Hab.	Habakkuk
Esth.	Esther	Zeph.	Zephaniah
Job	Job	Hag.	Haggai
Ps.	Psalms	Zech.	Zechariah
Prov.	Proverbs	Mal.	Malachi

Books of the New Testament (NT)

Matt.	Matthew	2 John	2 John
Mark	Mark	3 John	3 John
Luke	Luke	Acts	Acts
John	John	Rom.	Romans
1 John	1 John	1 Cor.	1 Corinthians

2 Cor.	2 Corinthians	Tit.	Titus
Gal.	Galatians	Philem.	Philemon
Eph.	Ephesians	Heb.	Hebrews
Phil.	Philippians	Jas.	James
Col.	Colossians	1 Pet.	1 Peter
1 Thess.	1 Thessalonians	2 Pet.	2 Peter
2 Thess.	2 Thessalonians	Jude	Jude
1 Tim.	1 Timothy	Rev.	Revelation
2 Tim.	2 Timothy	Apoc.	Apocalypse (Revelation)

Abbreviating Titles of Works by Shakespeare

If you are referring to the same work repeatedly or to a number of works by Shakespeare or another author, give the title in full the first time you refer to the work, and inform your reader in parentheses that hereafter you will refer to the work using an abbreviated form of the title: Shakespeare's *Romeo and Juliet* (*Rom.*)

You may use the MLA-recommended abbreviated forms for titles listed here. If no abbreviation is specified by MLA for a particular work, you may create your own shortened form as long as it will be clear to your reader and as long as you have informed your reader in parentheses what the shortened title will be. Italicize titles of plays, poetry collections, and long poems that have been published as separate entities. Use double quotation marks around the titles of short poems, such as the titles of Shakespeare's sonnets.

Shakespeare's Plays

All's Well That Ends Well	*AWW*
Antony and Cleopatra	*Ant.*
As You Like It	*AYL*
The Comedy of Errors	*Err.*
Coriolanus	*Cor.*
Cymbeline	*Cym.*
Hamlet	*Ham.*
Henry IV, Part 1	*1H4*
Henry IV, Part 2	*2H4*
Henry V	*H5*
Henry VI, Part 1	*1H6*

Henry VI, Part 2	2H6
Henry VI, Part 3	3H6
Henry VIII	H8
Julius Caesar	JC
King John	Jn.
King Lear	Lr.
Love's Labour's Lost	LLL
Macbeth	Mac.
Measure for Measure	MM
The Merchant of Venice	MV
The Merry Wives of Windsor	Wiv.
A Midsummer Night's Dream	MND
Much Ado about Nothing	Ado
Othello	Oth.
Pericles	Per.
Richard II	R2
Richard III	R3
Romeo and Juliet	Rom.
The Taming of the Shrew	Shr.
The Tempest	Tmp.
Timon of Athens	Tim.
Titus Andronicus	Tit.
Troilus and Cressida	Tro.
Twelfth Night	TN
The Two Gentlemen of Verona	TGV
The Two Noble Kinsmen	TNK
The Winter's Tale	WT

Shakespeare's Poems

A Lover's Complaint	LC
The Rape of Lucrece	Luc.
The Phoenix and the Turtle	PhT
The Passionate Pilgrim	PP
Sonnets	Son.
Venus and Adonis	Ven.

Abbreviating Titles of Works by Chaucer

If you are referring repeatedly to a single work or to a number of works by Chaucer or another author, give the title in full the first time you refer to the work, and inform your reader in parentheses that hereafter you will refer to the work using an abbreviated form of the title: "The Nun's Priest's Tale" ("NPT").

You may use the MLA-recommended abbreviated forms for titles listed here. If no abbreviation is specified by MLA for a particular work, you may create your own shortened form as long as it will be clear to your reader and as long as you have informed your reader in parentheses what the shortened title will be.

Italicize the titles of works published as separate entities (*The Canterbury Tales*, a collection of short tales or stories) and long poems (*The Parliament of Fowls*) or poetry collections. Use double quotation marks around the titles of short works and short poems published as parts of longer works ("The General Prologue," "The Clerk's Tale").

Chaucer's *Canterbury Tales*

"The Canon's Yeoman's Tale"	"CYT"
The Canterbury Tales	*CT*
"Chaucer's Retraction"	"Ret"
"The Clerk's Tale"	"ClT"
"The Cook's Tale"	"CkT"
"The Franklin's Tale"	"FranT"
"The Friar's Tale"	"FrT"
"The General Prologue"	"GP"
"The Knight's Tale"	"KnT"
"The Manciple's Tale"	"ManT"
"The Man of Law's Tale"	"MLT"
"The Merchant's Tale"	"MerT"
"The Miller's Tale"	"MilT"
"The Monk's Tale"	"MkT"
"The Nun's Priest's Tale"	"NPT"
"The Pardoner's Tale"	"PardT"
"The Parson's Tale"	"ParsT"
"The Physician's Tale"	"PhyT"

"The Prioress's Tale"	"PrT"
"The Reeve's Tale"	"RvT"
"The Second Nun's Tale"	"SNT"
"The Shipman's Tale"	"ShT"
"The Squire's Tale"	"SqT"
"The Summoner's Tale"	"SumT"
"The Tale of Melibee"	"Mel"
"The Tale of Sir Thopas"	"Th"
"The Wife of Bath's Tale"	"WBT"

Chaucer's Poems

Anelida and Arcite	*AA*
The Book of the Duchess	*BD*
The House of Fame	*HF*
The Legend of Good Women	*LGW*
The Parliament of Fowls	*PF*
Troilus and Criseyde	*TC*

CHAPTER 23

Shortening the Names of Publishers

1. Shorten the names of well-known publishers:

Cengage	Cengage Learning
Prentice	Prentice Hall, Inc.
Random	Random House, Inc.

2. Be sure, however, to give enough information to allow your reader to find the full name and address of the publisher in references such as *Books in Print* or *Literary Market Place* if more information is needed.

3. If a well-known publisher's name includes one person's name and initials, shorten it to the last name:

Knopf	Alfred A. Knopf, Inc.
Norton	W. W. Norton and Co., Inc.

4. If a well-known publisher's name includes the last names of two or more persons, shorten it to the last name of the first person listed:

Farrar	Farrar, Straus and Giroux, Inc.
Simon	Simon and Schuster, Inc.

5. For less well-known publishers, you may give a more complete name (e.g., *Public Citizen Health Group* rather than *Public, Health Communications* rather than *Health*).

6. If you are not sure that your reader will recognize a publisher's name when it has been shortened, give the name in full or write out any part of it that might cause confusion. For example, if you shortened *Friends United Press* to *Friends UP*, your reader might assume the publisher was Friends University Press. For this entry, use *Friends United*.

7. If you believe the additional information would be useful to your readers (e.g., other students in your class or a general readership not familiar with the world of publishing) or if your professor requests it, you may give the full name of a publisher, but you should omit the following from the publisher's name:

The	NEA or Natl. Educ. Assn. for The National Education Association
Co.	Company
Corp.	Corporation
Inc.	Incorporated
Ltd.	Limited
Books	Basic Books → Basic
Press	Da Capo Press → Da Capo
House	Random House, Inc. → Random
Publishers	Harper and Row, Publishers, Inc. → Harper

8. Because universities often publish materials separately from their university presses, use the abbreviation *U* for *University* and *P* for *Press* when you cite a university press. For example, a book could be published by the University of South Carolina or by the University of South Carolina Press:

University of South Carolina → U of South Carolina

University of South Carolina Press → U of South Carolina P

9. If you are not certain that your readers will recognize the acronym for a publisher's name (*SIRS* for *Social Issues Resources Series, Inc.*; *MLA* for *Modern Language Association of America*; *GPO* for *Government Printing Office*), give the publisher's name in full or use a more recognizable abbreviation (e.g., *Mod. Lang. Assn.* instead of *MLA*).

Here are some examples of how publishers' names may be shortened:

Abrams	Harry N. Abrams, Inc.
Addison	Addison Wesley Higher Education Group
Addison	Addison Wesley Longman, Inc.
Allyn	Allyn and Bacon
Barron's	Barron's Educational Series, Inc.
Basic	Basic Books
Bruccoli	Bruccoli Clark Layman Publishers

Cambridge UP	Cambridge University Press
Cengage	Cengage Learning
Crown	Crown Publishing Group
Da Capo	Da Capo Press, Inc.
Duke UP	Duke University Press
ERIC	Educational Resources Information Center
Faber	Faber and Faber, Inc.
Facts	Facts on File, Inc.
Farrar	Farrar, Straus and Giroux, Inc.
Gale	Gale Research, Inc.
GPO	Government Printing Office
Harcourt	Harcourt Brace Jovanovich
Harcourt	Harcourt, Brace, and World
Harcourt	Harcourt College Publishers
Harcourt	Harcourt, Inc.
Harper	HarperCollins Publishers, Inc.
Harper	Harper and Row, Publishers, Inc.
Harvard UP	Harvard University Press
Heath	D. C. Heath
Heinle	Heinle and Heinle
Hill	Hill and Wang
HMSO	Her (or His) Majesty's Stationery Office (British)
Houghton	Houghton Mifflin Co.
Knopf	Alfred A. Knopf, Inc.
Little	Little, Brown and Company, Inc.
Longman	Longman Publishing
Louisiana State UP	Louisiana State University Press
Macmillan	Macmillan Publishing Co., Inc.
McDougal	McDougal Littell, Inc.
McGraw	McGraw-Hill, Inc.
MLA	The Modern Language Association of America
NCTE	The National Council of Teachers of English
NEA	The National Education Association
Norton	W. W. Norton and Co., Inc.
Oxford UP	Oxford University Press
Pearson	Pearson Education

Penguin	Penguin Putnam, Inc.
Prentice	Prentice Hall, Inc.
Putnam's	G. P. Putnam's Sons
Random	Random House, Inc.
Scribner's	Charles Scribner's Sons
Simon	Simon and Schuster, Inc.
SIRS	Social Issues Resources Series
St. Martin's	St. Martin's Press, Inc.
Time	Time Life, Inc.
UMI	University Microfilms International
U of Chicago P	University of Chicago Press
U of South Carolina P	University of South Carolina Press
U of Texas P	University of Texas Press
UP of Mississippi	University Press of Mississippi
Vanderbilt UP	Vanderbilt University Press
Wadsworth	Wadsworth Group
Wadsworth	Wadsworth Publishing Co.
Wiley	John Wiley and Sons, Inc.
Yale UP	Yale University Press

WORKS CONSULTED

Baym, Nina. "[Plot in *The Scarlet Letter.*]" "Plot in Hawthorne's Romances." *Ruined Eden of the Present.* Ed. G. R. Thompson and Virgil L. Lokke. West Lafayette, IN: Purdue UP, 1981. 49-70. Rpt. in Gross et al. 402-07.

Blake, William. "The Tyger." Kennedy and Gioia 1026-27.

Carpenter, Frederic I. "Scarlet A Minus." *College English* 5.4 (1944): 173-80. Rpt. in Gross et al. 291-300.

Colacurcio, Michael J. "Footsteps of Ann Hutchinson: The Context of *The Scarlet Letter.*" *English Literary History* 39.3 (1972): 459-94. Rpt. in Gross et al. 213-30.

Crane, Stephen. "The Open Boat." McMichael et al. 1491-1508.

Crews, Frederick C. "The Ruined Wall." *The Sins of the Fathers: Hawthorne's Psychological Themes.* New York: Oxford UP, 1966. 136-53. Rpt. in Gross et al. 361-71.

Donne, John. "Death Be Not Proud." Kirszner and Mandell 1148.

Fogle, Richard Harter. "[Realms of Being and Dramatic Irony.]" *Hawthorne's Fiction: The Light and the Dark.* Norman: U of Oklahoma P, 1952. 106-18. Rpt. in Gross et al. 308-15.

Gross, Seymour, et al., eds. *The Scarlet Letter: An Authoritative Text, Essays in Criticism and Scholarship.* By Nathaniel Hawthorne. 3rd ed. New York: Norton, 1988. Print. Norton Critical Editions.

Harnack, Andrew, and Eugene Kleppinger. *Online: A Reference Guide to Using Internet Sources.* Boston: Bedford-St. Martin's, 2000. Print.

Hawthorne, Nathaniel. *The Scarlet Letter.* Gross et al. 1-178.

---. "Young Goodman Brown." Kennedy and Gioia 420-28.

Herbert, George. "Easter Wings." Kennedy and Gioia 842.

Herrick, Robert. "To the Virgins, to Make Much of Time." Kennedy and Gioia 1052.

Keats, John. "Ode on a Grecian Urn." Kirszner and Mandell 1171-72.

Kennedy, X. J., and Dana Gioia, eds. *Literature: An Introduction to Fiction, Poetry, Drama, and Writing.* 11th ed. New York: Longman-Pearson, 2010. Print.

Kirszner, Laurie G., and Stephen R. Mandell, eds. *Literature: Reading, Reacting, Writing.* 7th ed. Boston: Wadsworth-Cengage, 2010. Print.

McLaurin, Ken. "The Bee Constellation." *Poet and Critic* 25.1 (1994): 13. Print.

---. "Cancer." *45/96: The Ninety-Six Sampler of South Carolina Poetry.* Ed. Gilbert Allen. Greenville, SC: Ninety-Six Press, 1994. 150. Print.

---. "Storm Pit." *Beloit Poetry Journal* 32.2 (1981-82): 43. Print.

McMichael, George, et al., eds. *Concise Anthology of American Literature.* 7th ed. Boston: Longman-Pearson, 2011. Print.

McNamara, Anne Marie. "The Character of Flame: The Function of Pearl in *The Scarlet Letter.*" *American Literature* 27.4 (1956): 537-53. Print.

Miller, Arthur. *Death of a Salesman.* Kennedy and Gioia 1772-1836.

MLA Handbook for Writers of Research Papers. 7th ed. New York: Mod. Lang. Assn., 2009. Print.

MLA Style Manual and Guide to Scholarly Publishing. 3rd ed. New York: Mod. Lang. Assn., 2008. Print.

Shakespeare, William. "My mistress' eyes are nothing like the sun." Kennedy and Gioia 1084.

Stubbs, John Caldwell. "*The Scarlet Letter:* 'A Tale of Human Frailty and Sorrow.'" *The Pursuit of Form: A Study of Hawthorne and the Romance.* Urbana: U of Illinois P, 1970. 81-102. Rpt. in Gross et al. 384-92.

Trimmer, Joseph F. *A Guide to MLA Documentation.* 8th ed. Boston: Wadsworth-Cengage, 2010. Print.

Twain, Mark [Samuel Langhorne Clemens]. *The Adventures of Huckleberry Finn.* McMichael et al. 1187-1365. Print.

Whitman, Walt. "The Wound-Dresser." *Complete Poetry and Selected Prose.* Ed. James E. Miller, Jr. Boston: Houghton, 1959. 220-22. Print. Riverside Editions.

INDEX

A Quick Reference: Annotated Citations

For a quick reference guide to all the annotated citations that appear in this book, see page 309.

A QUICK REFERENCE:
ANNOTATED CITATIONS

A Book with One Author

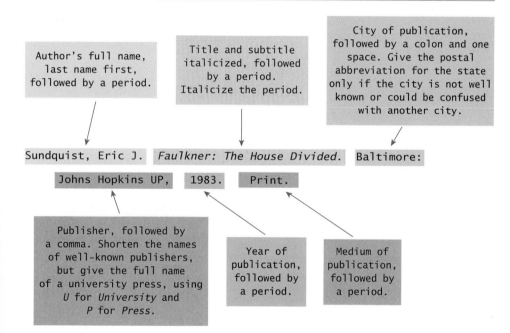

Author's full name, last name first, followed by a period.

Title and subtitle italicized, followed by a period. Italicize the period.

City of publication, followed by a colon and one space. Give the postal abbreviation for the state only if the city is not well known or could be confused with another city.

Sundquist, Eric J. *Faulkner: The House Divided.* Baltimore:

Johns Hopkins UP, 1983. Print.

Publisher, followed by a comma. Shorten the names of well-known publishers, but give the full name of a university press, using *U* for *University* and *P* for *Press*.

Year of publication, followed by a period.

Medium of publication, followed by a period.

A Book in a Series

Full name of editor,
last name first, followed
by abbreviation *ed.*
(*editor*).

Title and subtitle in
italics, followed by
an italicized period.

Cox, Leland H., ed. *William Faulkner: Biographical and Reference Guide*. Detroit: Bruccoli-Gale, 1982. Print. Gale Author Handbook 1.

Series name
and number,
not
italicized,
followed by a
period.

City
of publication,
followed by a colon
and one space.
Give the postal
abbreviation for
the state only
if the city is not
well known or could
be confused with
another city.

Publisher's
imprint,
hyphen, and
publisher,
followed by
a comma.

Year of
publication,
followed by
a period.

Medium of
publication,
followed by
a period.

A Short Story in an Anthology

Author's name, last name first, followed by a period.

Short story title in double quotation marks with a period typed inside the final quotation marks.

Title and subtitle separated by a colon, italicized, and followed by an italicized period.

Editors of the anthology (names not inverted), preceded by *Ed.* (*Edited by*) and followed by a period.

Faulkner, William. "A Rose for Emily." *Literature: An Introduction to Fiction, Poetry, and Drama.* Ed. X. J. Kennedy and Dana Gioia. 8th ed. Interactive ed. New York: Longman, 2002. 28-35. Print.

Edition number (given only if the book is not a first edition).

Specialized edition (comes with CD-ROM and Web links).

City of publication, followed by a colon and one space. Give the postal abbreviation for the state only if the city is not well known or could be confused with another city.

Publisher, followed by a comma.

Year of publication, followed by a period.

First and last page numbers of story, separated by a hyphen and followed by a period.

Medium of publication, followed by a period.

An Article from a Scholarly Journal with Continuous Pagination

Author's full name, last name first, followed by a period.

Title and subtitle, separated with a colon and typed in double quotation marks with a period typed inside the final quotation marks. Novel title italicized.

Adams, Jenny. "Marketing the Medieval: The Quest for Authentic History in Michael Crichton's *Timeline*." *Journal of Popular Culture* 36.4 (2003): 704-23. Print.

Volume number, followed by a period and no space, and the issue number, followed by one space.

Year of publication in parentheses, followed by a colon.

First page, a hyphen, and last page of article (second number shortened if appropriate), followed by a period.

Medium of publication, followed by a period.

Journal title italicized (not followed by a period).

An Article from a Popular Monthly or Bimonthly Magazine

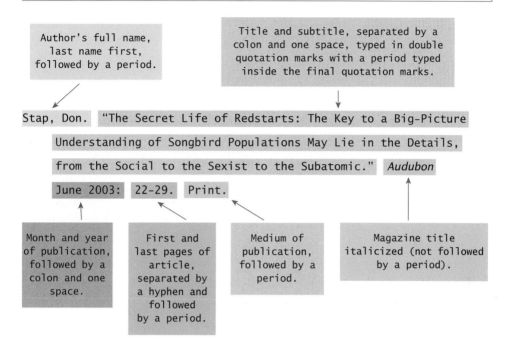

Author's full name, last name first, followed by a period.

Title and subtitle, separated by a colon and one space, typed in double quotation marks with a period typed inside the final quotation marks.

Stap, Don. "The Secret Life of Redstarts: The Key to a Big-Picture Understanding of Songbird Populations May Lie in the Details, from the Social to the Sexist to the Subatomic." *Audubon* June 2003: 22-29. Print.

Month and year of publication, followed by a colon and one space.

First and last pages of article, separated by a hyphen and followed by a period.

Medium of publication, followed by a period.

Magazine title italicized (not followed by a period).

A Newspaper Article with an Author Given and Lettered Sections

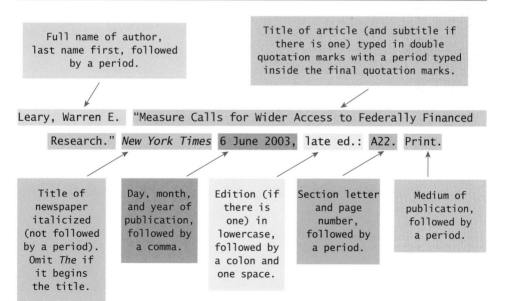

Full name of author, last name first, followed by a period.

Title of article (and subtitle if there is one) typed in double quotation marks with a period typed inside the final quotation marks.

Leary, Warren E. "Measure Calls for Wider Access to Federally Financed Research." *New York Times* 6 June 2003, late ed.: A22. Print.

Title of newspaper italicized (not followed by a period). Omit *The* if it begins the title.

Day, month, and year of publication, followed by a comma.

Edition (if there is one) in lowercase, followed by a colon and one space.

Section letter and page number, followed by a period.

Medium of publication, followed by a period.

A Review of a Book Taken from a Newspaper

Author's full name, last name first, followed by a period.	Title of review (and subtitle if there is one) in double quotation marks with a period typed inside the final quotation marks.	Author of book being reviewed, preceded with *by*, followed by a period.

Maslin, Janet.   "The Founder of Healthy, Wealthy, and Wise, Inc."

Rev. of *Benjamin Franklin: An American Life,*   by Walter Isaacson.

New York Times   3 July 2003,   late ed.:   E3+.   Print.

Rev. of (*Review of*), followed by title and subtitle of book reviewed (separated by a colon, italicized, and followed by a comma).	Newspaper title italicized (not followed by a period). Omit *The* if it begins the title.	Day, month, and year review was published, followed by a comma.	Edition (if there is one), followed by a colon.	Section and page number, followed by a period or plus sign and period if article jumps to a second page.	Medium of publication, followed by a period.

A Web Page from a Print Source with an Author Given

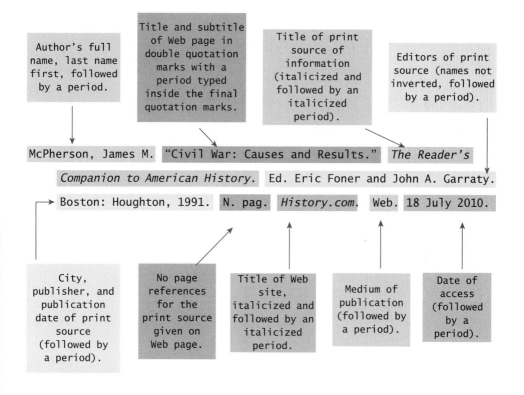

An Article with an Author Given from an Online Scholarly Journal

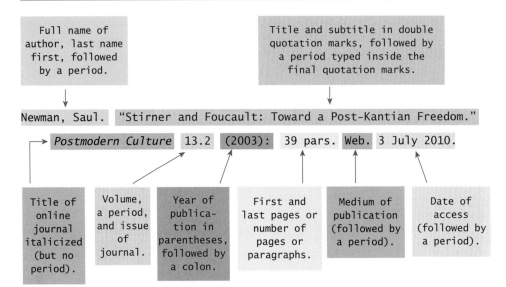

An Article from an Online Newspaper

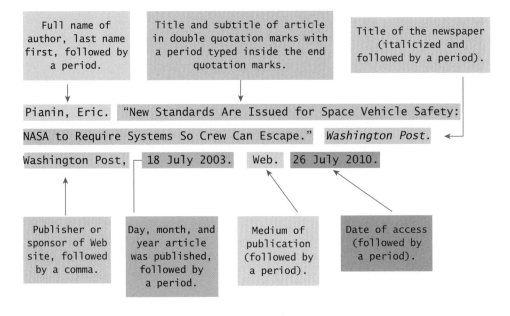

A Scholarly Journal Article from a Personal Subscription Database

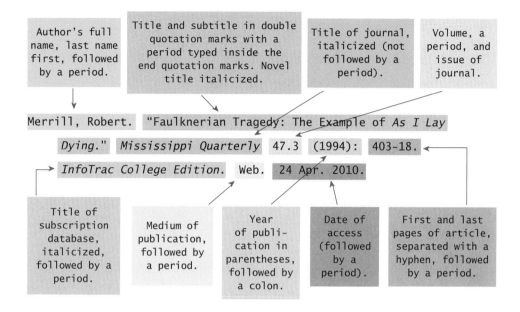

| Author's full name, last name first, followed by a period. | Title and subtitle in double quotation marks with a period typed inside the end quotation marks. Novel title italicized. | Title of journal, italicized (not followed by a period). | Volume, a period, and issue of journal. |

Merrill, Robert. "Faulknerian Tragedy: The Example of *As I Lay Dying*." *Mississippi Quarterly* 47.3 (1994): 403–18.
InfoTrac College Edition. Web. 24 Apr. 2010.

| Title of subscription database, italicized, followed by a period. | Medium of publication, followed by a period. | Year of publication in parentheses, followed by a colon. | Date of access (followed by a period). | First and last pages of article, separated with a hyphen, followed by a period. |

A Scholarly Journal Article from *InfoTrac OneFile*

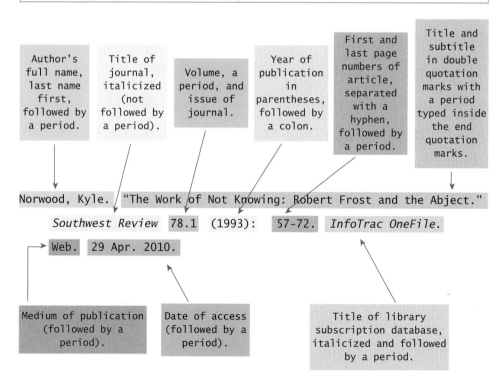

| Author's full name, last name first, followed by a period. | Title of journal, italicized (not followed by a period). | Volume, a period, and issue of journal. | Year of publication in parentheses, followed by a colon. | First and last page numbers of article, separated with a hyphen, followed by a period. | Title and subtitle in double quotation marks with a period typed inside the end quotation marks. |

Norwood, Kyle. "The Work of Not Knowing: Robert Frost and the Abject."
Southwest Review 78.1 (1993): 57–72. *InfoTrac OneFile*.
Web. 29 Apr. 2010.

| Medium of publication (followed by a period). | Date of access (followed by a period). | Title of library subscription database, italicized and followed by a period. |

QUICK LIST OF BOXES